# LIVE
# SOUND
# MIXING

D U N C A N   R   F R Y

F O U R T H • E D I T I O N

# Contents

This is the fourth revision of a book I originally thought might have a shelf life of a couple of years or so, given that the live sound industry is continually moving forwards, and the rate of change is constantly accelerating. But I still walk into gigs large and small and see the same equipment I saw five or even ten years ago.

However the Digital Live Sound express is just pulling into the station, so along with tried and true existing technology, I've included as much information as possible on the digital equipment that you'll need to know and love!

Rewriting a book like this is an enormously time consuming task, and it has only been made possible through the help of a great number of people. In particular my ARX partners Colin and David Park, for their invaluable help and technical advice (whether I took it or not!).

Special thanks also to Les Marton, John Elsdon, and Trevor Cronin, for their stories and practical suggestions, and also to all those people who took the time to write to me saying how much the book has helped them. Once again I hope they find something to like in this new edition.

Duncan R. Fry
July 2005

Published by **Dunkworld Communications**
33 Advantage Road,
HIGHETT, 3190,
Victoria, Australia
Fax: (03) 9555 6747   International Fax: +61 3 9555 6747
E-mail:  dunk@dunkworld.com     Website: www.dunkworld.com

## Introduction

Do you like the sound of live music? If you do, then here are some things to think about.

1. You walk into a concert to see your favourite act. The lights dim, the band comes on, the floor shakes as the giant sound system roars into life. You see the sound engineer at the controls of an enormous mixing console, surrounded by banks of equipment with flashing lights, and you think, "Wow, I'd like to do that."

2. You head off to a club to see a band you've heard about. The sound is terrible, with squeals and rumbles all night, lost vocals and drowned solos. The sound engineer seems more concerned with his drink level than the instrument levels, and you think, "Hey, I'm sure I could do better than that."

3. Your friends start a band and they need someone to mix; or perhaps your work, school or church need someone to do sound, and they decide that it's going to be you. So where do you start, who do you ask, what do you do?

Sound familiar? If any of these situations strike a responsive chord, then this book is for you. There is no guarantee it will get you a gig mixing either of the first two bands (although it might!), but it's a great start for the third. It should make you aware of just what a sound engineer is trying to do, the problems he (or she) faces, and how to solve those problems.

This is not a technical book. Technical books on sound theory can often be so intimidating that you are reluctant to risk twiddling a knob in case it's the wrong one. Well relax, because this book is not one of those. But if you have an ear for music, then this book will show you how to link those ears to your fingers, and pull the best sound possible sound out of any live sound system.

# 1      *Basic Principles*

## What is a Live Sound System?

A Live Sound system, or Sound Reinforcement system, is a collection of equipment designed to amplify voice and music so that they can be heard by a larger number of people. From the small speaker that makes the announcements at school to the truckloads of equipment used by big touring acts, the principle remains exactly the same:

1. The original sound travels to one or more microphones

2. The microphone converts the sound to electrical impulses (commonly called a signal) and sends it down a wire to a mixing console

3. The mixing console mixes all the signals together in the correct balance and sends this 'mixed' signal down another wire to an amplifier

4. The amplifier converts the electrical signals into much larger ones and sends them down another wire to the speaker(s)

5. The speaker converts the electrical signals into mechanical vibrations, setting up sound waves

6. The audience hears these sound waves

That's it. That's all the mystery there is to a PA system. Try to think of it as a directional chain when you're wiring things together and you can't go far wrong:

The microphone leads run OUT of the microphone, IN to the console

The mixed signal runs OUT of the console, IN to the amplifier

The amplified signal runs OUT of the amplifier, IN to the speakers.

When you're confused about what lead goes where, refer back mentally to this simple chain of events and you'll find that everything falls into place.

Some systems may have the amplifier inside the console - this is called a 'powered mixer'; others may have the amplifier inside the speaker box - a 'powered speaker'.

Nevertheless, the chain remains the same. *No matter how large or small the system, it will always follow this same basic layout.*

## *A Simple System*

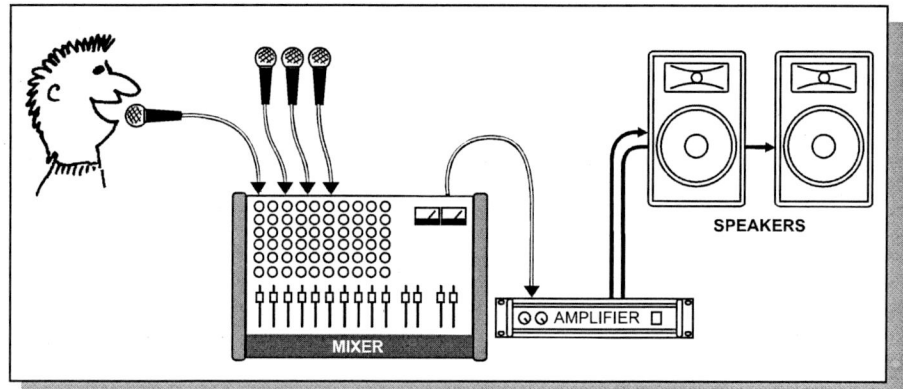

In practice this simple setup is as follows:

1. The microphones plug into leads which run to the mixing console, which is usually set up at the side of the stage. Each mic has its own channel.

2. Each channel often has basic tone controls (more commonly known as the EQ section - more on this later). These are usually LOW and HIGH, which act pretty much like the ones on your home stereo. As well, each channel has a knob or a slider which controls the volume on that one channel only.

3. The mixer has a Master volume control, again a knob or slider, which mixes all the channel volumes together and sends it out as one 'mixed' signal from the mixer's Main Output.

5. Speaker leads run from the Output of the amplifier to the Main speakers; for example one each side of the stage.

4. This signal then runs down a lead to the Input of an amplifier. This amplifier is known as a Power Amp, as it does not have a pre-amp section - your mixer is supplying that function.

That's it. To get a sound out, set the Master volume at about 7, or two thirds the way up, and talk into the microphone as you gradually bring up the level of the channel volume control until it is as loud as you want. If everything is working and has been plugged up correctly, then you should hear yourself going "Check ONE - TWO", the timeless chant of the sound engineer!

*Check ONE-TWO, the timeless chant of the sound engineer!*

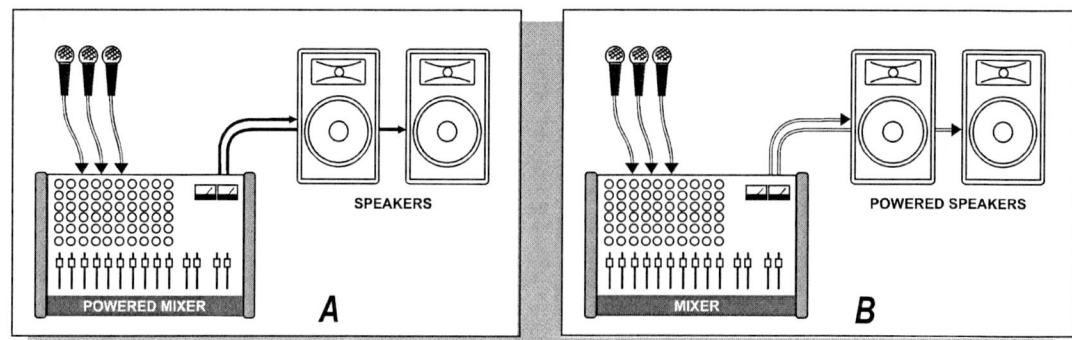

If you have a powered mixer, (Diagram A) with the amplifier inside the console, it's even easier. You only have to plug in the microphones, and plug the speaker leads from the mixer's amp section to the speakers.

Note: These powered mixers also have standard mixer outputs, marked Left Out/Right Out or similar, as well as the amp section outputs. Make sure you plug the speaker leads into the correct connectors, usually marked Left AMP Out/Right AMP Out or similar.

If you have powered speakers (with the amplifiers inside - Diagram B), you send the mixed signal from the normal Left and Right outputs of the mixer down to the inputs of the speakers. These leads will need to be Shielded signal leads, NOT SPEAKER LEADS. More on this in *Chapter 4 - Cables and Connectors.* You will also need to plug in AC power connectors to the back of the powered speakers, switch them on, and turn up any volume controls (if they have them).

### *A Bigger System*

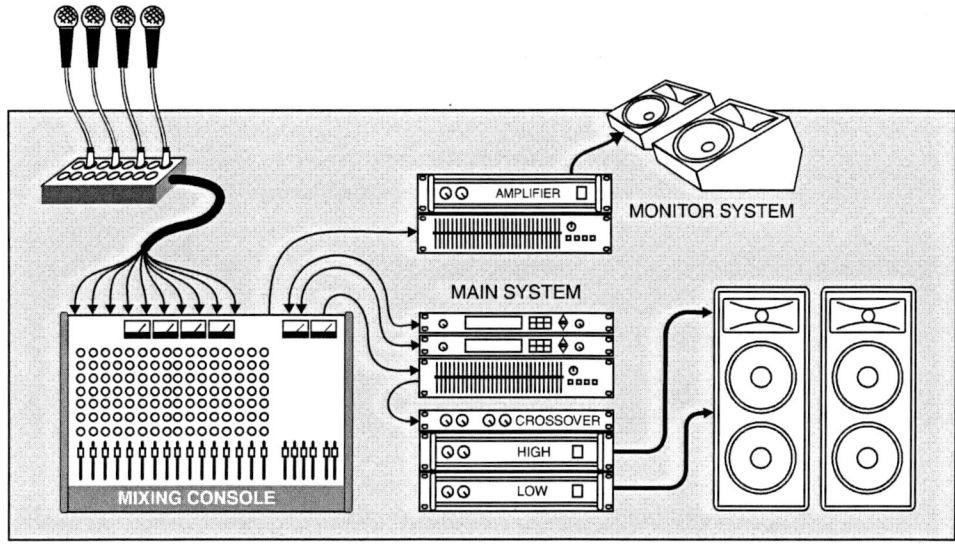

OK, that's a simple system.  Now let's have a look at a more complicated system layout, one which is used by a lot of sound systems in pubs, clubs, and medium sized venues.  It's a bit of a jump from the previous system, but still conforms to the 6 basic functions of a sound system as described earlier.

1. This time the mixing console is out in the audience so that the sound engineer can hear the band the same way the audience does.

2. The individual mic leads plug into a box on stage (appropriately called a Stage Box!), and a thick cable runs from this box down to  the mixer. This is called a Multicore cable, or Snake, and is virtually a long extension of each mic cable, grouped together inside a thick plastic sheath to protect it from damage.

3. The mixing console this time is a bit more complicated than the previous one we looked at, but it still performs the same basic functions, plus a few more:

   So that the band can hear itself on stage there is a Monitor control on each channel. This sends a separate signal to extra amps and speakers on the stage so that the singer(s) can hear themselves above the band. (See Chapter 11 - Monitors)

   There are also a couple of Effects units (Delay/Reverb) running off Effects controls on each channel, to fatten up vocals or drums or for special effects. (See Chapter 6 - Effects). The EQ section is also more comprehensive, split into Low, Mid and High with maybe an extra Frequency control for the Mids. (See Chapter 2 - Mixing Consoles)

4. The Main signal from the Mixer runs into a Graphic Equalizer.  This lets the engineer 'tune' the system to compensate for acoustic deficiencies in the room, which can cause feedback and other unwanted sounds. *(See Chapter 3 - Equalizers and Equalizing)*

5. This sound system has separate speakers for Bass and Treble (LOW and HIGH) and needs an amp for each one, with an Active crossover splitting the signal into LOW and HIGH frequencies. This type of system would be called Bi-Amped, or Active 2 way system.

Next step up would be a 3 way, LOW, MID and HIGH, with a 3 way Active Crossover and 3 separate amps.

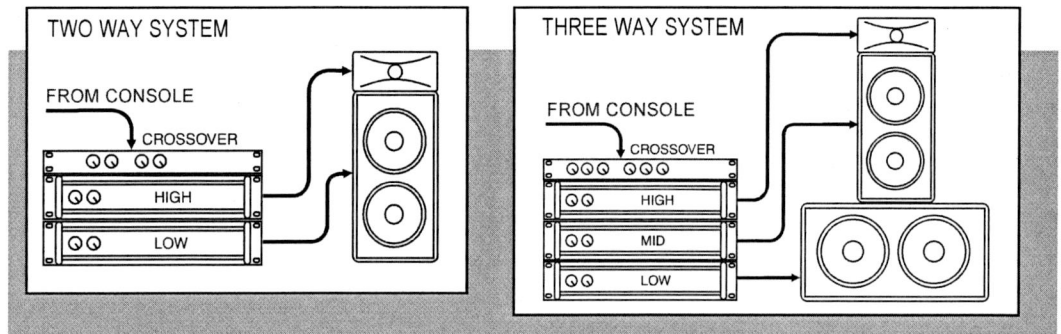

## *A Typical Touring System*

From this size of system we jump to one that many touring bands would use. It has a lot more in it than our previous system, for more volume and more control over the sound.

However, it still works on our basic 6 sound reinforcement principles: Band to Microphones to Mixer to Amplifiers to Speakers to Audience.

1. The mixing console has at least 24 channels, often up to 56, and it is frequently run in Stereo. There are no monitor controls on each channel, just a number of what are called Auxiliary sends. These send signals to various effects units - Delays, Reverbs - and these are housed in an Effects Rack next to the console. The EQ section is often much more comprehensive, with sweepable Low Mids and High Mids, plus extra switches and controls.

2. This effects racks will contain 2 Graphic Equalizers (remember we're in stereo now), multiple delays and reverbs, compressors, noise gates, Aural Exciters, enhancers, tube mic pre-amps, all sorts of gadgets to give the sound engineer absolute control over the sound.

3. The monitors on stage are now run from a *separate* mixer at the side of the stage.

   The multicore snake from the Stage Box is split so that one line runs to the Mixing console in the audience, the House mixer, and another runs across the stage to the Monitor mixer. This Monitor mixer can have from 6 to 20 or more outputs, and if necessary can send a different mix to each of the musicians on stage.
   Some musicians will be using 'in-ear monitors'(small 'walkman-type' headphones in each ear) which are usually wireless and come with their own specific mixing requirements to operate correctly. *See Chapter 11 - Monitors,* for more on these.

   Each output from the monitor mixer will run into its own Graphic Equalizer, for feedback control, and then to its own amplifier. Needless to say there is a monitor engineer to look after all this!

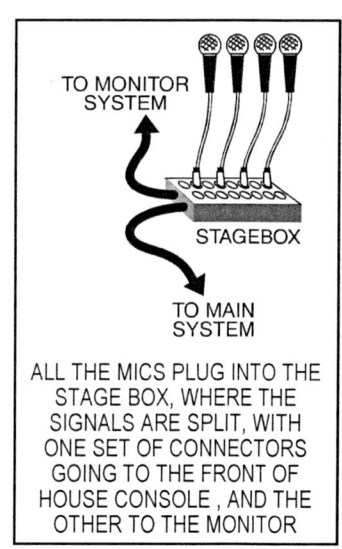

TO MONITOR SYSTEM

STAGEBOX

TO MAIN SYSTEM

ALL THE MICS PLUG INTO THE STAGE BOX, WHERE THE SIGNALS ARE SPLIT, WITH ONE SET OF CONNECTORS GOING TO THE FRONT OF HOUSE CONSOLE , AND THE OTHER TO THE MONITOR

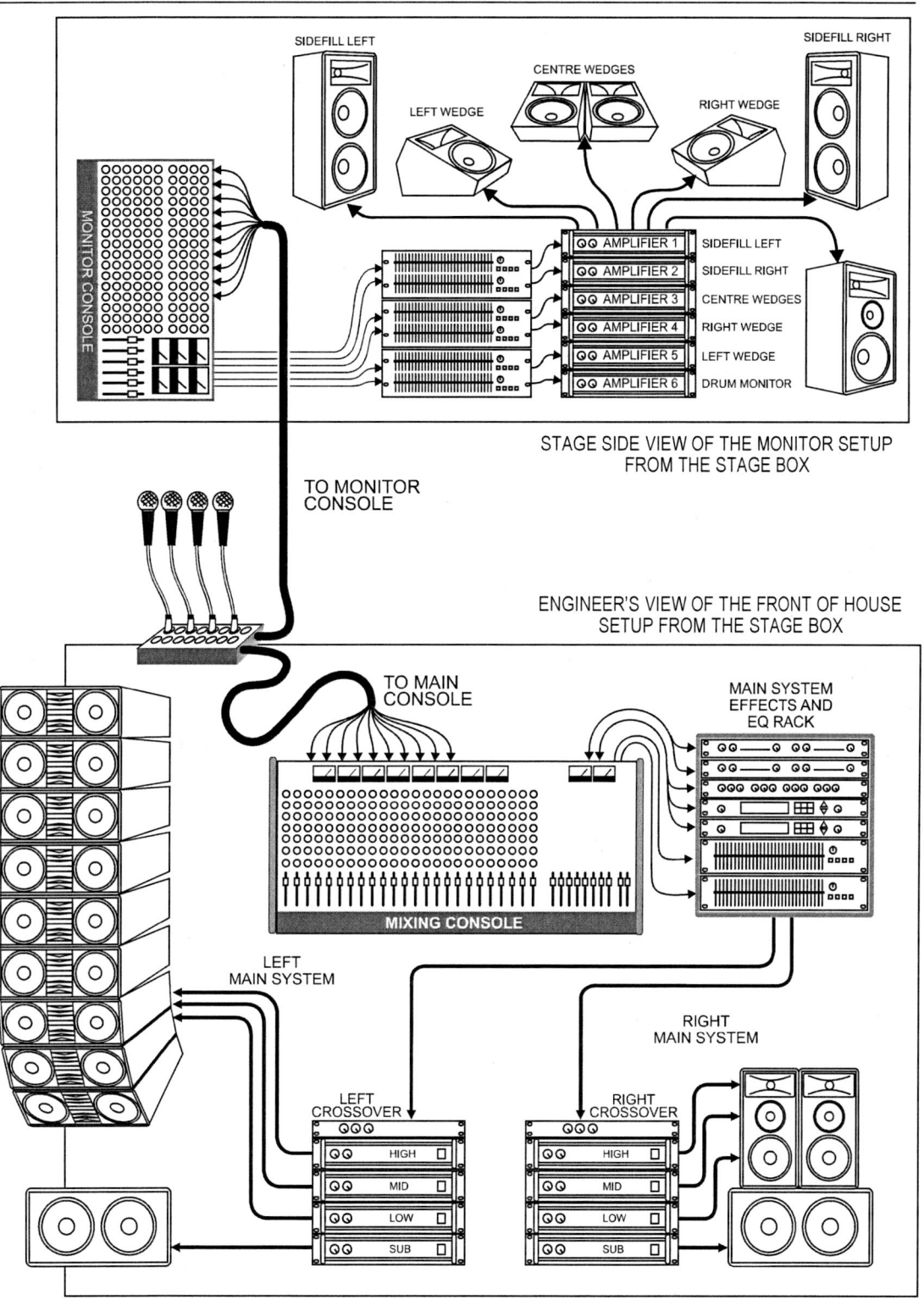

STAGE SIDE VIEW OF THE MONITOR SETUP
FROM THE STAGE BOX

ENGINEER'S VIEW OF THE FRONT OF HOUSE
SETUP FROM THE STAGE BOX

4. There will be multiple amp racks to drive a large number of speakers.  The system may
be run 3, 4 or even 5 way: Sub Bass, Low, Low Mid, High Mid, High.
The speakers may also be a Line Array system, (see Left side of picture) where multiple boxes are hung or stacked on top of each other in a vertical line, to provide a

continuous beam of sound, one that ideally will cover the whole audience area in the venue. *(See Chapter 10 - Speakers)*

Still, as you can see, the principle remains the same in these 3 very different PA systems; only the amount of equipment changes. Our 6 basic functions of sound reinforcement still apply. A mixing console is still a mixing console, whether it has 6 channels or 56!

In the next few chapters we'll work our way through the various sound system components and how to use them, work out how we're going to put it all together, and then what we can do to pull a decent sound out of it.

And after that we'll have a close look at what you can do when things don't go according to plan!

### The Way we Were

Next time you complain about not having enough channels, here's a mid 60's Kustom (USA) console with a whopping 6 channels! Two way EQ, plus onboard 7 band Graphic EQ, Spring Reverb and a 2 way crossover. And about the size of a 24 channel 8 bus console of today!

*Thanks to Peter at Nova Sound for uncovering this for me. Yes, it still works!*

If you thought that all in one systems like the JBL Eon and others were a new idea, think again. This Watkins (U.K.) unit from the early 60's is a complete system in one box.

3 microphone channels, plus tape delay, plus Front of House speakers *and* Stage Monitors! The open backed cabinet lets the vocals project backwards to the stage as well as out front!

*Special thanks to Brad Coates from Melbourne Music Centre (www. melmusic.com.au) for digging out this classic!*

## 2 Mixers

A mixer, mixing console, or desk, or board, collects up *all* the microphone signals, *all* the line signals, *all* the effects, then mixes them all into one signal and sends it off to the amps. These days they can either be Analog or Digital, but they all still perform the same tasks. A mixer has to cope with tremendously varied signal levels, from very loud to very soft, and bring them all to a convenient common operating level.

The level of this signal path through the mixer (and the whole system) is known as the Gain Structure. Keeping all parts of this gain structure at their ideal level is the key to making the whole sound system work as efficiently as possible.

If you think of the multicore snake as your system's lifeline, then the mixer is the heart. If something goes wrong with it then the system is in big trouble, since every part is connected in some way to it. And if you don't set the it up right, then you'll find it almost impossible to pull a good sound out of the system.

The basics of every good mixer are quiet Input gain and good EQ control. The more control you can exert over each microphone, the better your sound will be.

Let's have a look at some typical controls on a mixer, what they do and how they work.

### Gain

Also called Input level, or Trim.

This knob determines how sensitive the Input is to the incoming signal, whether it's a microphone signal or a line signal (Keyboards, Tape decks, CD players, Effects returns). It's probably easier to think of it as controlling how much signal you are letting in to the mixer channel - if it's a soft signal you let more in, if it's a loud one then you let less in. For example, a soft background vocal will need more gain, while the 'thump' of a Kick drum will need less gain.

We do all this to keep the Input stage of the mixer at its optimum gain setting. Too loud a signal will overload it and cause distortion, and too soft a signal will mean the rest of the signal path will need to be driven harder, increasing the noise level. The Input Gain stage is the most critical stage in achieving a good console gain structure, and the signal must be kept as clean and clear as possible, because ***any noise or distortion at this point will flow on through the whole system.***

Because of this, nearly every mixer will have an LED (usually Red) on each channel, marked Clip or O/load or Peak that lights up when the level going through the channel is too high.

*Analog or digital, the mixing console is the heart of every system*

---

On a Gain control with a scale of 0 to 10, 0 is not usually Off but Low. If it is not low enough there should be a PAD switch to drop the Input Signal by 20 dB. If there is no Pad switch, see Page 16 for a simple Pad design, suitable for mounting inside a pair of XLR type connectors.

### *If it's so critical, then how do you set it up?*

Here's the easiest way. Set the Gain control hard left (minimum), and put the channel fader on 0 dB (or U for Unity) which is about 3/4 of the way up. Press in the PFL/Solo button and watch its meter. Talk, sing, or yell into a microphone plugged into that channel, and slowly bring up the Gain control until it is peaking at around -6 to -3dB on the meter.

You then do this for each channel, either with an assistant on stage to run though each mic, or when the band comes on for the sound check (see Chapter 12: Setting Up). With drums, you could probably set the Gain at a little less for Kick and Snare as your average meter is not going to see the actual peak level of the drum signal until it's too much.

Keep checking the Gain controls as you build the mix (especially if you add much channel EQ) to make sure nothing has got out of control, and you're halfway there. If you have set them correctly, then each channel fader should ideally hover around the 0 dB point during your mix.

### *Channel EQ*

EQ is short for Equalizer, and the EQ section of the channel is one big Tone control. It lets you modify the sound coming from whatever is plugged into this particular channel, either a microphone or a line signal.

You will need to modify the sound of the voice or instrument for basically 2 purposes:

1. As a creative tool, to change the sound of the instrument or voice to a sound that you prefer.
2. As a control tool, to remove the frequencies from the voice or instrument's sound that are causing acoustic problems - feedback, overtones, muddiness, ringing.

These EQ controls can be basic, for example one knob to cut and boost LOW (Bass) and another one for HIGH (Treble); or they can be very complex, with four way full parametric functions.

But no matter what type of EQ you have on the mixer, its purpose is the same - to give you control over the sound.

### *Fixed EQ*

As its name suggests, this has fixed frequency bands that can be either cut or boosted, depending on the requirements. The frequencies are split up in a similar way to crossovers:-

LOW and HIGH - 2 way EQ

LOW, MID and HIGH - 3 way EQ

LOW, LOW MID, HIGH MID and HIGH - 4 way EQ

Turning each knob boosts or cuts that frequency band by up to 12 or 15dB. The advantages of fixed EQ are low cost, less margin for error in inexperienced hands, and speed of use. The disadvantages are that it is basically 'near enough is good enough'. You can't cut a particular frequency in the LOW MIDS on a drum, for example; you end up having to pull down ALL the LOW MIDS, which can take all the power out of the sound (see Gates in Chapter 7).

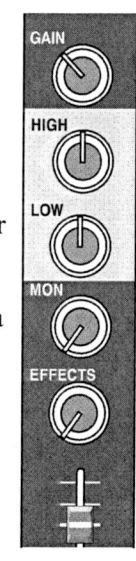

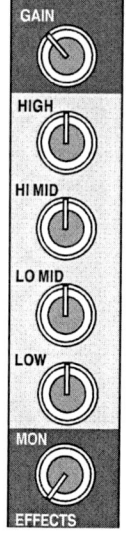

### *Sweepable EQ*

Usually available as 'Quasi' Parametric (which means not quite parametric - no Bandwidth control). Full Parametric EQ means that you have control over every parameter; Frequency, Bandwidth, and Level.

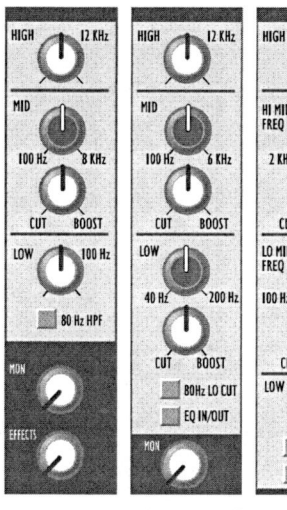

Sweepable EQ is a very flexible set up, and is usually available on the Mid range controls in 3 and 4 way EQ systems. How it works is like this:

Rather than having to cut or boost the whole of a frequency band, as you do in Fixed EQ, sweepable EQ lets you target the particular frequency that needs adjusting. To use our previous example, rather than having to pull down the complete LOW MID area on drums, leaving them with that sort of hollow flat sound, you can pick the exact frequency that sounds boomy (often in the 250 to 300 Hz area) and reduce that only.

You can also give vocals a bit of a kick in the 3.5 KHz area without having to boost the whole of the HIGH MIDs, something that can lead to terrible feedback problems, especially in monitors.

A single MID sweep control is common on mid price bracket mixers, others will have sweepable LOW as well, while more expensive versions will have sweepable LOW MID and HIGH MID, plus fixed HIGH and LOW.

### How do you use it?

Well, let's go back to our drum example. Get the drummer to hit the drum steadily, and listen for the 'boing' sound that you want to remove. Without touching the Frequency control, cut the Level control about 6 dB. Then, sweep the Frequency control slowly around until the frequency that is causing the overtone suddenly drops in level.

Rock the control each side of the frequency until you get it exactly right. Now check the Level control; if all the life has been pulled out of the sound, bring some level back - if it still boings a bit, then cut it some more.

Just remember that a little is a lot. *Never* make sudden, drastic EQ changes - always move the controls slowly so that you can easily identify any unwanted side effects that may appear.

The Frequency sweep knob can be placed above or below the Cut/ Boost control, or they can both be on the same central shaft. The outer knob will be the Frequency sweep, and the inner one the Cut/ Boost. For reasons of space, this last type of layout is common on 'up market' consoles that may have Full parametric 4 way EQ.

Space is an important consideration in mixer design. Check out the size of the 3 typical channels down the edge of these pages. Everything has to be within easy reach of the engineer.

**The more you have to lean over to get to the control you want, the more the risk of accidentally moving something else as you do.**

When you consider that full 4-way parametric EQ would have 12 knobs for the EQ section alone, you can see how the available space gets eaten away, especially if you have 16 Aux sends, 8 Subgroups and 40 input channels!

## Other Channel Controls

### 48 V Phantom

Some microphones - condenser microphones - need power to make them work. This switch sends 48 volts DC down the microphone line to the microphone, and is cancelled out at the balanced input stage of the channel.

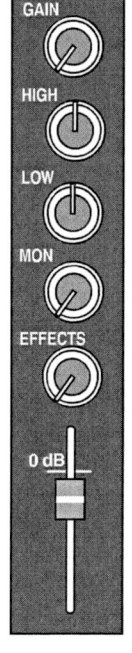

Be careful when using a mixer that doesn't have individual phantom power switches on each channel, but only has one switch for all channels (commonly known as Global Phantom power). It's either on all channels or it's off. If everything is balanced there should be no problem, but if not, then something unbalanced can fry.

Also bear in mind that plugging and unplugging phantom powered microphones during a changeover can send heart-stoppingly large bangs through the whole system!

### Pad

This is a switch that lowers the microphone Input gain by 20 to 30 dB. In effect it makes the microphone input a bit deaf to the signal coming in. You may have to switch the pad IN when the channel overload LED is coming on even when the Input gain is turned right down.

Just make sure you don't have too many of them, or all of them, switched in. The system will still work, but you will have to pick up the missing gain by driving everything else harder, increasing both the noise level and the risk of distortion.

If the mixer you are using has no Pad switch, here is a simple design that can be mounted inside 2 XLR connectors:

### A simple Pad design

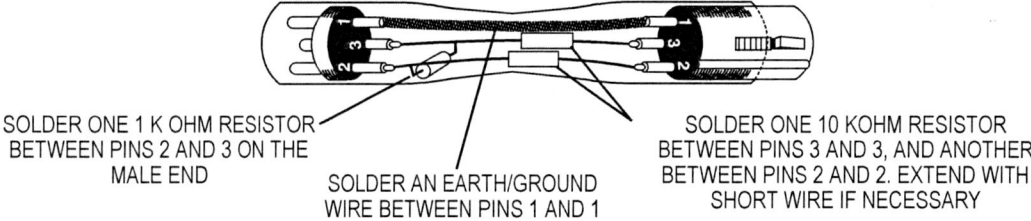

SOLDER ONE 1 K OHM RESISTOR BETWEEN PINS 2 AND 3 ON THE MALE END

SOLDER AN EARTH/GROUND WIRE BETWEEN PINS 1 AND 1

SOLDER ONE 10 KOHM RESISTOR BETWEEN PINS 3 AND 3, AND ANOTHER BETWEEN PINS 2 AND 2. EXTEND WITH SHORT WIRE IF NECESSARY

### Ø Reverse

Phase Reverse. This swaps over the + and − lines on a Balanced Input. It is useful for microphones that may be wired out of phase, or microphones that are too close together and causing phase cancellation, such as on the rack toms of a drum kit. They will sound hollow or dull with little or no low frequencies. Push the switch In and Out to compare; one will sound much better than the other. Refer to the 3 to 1 rule in *Chapter 5 - Microphones/Drums*

### Mic/Line

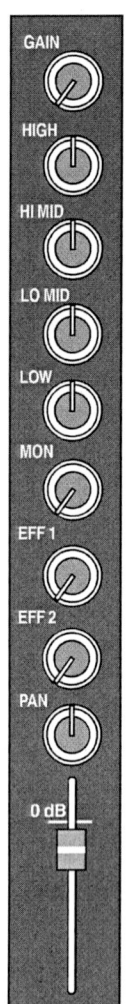

This switch changes the gain control circuitry depending on whether you are plugging in a microphone, or a line level signal such as an Effects return, CD player, DAT or tape deck.

On many mixers there are separate Microphone and Line inputs, the microphone usually being a 3 pin XLR (Cannon) type and Line a guitar jack. This enables you to have two different things plugged into the one channel, switching between them as necessary.

For example, you could have an effects return plugged into a Microphone input, with the gain turned right down, and a CD or tape deck plugged into the Line input on the same channel. This way you could use the effect during the set, and play a CD or tape in between sets. It saves on channels if you are running short.

### High Pass Filter (Lo Cut)

This rolls off the low frequencies from about 80 or 100 Hz down. It should be switched IN on any channels where you don't need that kind of low frequency information which will only muddy up your signal: Hi Hats, Vocals, some guitars (especially acoustic). It should be switched OUT on Drums and Bass guitar.

### EQ In/Out

This switches out the EQ section of the channel to enable you to make comparisons between the sound with the EQ switched In or Out.

Headline band engineers have been known to switch OUT the EQ on vital channels just to have a little fun at the support band engineer's expense! If you're the person mixing the support band, check that these switches are IN.

Live Sound Mixing 4th Edition  ©2005 D.R.Fry

## Group Assigns

*Also called Subgroup assigns, Bus assigns, Submaster assigns.*

These switches are only on mixers that have Groups. If the one you are using is, say, a 16 into 2, it won't have these. If it is a 16 into 4 into 2, then it will.

Group assign switches determine where the signal from the channel goes - either straight to the Left/Right masters, or to a Group master to be linked up with similar signals.

For example, on a 4 group mixer, you could assign all the drums to Group 1, the guitars and bass to 2, vocals to 3, and maybe keyboards to 4. With an 8 group console you could do the same in stereo.

This may sound unnecessarily complicated, but in reality it's not. These group masters run directly to the Left/Right masters, and in this way you can use one (or two if you have enough) slider to control the overall level of the drums, one the instruments, one the vocals, and so on.

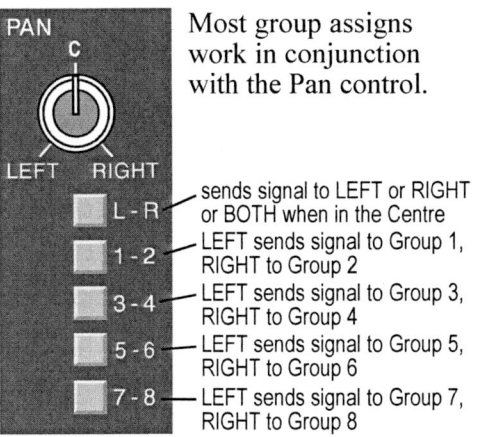

Most group assigns work in conjunction with the Pan control.

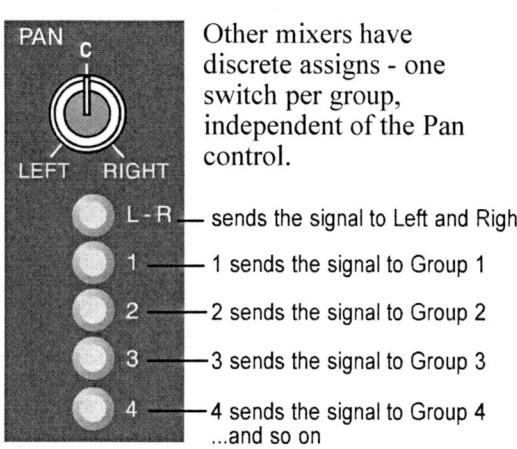

Other mixers have discrete assigns - one switch per group, independent of the Pan control.

A typical 8 Group (8 Bus) Master section. Each group Master has a Pan control, to vary how much of its signal goes to the Left or Right Master. There may also be switches to send each group to its own output, and group Mute switches.

 No matter what you do on a mixer that has groups, remember this:

***If you haven't pressed down one of the switches, the signal will not leave the channel!*** You haven't told it where to go.

The groups are there to make life easier for you. You can run any channel to any group or straight to the L/R masters, in whatever arrangement suits your needs. You could run your Lead Vocal straight to L/R, and just send the backing vocals to a group so you can put a gate across them.

We'll take a look at some suggested set ups in *Chapter 12 - Setting Up*, as using groups to control the mix can really lighten your load.

### PFL and SOLO

*Sometimes called Cue*

On most mixers other than really basic ones, each channel will have a switch marked PFL or SOLO, and the Master section should also have a meter with the same words.

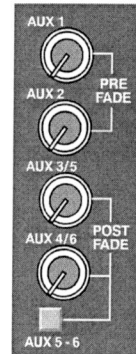

This switch lets you listen in the headphones to each channel individually. As a *general* rule (but not always, as you'll no doubt find):

> PFL stands for Pre Fade Listening, and lets you listen to the channel irrespective of where the channel fader is positioned.

> SOLO lets you listen to the channel Post Fade, so you will have to push the channel fader up to hear something. On some consoles there is a Global (meaning 'affects the whole console') switch to change the Solo from AFL (After Fade Listening) to PFL

This control is very handy when you need to listen to something on its own during the gig, to identify a problem, or just to check that something is coming through to the channel

Some mixers will also have a switch in the Master section marked PFL (SOLO) to Left/ Right, Solo In Place or something similar. This is for listening to individual channels **through the system** during a sound check. When it is switched IN and you press a PFL/ SOLO switch, it sends that individual channel straight to the L/R masters, shutting off every other channel.

Speaking from bitter experience, make sure this switch is OUT when the band starts to play, otherwise the first PFL/SOLO switch you hit will turn off everything but that channel! Very embarrassing.

### Channel On/Off

This should be self explanatory! If the channel has this switch, then there should be an LED next to it to indicate the channel has been switched on.

### Auxiliary Sends

An Auxiliary send is a control that sends the signal from the channel out of the mixer, separate from the main channel fader. It can send the channel signal out to the monitor/foldback amps and speakers, or to various effects units, which can then send the signal back into the mix via either the effects returns or a spare channel.

Basic mixers have one or maybe two aux sends - one for monitors, one for effects (Echo, Reverb). Larger mixers have 4, 6 or more, often designated as being Pre Fade or Post Fade, with Pre Fade usually being used for monitors and Post Fade for effects.

### Pre Fade

Means that the position of the channel fader has no effect on the Aux Send. It should ideally be Pre EQ as well if it is to be used to run the monitors. More on this in the MONITORS section.

### Post Fade

Means that the channel fader has to be up before anything gets sent out of the Aux Send. It is usually used as an Effects send, so that when correctly set up the channel fader can control the effects send as well. This may sound fiddley, but if you have 32 microphone channels plus stereo effects returns to keep a close eye on during the mix, it can save your fingers a lot of walking!

Since Post Fade sends follow the channel fader exactly, they can also be used to send a separate mix, based on your House mix, to something else - TV or Radio feed, for example, or when running a central cluster of speakers plus the normal Left and Right.

There are no hard and fast rules for using Auxiliary sends - you should just use them whichever way suits your needs. For example, using a Pre Fade send on effects lets you keep the effect level up while dropping the original signal (great for singers who go flat on long notes!). Using a Post Fade send lets you control the original signal and the effect at the same time. When you fade down a solo, for example, you fade down the effect as well.

Some mixers, for reasons of economy and space, might have 6 Aux sends but only 4 knobs. A switch near Aux 3 and Aux 4 changes them to Aux 5 and Aux 6. Great for when you need to run a lot of effects on different channels.

### Using Aux Sends with Subs

A post fade auxiliary is also useful to run as a Sub Bass send. Sub Bass is a very powerful thing to use; but you don't necessarily want it in every song, or on every instrument.

By running your Sub speakers on a post fade auxiliary send you can control them much better. You can add Sub Bass on the Bass, Drums, Gongs, maybe some Keyboards, and keep it out of acoustic guitar and Vocals, except as a special effect. Bring it in by pushing up the auxiliary master, pull it out by bringing down the master; and since it is post fade it follows the position of the faders in the mix.

Since you won't be using your existing System crossover or processor, the only extra thing you'll need to do this is a separate crossover to provide a Sub Bass signal to run into the Sub amp(s). For easy access I'd also choose the post-fade auxiliary send closest to the main channel fader, to reduce the risk of turning the wrong knob.

### Auxiliary Returns

The signals that you send off to your effects (delays, reverbs, etc) need to be returned to the mixer so they can be mixed in with the original signals at the appropriate levels.

Although most mixers have specific Effects Return Inputs and controls, these controls are not usually sliders. If you have the spare channels available it is often easier from a mixing point of view to bring the effects back in via a standard microphone input channel. In this way you can control the level of the effect with a slider, the same as the original signal. It also makes it much easier to pull down the effects in between songs.

**Most Important:** If you decide to bring the returns back via microphone channels, remember this. You must make sure that the Aux send that you are using to send the signal OUT on is completely turned OFF on the channel you are bringing the effect

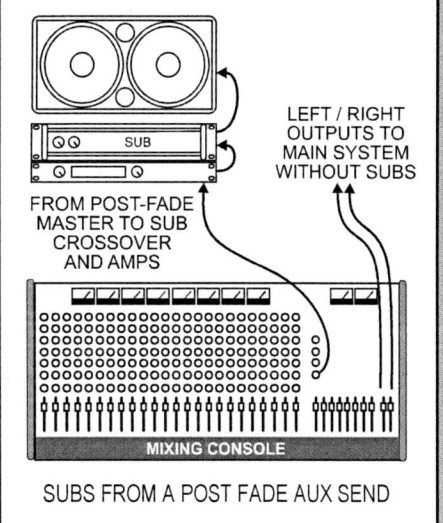

SUBS FROM A POST FADE AUX SEND

DIAGRAM SHOWING SIGNAL PATH OF PRE AND POST FADE SENDS, AND ALSO THE DIFFERENCE BETWEEN PRE EQ AND POST EQ

back IN on. Yes, appalling grammar, I know, but have a look at the example on the right and it should be clear.

Be careful. Even if it is turned up just a little bit, it can feed the effect back into itself causing uncontrollable squeals. It's hard to track down in a hurry and, once again, it's very embarrassing!

### Auxiliary Masters

These are overriding Master controls for the Auxiliary sends. There will be one of them for each Aux send, and they should be located somewhere on the console, usually in the Master section.

Look for knobs (or faders) called Aux Masters, Effects Masters, Monitor Masters or something similar. Find them and set them at about 2 o'clock for a start. If that's not enough, wind them up; if it's too much, pull them back.

### Differences

We've worked our way through just about all the basic controls you can expect to find on an analog mixer, but remember, they won't necessarily be laid out in the same order. Each manufacturer has their own design and layout ideas.

AUX SEND **4**, GOING TO THE DELAY... **...MUST** BE TURNED **DOWN** ON RETURN CHANNEL

For example, some Yamaha mixers have a multi position rotary switch for Gain trimming instead of a continuously variable control, and instead of being near the top of the channel, it's down near the fader.

Others have the EQ section nearest the fader, and the auxiliaries up near the top of the channel along with the channel Group assign controls. The theory is that once these are setup you rarely change them during the set, whereas you are continually adjusting the EQ so it's placed closer to you.

These variations in layout don't necessarily mean that the mixer works differently - all it means is that if you're unused to a particular layout you have to concentrate harder until you're familiar with it.

## Mixing Console Rear Panel

This is the back of the mixer where the leads all plug in - the multicore snake, the effects sends and returns, and the Main outputs.

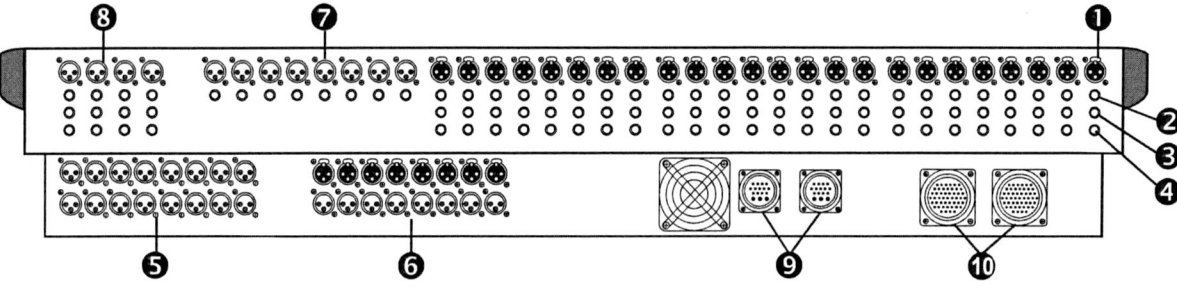

Each channel will have some or all of the following:

❶ A microphone input (usually XLR type)

❷ A separate Line input (usually a guitar jack, but sometimes another XLR)

❸ An Insert jack or jacks. If there are two, they are marked Insert IN and Insert OUT. If there is only one, it is a TRS jack (stereo jack - it stands for Tip, Ring, Sleeve), and Tip is usually IN, Ring is OUT, and Sleeve is Earth/Ground for both of them. Tip and Ring functions may be reversed on some desks (Mackie for one), but in either case the configuration is usually printed on the rear panel.

Live Sound Mixing 4th Edition  ©2005 D.R.Fry

The Insert point is used to insert an Effect, a Gate, a Compressor, an EQ, a De-Esser or any other signal processor into the channel. It breaks the signal flow of the channel after the Gain stage, sends the signal OUT to the Effect etc, then brings the Effect etc back IN to the channel.

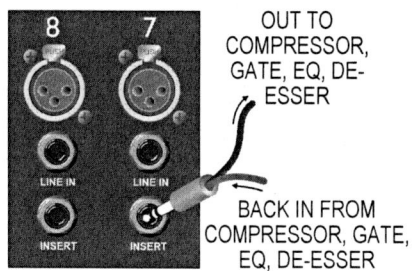

OUT TO COMPRESSOR, GATE, EQ, DE-ESSER

BACK IN FROM COMPRESSOR, GATE, EQ, DE-ESSER

This is useful if you want to use the effect or whatever on ONE channel only. It saves tying up the Auxiliary sends, leaving them free for effects that may be needed on more than one channel. The Insert point is a very common place to put Noise Gates.

❹ There can also be a separate Line Out or Direct Out jack, usually used for recording. This can be Pre Fade or Post Fade, depending on the console.

❺ Over in the Master section there will be the Auxiliary Outputs, either marked by number - Aux 1 Out, Aux 2 Out, etc, or by name - Effects Out, Monitor (or Mon) Out; it depends on what is written on the channel knobs.Big consoles like the one pictured may have 16 Aux sends so they can also double as Monitor consoles.

❻ There will also be the Auxiliary Returns, marked Aux 1 Return (Ret) or Effects Return (Eff Ret), again depending on what is on the channel.

❼ Each Group can have an Insert point as well (Group 1 Ins, Group 2 Ins, etc) which is set up and used the same way as the channel Inserts, and there can also be separate Group Outputs, which can be used for recording purposes, or for running a Front of House console as a Monitor one.

❽ The Master Left and Right Outputs will either be XLR type or Jack (or sometimes both), and there may be a separate Mono Out. This will be the sum of the Left and Right outputs, and may have its own fader on the front panel. Don't confuse it with the MON (Monitor) output when you are plugging everything up. Plus, like the channels and the groups, there may also be Insert points on these Master outputs.

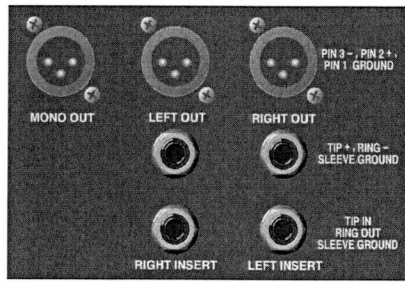

MONO OUT    LEFT OUT    RIGHT OUT

PIN 3 – , PIN 2 + , PIN 1 GROUND

TIP + , RING – SLEEVE GROUND

TIP IN RING OUT SLEEVE GROUND

RIGHT INSERT    LEFT INSERT

## Power Supply

❾ Some mixers plug straight into the main AC power, but others don't. If the mixer has a separate External power supply, then there will be a multipin connector of some kind where it will plug in. This will supply the different voltages that the mixer needs.

An external power supply like this is an amplifier shaped unit that may be either loose or mounted in the effects rack. If it is loose, make sure you don't leave

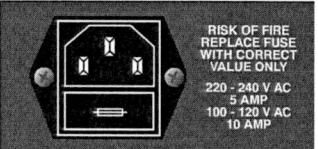

RISK OF FIRE REPLACE FUSE WITH CORRECT VALUE ONLY

220 - 240 V AC 5 AMP 100 - 120 V AC 10 AMP

INTERNAL POWER SUPPLY - A 110/240V AC INPUT CONNECTOR

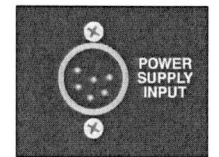

POWER SUPPLY INPUT

EXTERNAL POWER SUPPLY - A LOW VOLTAGE DC MULTIPIN CONNECTOR

it behind when you pack up after the gig. It's a real nuisance to have to drive back the next day and pick it up!!

## Multipin Connectors

❿ Larger mixing consoles for touring systems often have multipin connectors so that all the multicore snake lines can be plugged in at once, saving a lot of time and ensuring error free repeatability.

Well, that's all the connections you need to get the system happening. All mixers are a little different, and there may well be more holes in the rear panel; if you can't work out what they are, then look them up in the Owner's Manual!

MIC IN

LINE IN

INSERT

DIRECT OUT (LINE OUT)

AUX 1 OUT (EFFECT OUT)

AUX 2 OUT (MON. OUT)

AUX 1 RETURN (EFFECT RET)

GROUP 1 OUT

GROUP 1 INSERT

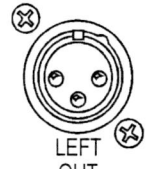

LEFT OUT

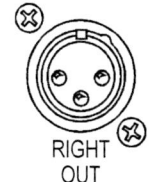

RIGHT OUT

## Digital Mixers

Digital audio for live sound is like a runaway train - it's unstoppable, and it's heading into the station right now! We already have digital effects units – delay, reverb, pitch shifting etc, plus digital signal processors - crossovers, equalizers and more, but Digital Mixers are finally reaching a point where they can take on Analog for Live Sound use.

### What's the difference?

Both Analog and Digital mixers are essentially control surfaces. The difference is that an analog mixer has one knob or switch per function per channel. Everything that the desk can control is right there in front of you - all the time.

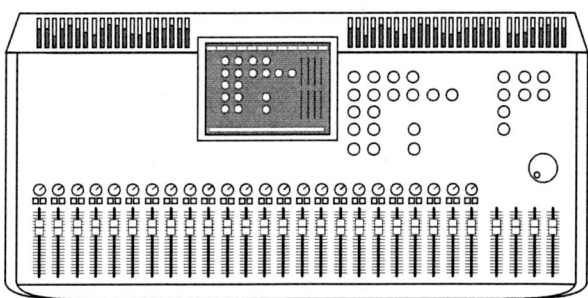

Digital mixers look a lot different. The only similarity with analog is a row of faders across the bottom edge. There are a lot less knobs, one or more computer screens, sometimes a computer keyboard, and maybe even a mouse!

Since digital mixers are an emerging technology, the major problem from a user point of view is the lack of a Common User Interface.

TYPICAL DIGITAL MIXER WITH METERS, FADERS, MULTI-PURPOSE CONTROLS AND ON-SCREEN DISPLAY

> *Instant access to all parameters is what keeps analog mixer manufacturers in business!*

No matter which analog mixer you walk up to, they all have Gain knobs, EQ knobs, Aux send knobs, bus routing switches, whatever. As a general rule if you've used one you can use any of them. Soundcraft, Midas, Allen & Heath, Yamaha, Mackie - they may move the channel EQ section up here or the Aux section down here, but they're all still there. **Instant access to all parameters is what keeps analog mixer manufacturers in business!**

Not so with digital. Each manufacturer has their own idea of what channel functions should be shown, and what should be hidden one or more menu layers down. Some previous knowledge of the type of digital mixer is pretty well essential if you expect to walk up to it and start mixing.

It's a similar situation to the way PCs were before Windows came along. Love it or hate it, it has at least provided an initial universal look and feel that enables most people to sit down and find their way around any program without reading a 400 page manual first!

### Multi purpose controls

This screen, or display, is the heart of the digital mixer, and shows different aspects of the system depending on which choices you make. Compared to an analog mixer, digital mixers look sparsely populated with knobs.

They will usually have just one actual set of channel controls, one set of group controls, one set of master controls. Along the bottom is a row of faders, each with a corresponding Input Gain control.

The one set of channel controls, for example, are used for every channel - you select which channel you want to use them for, it comes up on the screen, you physically turn the appropriate knobs, and these changes are applied onscreen.

For an input channel, the screen might initially show an overview of everything

ACTUAL CONTROLS AND ON-SCREEN VIRTUAL CONTROLS

to do with the channel. If it's a touch screen, touch the appropriate icon and it will switch to, say, the EQ section. The physical knobs will now control the on-screen knobs. Touch a different icon and the Aux sends will come up onscreen, and the physical knobs will now control the on screen aux sends. Touch another icon and the Group assigns or Effects controls will come up on screen, and the same knobs will now control those.

Can we see a pattern starting to emerge here? When you have finished with that channel, you can switch to the next and go through the same process. All your changes to the previous channel will be saved and applied, and the physical knobs will now control the next channel you've chosen to work on. The same process applies to the groups, and the masters. All the controls, switches and functions you'd expect on an analog desk are still there, and more, but they are not necessarily all there at the one time and in the same place. It takes a bit of getting used to, but what new thing doesn't?

For example, the DiGiCo D1 Live digital mixer differs from others by having 2 channel screens and one master screen. Each screen shows eight channels, for a total of 24, controlled by the knobs at the side of and below the screen. Touch the top of each onscreen channel and the knobs will control that channel and update its screenview. It is, perhaps, the most 'analog' of the digital mixers and many engineers find it an easy one to change to.

### *Default settings*

Luckily, when you switch a digital mixer on, you're not faced with a totally blank operating surface with nothing set up. They all have one or more default settings all ready to go, so that a lot of the intial setup is done for you. Pick the default that is closest to your needs, and then start modifying it to suit your particular setup. When it's the way you like it, save it, so that it can be your setup if you need it again.

For example, on a DiGiCo: On the Master screen, touch Session Files, then Load Session, then Projects, choose the template.ses file, then Load. The process is similar for any of the digital desks - Yamaha, InnovaSon, Mackie and probably many more soon.

If you know you're going to be using a specific digital mixer, I'd advise downloading a copy of the Owner's Manual from the manufacturer's website and studying it hard, so your learning curve at the gig will be much easier.

For this reason you'll often see digital mixers on large scale concerts featuring multiple bands and artists. Each band can have their own complete desk setup saved to the mixer's memory, making band changeovers much faster and less troublesome. When your band is up next, you just restore your settings from the afternoon's (or the day before's) soundcheck, and you're all set to mix.

### *Layers*

Many digital desks work in layers, or pages, or scenes. You might have only 24 faders across the bottom, even though the mixer has 48, 60 or more Inputs. Push a button, though, and those 24 faders now control a different layer/page of 24 channels. The settings - EQ, Gain, Aux sends, Bus routing - that you were using on your original 24 channels have been saved and are still working, but your faders can setup and control another 24.

However, now you have to remember which layer that booming conga drum mic was on, switch to it, pull up the channel settings for it, and adjust it. Not as fast as reaching out for the Lo Mid control on the channel marked Percussion/Conga on an analog mixer.

On the other hand, having every knob, switch, fader and associated expensive circuitry there all the time means that you might need a 56 channel console, even though you'll only ever use 24 mic channels at any one time.

For example, although our booming conga drum might only ever be used on the one song, it

=**"**=
*Luckily you're not faced with a totally blank operating surface*
=**"**=

still needs to have its own channel even if it's only getting hit three times and not used again for the whole show. On a digital console, that channel can be the conga (with special conga effects and EQ!) just for that song. It can then be routed back to be the cowbell or guest guitarist or anything, along with any specific EQ setting, for the next song.

What's more, all this can be saved and used again next time. All the parameters on every channel on every song can usually be copied to a plug in PC card or a removable USB drive, then taken away with you, plugged in and brought up again for the next night's show!

***This* is what keeps digital console manufacturers in business!** It will also keep promoters in business, because if you happen to step under a bus on the way to the show that night, another engineer can step in, pull up your settings and get the show going while you relax in intensive care! (We'll let the lawyers work out who actually owns your mix!)

Having the ability to control lots of channels from the one small footprint surface can mean that the space on the rear panel gets a little crowded for all those XLR inputs, and so there are multipin connectors (like analog consoles) to save space, or even connections for a digital multicore snake *(See Chapter 4: Cables and Connectors).*

A digital console can also let you halve or maybe throw away your effects rack! Depending on the size of the console, it will most likely have compressors and gates available for every channel and possibly outputs as well. The settings for them will come up on the display screen, which you then control with a set of knobs laid out in the same way as the onscreen display.

Likewise for Effects, like Delay and Reverb, which can be called up and modified with real and virtual knobs, or nudge buttons like external effects units. Since most of these are already digital, it makes sense to include the circuitry in the mixer. Of course, you can still have your favourite Widgetron and run in and out of it as you would on an analog desk.

Digital mixers are an emerging technology, and will be subject to a lot of change until they are at the same level of Common User Interface as Analog ones. Learn to love them, because they're here to stay!

*Saving and repeating settings is what keeps digital console manufacturers in business!*

### Mixers Quick Reference

☑ Make sure the Channels are switched ON and the EQ switched IN

☑ Make sure the Groups are selected and switched ON

☑ If you're suddenly faced with a 56 channel monster console and you've only used a 12 channel before, don't panic. Remember it's only the same thing 56 times. Just work your way from the top of the channel down to the fader. Concentrate and be methodical - don't try and hurry too much.

☑ Allow yourself plenty of time

☑ With an unknown console, don't do anything drastic to the channel gain or the EQ until you've become familiar with the way the console sounds

☑ If in doubt - ask!

## 3      *Equalizers*

## Graphic Equalizers

A Graphic Equalizer is a giant tone control. It runs from very LOW (Bass) through to very HIGH (Treble), and covers the whole audio sound spectrum, usually agreed to be 20 Hertz (20 cycles per second) to 20 Kilohertz (20 thousand cycles per second).

Depending on its design it will have 10, 15, 30 or more slider controls which indicate the relative amount of Cut and Boost per frequency, rather like a graph; hence the name Graphic Equalizer. Or it could be digital, with nudge buttons and rows of LEDs

A 10 band Graphic EQ has 1 octave between sliders, a 15 band has $^2/_3$ of an octave between sliders, and a 31 band has $^1/_3$ of an octave between sliders. Thus the more sliders, the more accurate control you have, enabling you to target the specific frequency you want to cut or boost, and leave the rest unchanged.

Note that a third octave equalizer may not always have 31 sliders. A lot of manufacturers feel that the frequencies at each end of the scale are not ones that need a lot of control, so they leave them out. For example, a 30 band will usually leave out 20 Hz, which is generally considered subsonic (something you feel more than hear), and a 27 band will leave out the 20Hz, 25 Hz and 31.5 Hz down the LOW end, and the 20 KHz slider on the HIGH end.

Digital Graphic Equalizers can be stand-alone units, or more often as a module built into Digital Mixers or Speaker Management Systems. They have a screen with a Graphical representation of the sliders on the front panel. These virtual sliders will either be controlled by selecting the slider you want to cut or boost, then using an Up or Down arrow button to adjust it, or by pressing any of a collection of nudge buttons across the bottom of the front panel.

NUDGE
BUTTONS

### *Why do we need one?*

We need an equalizer to make what comes out of the speakers 'equal' what went in. In other words, to make sure that the sound the audience hears is not affected by the sound of the room (not too much, anyway).

Every room, or area, has a 'sound' all of its own. Different surfaces reflect or absorb different frequencies and add peaks or dips in the sound that weren't there in the original sound. These changes can cause the system to sound boomy, ringy, dead or thin. By identifying the

---

frequencies that are causing these overtones, and reducing (or increasing) them by the right amount, we can smooth out the response of the system and make it sound much more pleasant to listen to.

We can also make it louder before it feeds back, which is very useful in stage monitors.

Our diagram shows a typical 31 band Graphic Equalizer, and for our purposes it has just about every feature that you might find on one. Not every Graphic EQ will have all these features, but they will all have some of them.

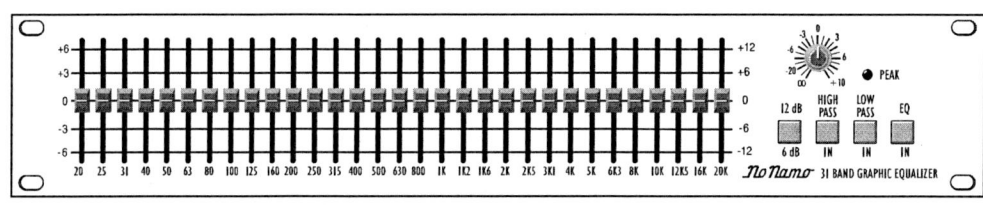

SUB/LOW    LOW MID    MIDS    HIGH MID    HIGH

### Range

This changes the maximum amount of cut and boost of each slider, from 12 or 15 dB, to 6 dB for fine tuning. This way you can have a lot of control (12 or 15 dB) for tricky monitor tuning, or more subtle EQ (6 dB) for the main speaker system.

### High Pass Filter

Also known as Low Cut, or Subsonic filter. If it is a switch, it is usually preset and rolls off frequencies from 30 - 40 Hz downwards. On some equalizers it is a knob or a slider, and the frequency is adjustable.

### Low Pass Filter

Also known as High Cut. Once again, if it is a switch, it is usually preset between 8 - 10 KHz, and rolls off frequencies above that. It may also be a knob or slider, and the frequency is adjustable.

### Bypass

EQ IN/OUT. This switch lets you make comparisons between EQ'd and Non EQ'd program.

### Peak LED (or Clip or O/Load)

This will light up when the EQ circuitry is about to overload or distort. You may need to reduce the input level slightly, and increase the gain somewhere else after the EQ (usually on a compressor or the crossover) to compensate.

### Sliders (or Faders)

These cut or boost whatever frequency is marked on them, up to the maximum as determined by the Range switch (see Range above). Use them carefully; too much cut can make the sound 'dead', and too much boost can cause feedback ringing.

### Master Level

This gives you overall level control of the signal, and can be a rotary knob or a fader. You can usually turn it right down to nothing, or very soft, and also turn it up, to +6 dB or more. This is useful if you have cut a lot of frequencies, because you'll need to bring the overall level back up to avoid overdriving the mixer.

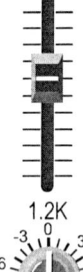

## Parametric Equalizers

### What are they?

We've already talked about quasi-parametric EQ on the channels of the mixing console, but these also come as stand alone units.

On a parametric Equalizer you can control *all* the parameters - the frequency, the amount of cut or boost of that frequency, and the bandwidth (Q), which can be adjusted as wide as, say, 3 octaves, to as narrow as 1/20th octave. This means two things:

TYPICAL PARAMETRIC EQ CONTROLS

1. You can effect a broad frequency band cut or boost - all the Mids up a little, centred around a particular frequency, for example.

2. You can zero in on a required frequency more exactly than you could on a Graphic Equalizer. For example, if 2.8K is troublesome, you pull that frequency alone out. This is known as notch filtering.

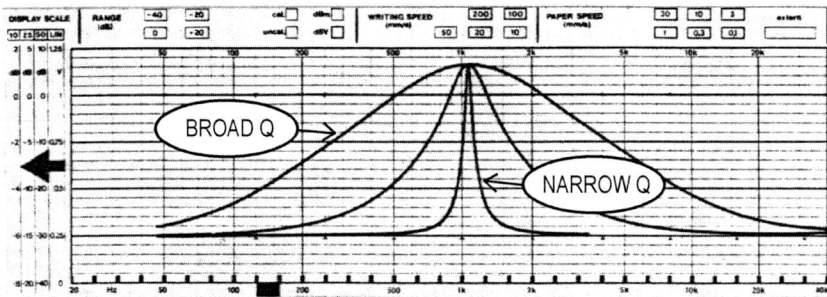

PARAMETRIC RESPONSE CURVES, CENTRED AROUND 1 KHZ

A narrow Q, signified by the symbol ⋀ , mean the frequencies either side of the one being cut or boosted remain unaffected. Only the one you have chosen is changed.

A broader Q, signified by ⌒ or ⋀ means that the cut or boost is spread over a wider range of frequencies, centred around the one you've dialled up.

Some parametrics have 3, 4, 5 or 6 sections, each either dedicated to a range of frequencies or able to be used over any frequency range. You will often find parametric EQs in monitor systems, inserted on each send, pulling out troublesome frequencies in the monitors.

### How do you use one?

To find a frequency you want to lose on a parametric, set up about 6 dB of cut, set the Q (Bandwidth) on medium, and slowly sweep the frequency control around until you hear the problem frequency disappear. Fine tune the cut and the Q until *only* the problem frequency has been pulled out.

A parametric equalizer offers the most accurate degree of control over the sound, which is why you will find them used in the most demanding situations. They are not difficult to use, with practice. If you can come to grips with the sweepable mid range controls on mixing consoles, then there's no reason why you shouldn't be able to handle a parametric EQ.

## Other EQ Tools

### Feedback Eliminators

Feedback Eliminators are digital signal processing devices that automatically hunt down feedback. They are automatic parametric equalizers that isolate the particular frequency that is feeding back and pull it out completely. Like most things in audio, some do it a lot better than others, and mixing engineers either love them or hate them, but they can really save your reputation on troublesome awards nights and corporate presentations..

SABINE 2400 FEEDBACK EXTERMINATOR. YOU'LL PROBABLY COME ACROSS THE EARLIER 2020 DUAL CHANNEL UNIT, AND MANY OTHER PRODUCTS WITH A SIMILAR CIRCUIT BUILT IN

The Sabine FBX Feedback Exterminator is a typical unit, with a patented circuit that works very fast.  It has filters that are one tenth of an octave wide, compared to one third of an octave on a 30 or 31 band Graphic EQ, so it has less of an effect on the overall sound.

### How do you get it to work?

Each model is different, but here are some general rules.

1. Set the microphones up as you would normally.
2. Adjust the Graphic Equalizer so that the system sounds the way you think it should. Don't pull out any feedback frequencies.
3. Push in the setup switch for a few seconds.
4. Gradually start to push up the master faders. As each feedback ring appears, the FBX will identify it and pull it down until the feedback stops.
5. Keep going until all the feedback rings (up to 9 on this Sabine) have been eliminated.

The FBX unit will leave an extra 3 filters floating to pull out any further feedback rings as they occur. For example, if the performer with a microphone walks in front of a speaker box it will pull out the inevitable squeal, and then go back to normal once they have moved away from the speaker.

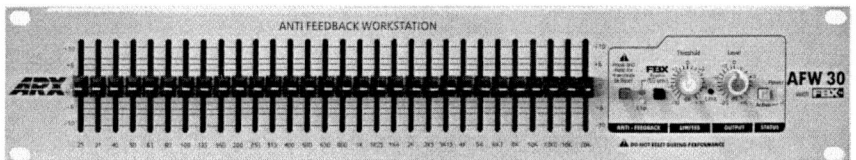

Feedback eliminators are made by several companies including Sabine, dbx, Shure; and ARX make the Anti Feedback Workstation, which combines an FBX module, a 30 band Graphic EQ, and a peak limiter all in the one package. Many of the digital equalizers on the market have some form of feedback elimination built in.

## Equalizers with Feedback indication

These are a combination of a simple analyzer (see below) and a Graphic EQ. Each EQ fader has an LED above it that lights up if that frequency is feeding back.

### How do you use it?

Use it as you would any other Graphic Equalizer. If you hear a feedback ring, and one of the LEDs lights up, pull down that frequency just enough to stop the ring. Don't be heavy handed - any more cut than is necessary will put a big hole in the sound at that particular frequency.

## Digital Graphic Equalizers

There are a few of these around as stand-alone units, from Klark Teknik, Ashly and others. Unlike analog EQs, there is no common interface or layout for any of them. They're all different, so if you come across one, you'll need to read its manual from cover to cover and to have used one before to be able to do much with it! They are popular in installed systems because their complexity makes them less likely to be fiddled with!

As I mentioned at the start of this chapter, though, they are becoming more common as a module in digital mixers and loudspeaker management systems.

## Onboard EQ

Many smaller mixers have a basic Graphic Equalizer already onboard. It is usually 5, 7 or 9 band depending on the quality and price of the mixer.

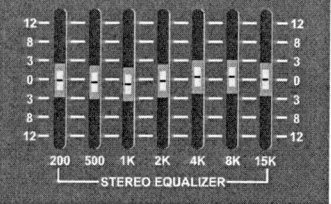

Should you use it? Well, if you have a fair idea of what you should be doing, it's better than nothing. However it's worse than doing nothing if you don't!

My feeling is that no EQ is better than bad EQ, especially if the band has had a go at it! A reasonable vocal-only speaker system, setup correctly, should be able to deliver a good sound without the aid of the onboard EQ. In smaller systems you need all the power that you can get, and poor EQ settings can rob you of valuable system range and dynamics.

The problem with them is that each fader covers too much of the audio spectrum to successfully pull out a feedback ring without pulling down a lot of frequencies either side.

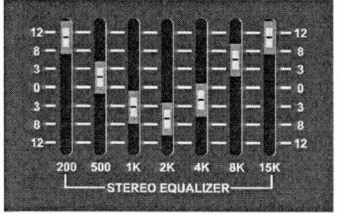

The end result is less volume and a 'dead' sound. For example, the very common settings on the right will suck all the life out of the vocals, but waste power trying to boost lower frequencies that small systems just can't handle without a Sub or two.

COMMON ONBOARD EQ CURVE
SET BY THE BAND!

If you're setting up a small vocal-only system, then using the onboard EQ with small (1-2dB or less) adjustments should be fine. Paying careful attention to the microphone placement will probably be a more worthwhile use of your time.

Just remember that it's just not possible for a 7 band EQ to have the resolution of a third octave (28 - 31 band) Graphic Equalizer, which is essential if you are miking up a complete band and need to do some surgical EQ tweaking.

## Spectrum Analyzer

Also known as Real Time Analyzers, or RTA's, these are very sophisticated devices, using rows of LEDs to give you a visual indication of the sound. Like Graphic EQs they are usually available in 28 to 31 band (1/3 octave) versions.

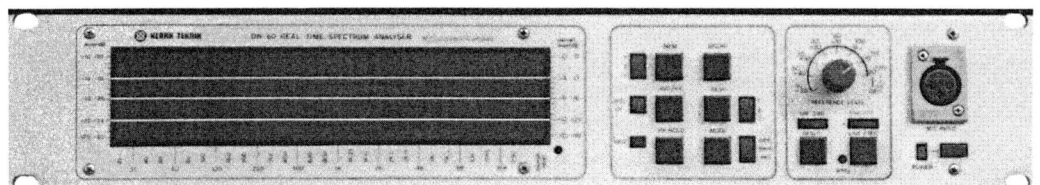

*Each fader covers too much of the audio spectrum, resulting in less volume*

An analyzer listens to the sound through its own microphone, and displays the exact level of each frequency that it hears.

### Why do we need one?

Well, your aim is to get the sound of the room and the system acoustically flat, removing all the peaks and dips in their combined response. Then, and only then, can you start to 'colour' the sound to the way you like to hear it. The analyzer is a useful tool for finding those peaks and dips quickly, so you can get to work faster.

The 28 to 31 band models are fairly expensive and come in hand held versions and rack mounted. Like most things in life, you get what you pay for. The best of them will have memories to store readings for later comparison, variable attack times, peak hold function, and 1, 2 or 3 dB settings. This last feature will give you a super accurate reading at 1 dB steps, and a more general reading at 3 dB steps, which is similar to the way your ears would hear things.

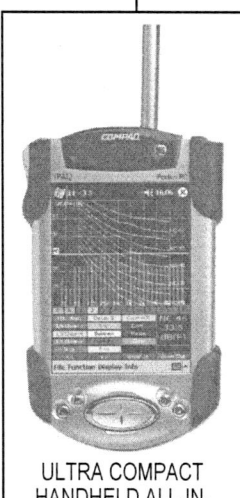

ULTRA COMPACT HANDHELD ALL-IN-ONE UNIT FROM IVIE

As an alternative to a rack mount unit, many of the audio recording/editing programs have a spectrum analyzer already built in. If you have a laptop computer that you take along to gigs, then by loading a program such as Sound Forge and a small amount of work you can get it to act as one for your sound system. Just make sure you have an XLR-to-minijack adapter lead so you can plug one of your vocal microphones into it.

## Setting up the Equalizer (Room Tuning)

Your main mix equalizer is the interface between the sound of the system and the sound of the room. Ideally it should be used to correct the room response, but in many cases it is used to correct deficiencies in the sound system as well.

Theoretical sound considerations are fine for the studio, because a studio is usually a near perfect acoustic environment.

A live gig, on the other hand, is about as far from a perfect acoustic environment as you can get. Drastic problems call for drastic solutions, and pretty quickly, too. There is no rolling the tape back in live sound! A polished hardwood stage with mirrors all around and a loud band playing on it is going to call for some pretty harsh EQ if the singer is ever going to hear himself or be heard by the audience. And, if he can't hear himself, no matter what the reason, you're going to get the blame!

Highly polished stages and dance floors, hard brick walls, galvanized iron roofing; combine these with a system that will often have a few good peaks of its own, and if you haven't got your EQ skills together you'd better hope and pray for a good sized crowd to help soak up some of that boom and bounce.

### Basic Room EQ methods

1. Plug a microphone into the console of the same type as the lead vocals, flatten out the EQ on that channel, put the microphone on a stand somewhere around the middle of the room, facing the stacks, pull down all the other channel levels, set the master L/R outputs at about -10dB, and bring up the channel level slowly. As the howls and squeals start to appear, bring down the appropriate sliders on the main equalizer. Keep going until you have the level you need.

This 'ringing out' method is very popular, because it works, but is prone to over EQing, leaving you with a PA that won't feed back, sure, but it won't sound any good either.

*Place mic slightly to one side of centre*

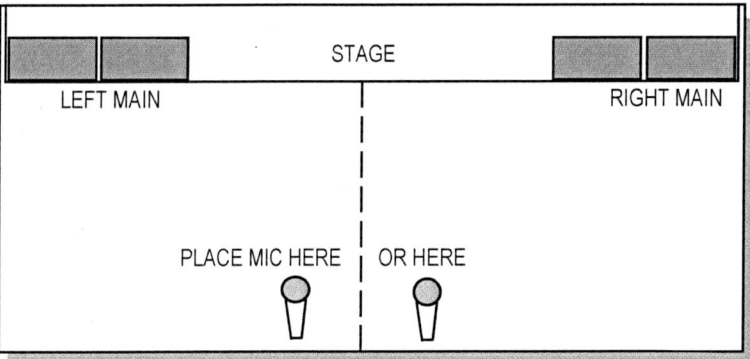

Remember that your microphones **won't** be out in front of the speaker stacks, they'll be behind them, and thus not quite so susceptible to setting up feedback squeals. ***Only pull the EQ sliders down just enough to stop the squeals***, or you'll take all the life out of the sound. Keep this one handy for monitor tuning, too.

2. Grab our microphone off the stand from method #1, and go "CHECK ONE - TWO" into it. Repeat this as you adjust the EQ sliders until you have a good crisp voice sound from the system, with plenty of 'punch' to it. I know these descriptions might be undefinable, but I'm confident that you'll know it when you hear it! Be alert for any honks or rings that hang on during or after your words, as these are the frequencies that are going to cause trouble.

3. Play a CD that you are very familiar with, and adjust the house EQ until the music sounds the way you think it should. Be very critical, and use the same CD and the same songs from them every night, until you know its sound inside out.

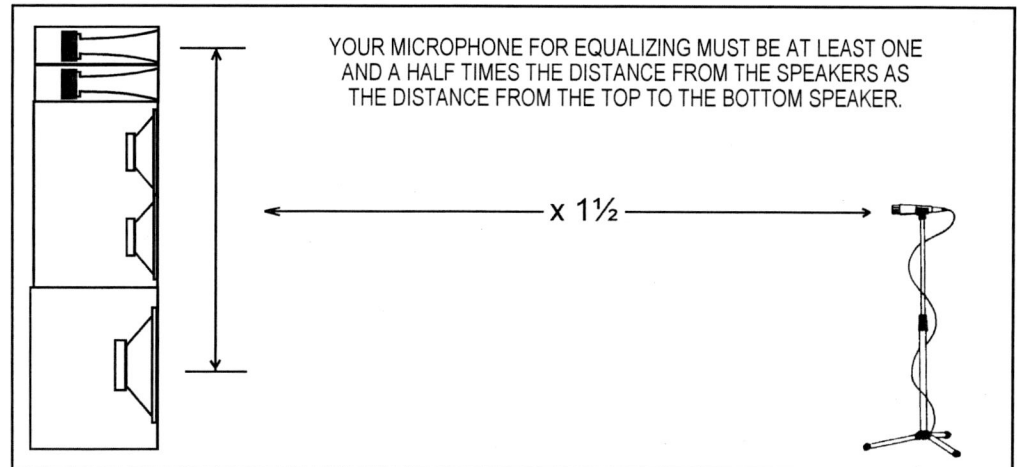

YOUR MICROPHONE FOR EQUALIZING MUST BE AT LEAST ONE AND A HALF TIMES THE DISTANCE FROM THE SPEAKERS AS THE DISTANCE FROM THE TOP TO THE BOTTOM SPEAKER.

x 1½

4. For this method you'll need a pink noise generator. This is a gadget that gives you equal amounts of each frequency from 20 Hz to 20 KHz. They either come together with a spectrum analyzer or you can make or buy one.

Put the microphone back into the same position as method #1, and bring up its level to just under feedback. Plug the pink noise generator into a channel, check that it's running OK, then switch the channel Off. Bring up its fader, switch the channel On for a split second and then Off again. You will clearly hear the room overtones hanging on for quite a while after the original signal stops. Locate the appropriate sliders on the EQ and adjust them until the 'hang on' is reduced as much as possible. Keep going until you have the microphone level you need.

The advantage of this method is that it simulates the way the room will sound when it's full of loud music, and isn't that what you really want to know?

5. A spectrum analyzer with a pink noise generator is the basis of this next method. With our microphone still in position #1, run some pink noise into the system as in #4, and read the response on your analyzer. If it is full of peaks and dips, adjust the corresponding sliders on your EQ until you get close to a straight line of dots along the 0 or centre line. The straighter the line, the flatter the response. And the flatter the response, the less chance of feedback squeals.

If you can't get close to a straight line, try adjusting the levels on the crossover first, **then** adjust the EQ. For example, if all of the low frequencies are way above the centre line, reduce the level of the low frequency crossover output until the line of LEDs hovers around the centre line - some above, some below. Then you can adjust the EQ to get a flatter response.

Although analyzers usually come with their own microphone, I like to use the same microphone that the lead singer does to run this sort of test, since this is the mic that is going to have the most gain applied to it. This gives you the most accurate picture of how the room, this microphone and the PA system will interact.

Two things here: One, if you've used the singer's microphone, don't forget to put it back!

And two, don't forget to unplug the microphone cable you've been using from the console and *plug the multicore snake channel back in.*

## Speaker Management Units

Digital mixers and digital speaker management units often have third octave qualization modules built in. When you run through the Setup program on a dbx DriveRack, for example, it will automatically analyze and tune the room for you if you plug a microphone into it. You can also override the settings with your own personal tweaks once it has have finished.

The dbx and other units also have a feedback eliminator module built in as well, which you

= *" =*
*Don't forget to plug the multicore snake channel back in*
= *" =*

can set up at the same time. For more on these units, see *Chapter 8 - Crossovers.*

When you are using any of these tools, remember what is acoustically flat to a microphone is not particularly musical to the human ear, and will sound a bit light in the LOW end and lacking sparkle in the HIGH end. Human hearing is most sensitive in the 3 to 4 KHz range (MIDs) and gets progressively less sensitive the higher or lower you go *(See Equal Loudness Contours, page 175)*

**A flat response is a starting point only.**

Always let your ears be the final judge of the best sound - that's what they are there for.

An analyzer is a good slave but a poor master, and not many of them buy tickets to see concerts!

### So where do you start?

I'd suggest using a combination of methods 1, 2 and 3, coupled with a LOT of practice in listening to sounds and picking the right frequency on the equalizer. There is no shortcut for this; it's just one of those things you have to learn.

### EQ'ing the Monitors *(See also Chapter 11 - Monitors)*

All of these methods work for monitors, but I'd suggest using methods 1 and 2 for tuning monitors quickly. They will instantly show you where the problem areas are, so you can pull them down on the graphics.

You'll find that tuning monitors frequently requires a heavier hand on the sliders, so you can remove as much chance of feedback as possible. With lead vocal, the microphone position rarely stays constant, so your EQ has to cope with the microphone often getting closer to the speakers than you'd prefer!

EQ'ing the monitors is the one area of mixing that people often have the most trouble with, so see also the troubleshooting section in *Chapter 14 - Problems.*

*Start with a combination of 1, 2, and 3 and LOTS of practice*

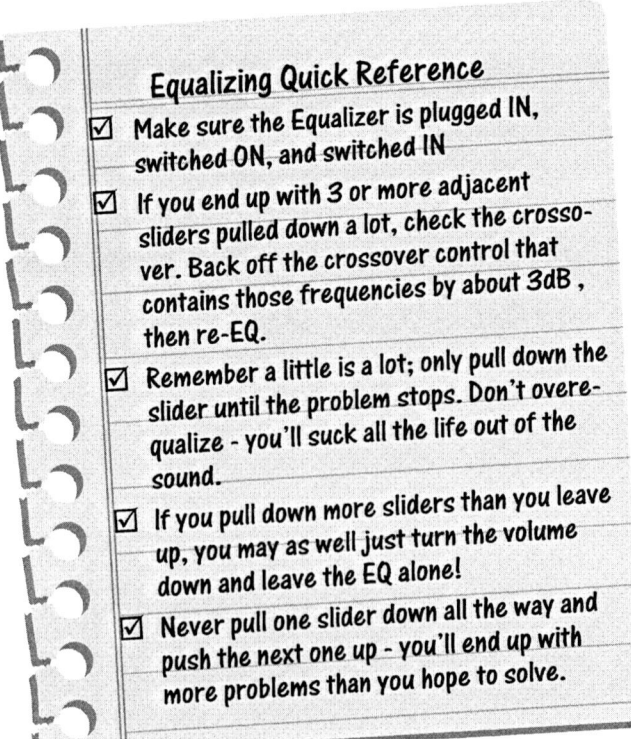

**Equalizing Quick Reference**

☑ Make sure the Equalizer is plugged IN, switched ON, and switched IN

☑ If you end up with 3 or more adjacent sliders pulled down a lot, check the crossover. Back off the crossover control that contains those frequencies by about 3dB, then re-EQ.

☑ Remember a little is a lot; only pull down the slider until the problem stops. Don't over-equalize - you'll suck all the life out of the sound.

☑ If you pull down more sliders than you leave up, you may as well just turn the volume down and leave the EQ alone!

☑ Never pull one slider down all the way and push the next one up - you'll end up with more problems than you hope to solve.

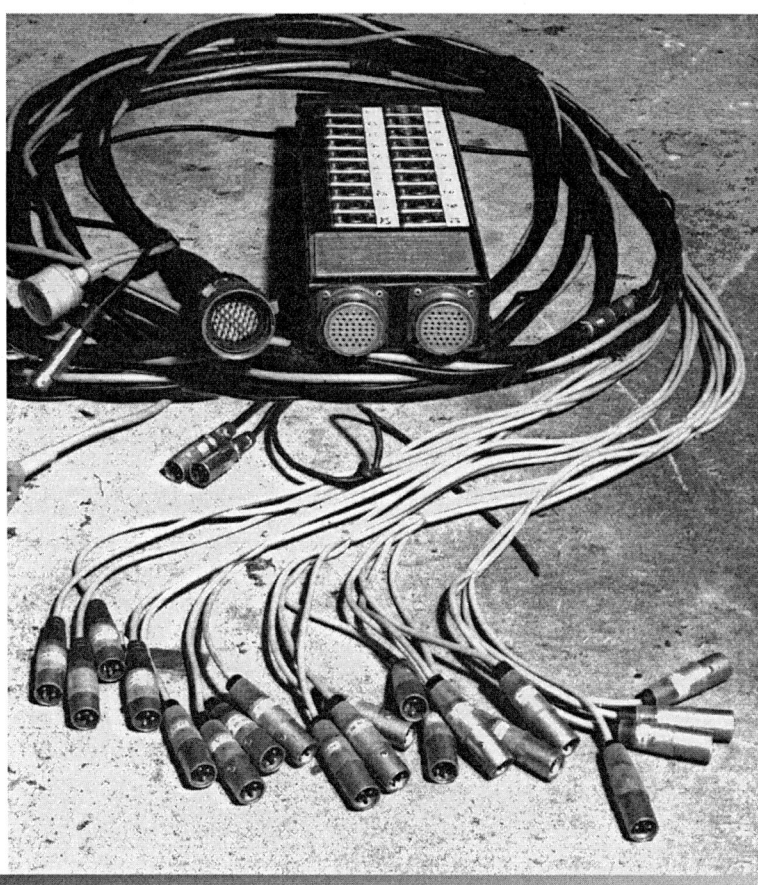

## 4     *Cables and Connectors*

### Lead Me To It

Lead and cables connect the whole system together, and faulty ones are the curse of the live sound business. They will all break down sooner or later, in strict accordance with Murphy's Law, but with reasonable care in their handling it can be much later rather than sooner. So the first thing to learn is:

### *How to coil up a lead*

**Rule #1:**

*"Never loop leads of any kind over your arm and elbow."* There are several ways that you can wind up leads safely, and the following is one of the most common.

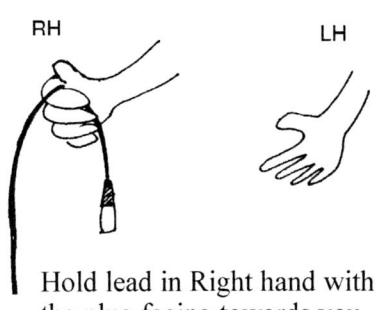

Hold lead in Right hand with the plug facing towards you.

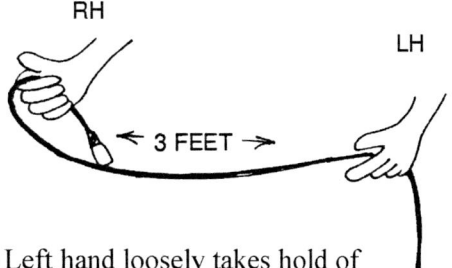

The Left hand loosely takes hold of the lead in front of the Right hand and slides along the lead until the hands are about 3 feet (1 metre) apart.

=❛❛=
*Never loop leads of any kind over your arm and elbow*
=❜❜=

---

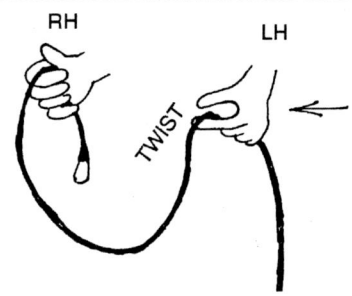

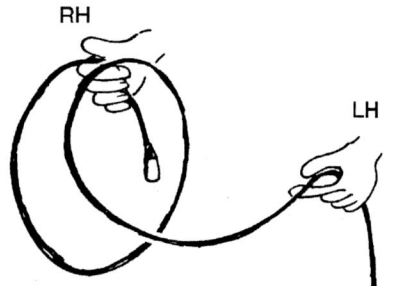

Hold the lead between the thumb and first finger of the Left hand and bring it towards the Right hand, giving the lead a small twist away from you as you do it.

Loop it up in the Right hand next to the existing lead and start again.

Sounds very complicated, but get someone to show you once and it's so straightforward that you'll never forget it. You'll also find that the lead has a particular way it wants to wind up, so try to follow what the lead wants to do. ***Don't force it***.

When all the lead is looped up in the Right hand, tie the loose end around the looped up lead in a very light half hitch knot. ***Not too tight*** - just enough to hold it all together. Alternatively you might use some Velcro or similar cable ties, which are permanently attached to one end (usually the male) then goes around the looped up cable and sticks to itself. Pull it apart to undo it.

Finally, put it in the leads case and find another.

Look after all your leads like this, and you lessen the chances of them dying on you at a crucial time.

### The Multicore Snake

This is the thick cable that runs all your microphone lines down to the mixer, and your outputs back up to the amplifiers. It is the system's lifeline, and you must look after it. Treat it very gently, let it coil up the way it wants to. Don't force it to coil up against the way that it wants to. Even a couple of non working lines in it can cause severe problems at the gig.

When you are packing up the snake, put the stage box end in first and start to lay the cable out in the bottom of the case in the biggest loop you can make. If it doesn't want to go one way, halve the loop size and make a figure-of-eight pattern until it starts to lay flat again. Continue looping it until it is all in the case. Don't tie any knots in it; just let it lie there. Don't try to loop it up on your arm; it's not good for it and it gets very heavy.

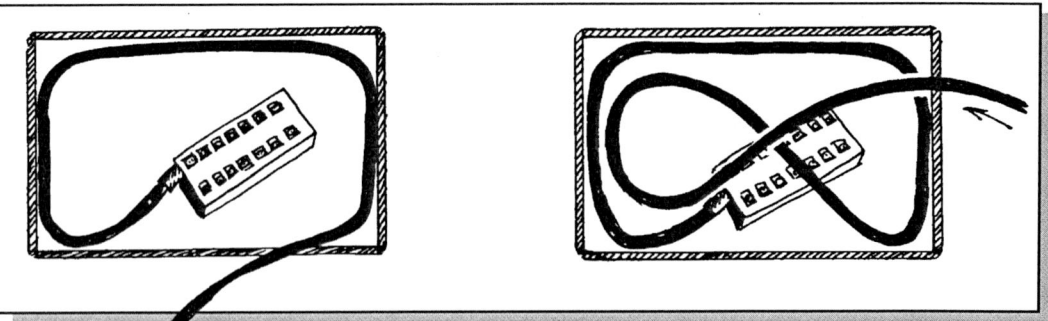

Although the multicore snake looks very thick and strong, in reality it is a lot of very thin leads. It consists of individually shielded multiple pairs of cables, and is known as 12 pair,

20 pair, 32 pair and so on. All these individual leads are sheathed in a thick layer of plastic for protection.

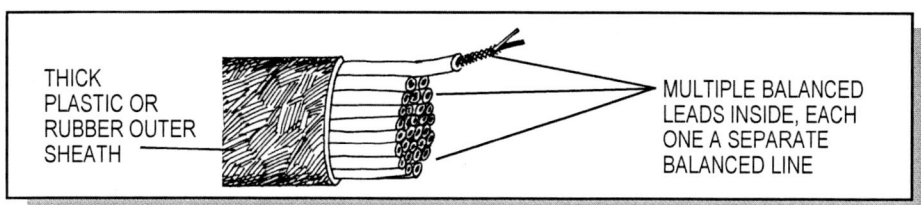

At one end the snake is connected to the stage box, either permanently or with a multi pin connector that enables the stage box to be disconnected for packing. This stops the cable being strained where it joins the stage box.

Just make sure you *remember to pack the stage box as well!*

The other end is fanned out into tails, each with a male XLR connector on it, that plugs into each channel on the mixing console. When you are plugging these in to the , make sure the weight of the cable is supported. Don't let the whole weight of the cable dangle from one connector, or you'll have problems when that one little solder joint gives way.

If you are fond of speedy setups, you could tape a separate pair of long microphone leads to the multicore snake as main Left and Right sends to the power amplifiers.

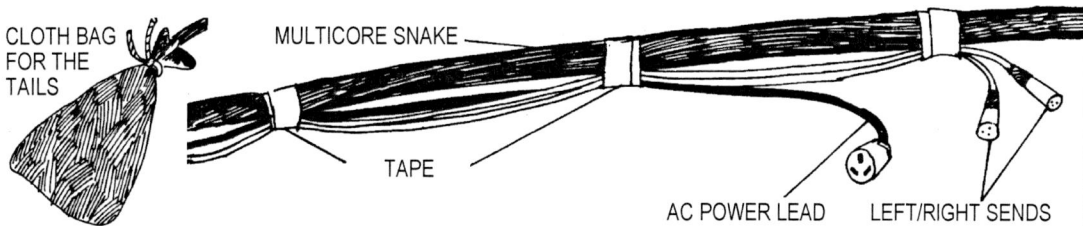

Purists will throw their hands up in horror, but since the mixer and the effects rack must be on the same AC power Earth/Ground as the rest of the system, you could also *loosely* tape a long power cable to the multicore snake as well. If you find it induces a lot of hum, well just untape it and don't do it again! Personally, though, I've done it for years with no problems at all. It's up to you.

Just remember to have the power cable turned around the right way! Socket at the mixer end, plug at the other. Its a lot of retaping if you get it wrong!

When you are packing up after the gig, don't just pull on the snake if it snags on something. Connectors often get stuck under table legs or chairs, and if you jerk on it, it could just rip away from its tail. A cloth bag that ties around the fan of tails is a good idea - it keeps the beer and post gig gunge out of them.

## Digital Multicores

Just as consoles are becoming digital, so are snakes, although they aren't multiple cores anymore. A single optical fibre or computer networking cable can carry all the necessary information down to the console, with an Analog to Digital converter at the stage end, and a Digital to Analog converter at the mixer end. If it's running to a digital console, then it doesn't need any converting. Some systems also have the pre-amps at the on-stage end, with the gain being remotely controlled from the mixer.

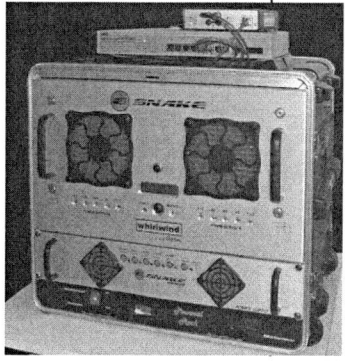

Their advantages include noise rejection, and light weight, so a fail-safe spare can be run alongside and still weigh less than a standard type. The disadvantages are high cost (although that is rapidly coming down) and proprietary interfaces, which can cause compatibility problems.

At the time of writing the analog multicore snake is the industry standard for analog mixers, but digital snakes are the logical interface for digital mixers.

## Signal Connectors

3 pin XLR type connectors, made by Cannon, Amphenol, Switchcraft, Neutrik and every second factory in China, are the industry standard.

They come in 2 sexes - Male and Female.

The male has 3 pins that stick out; the female has 3 holes that receive these pins.

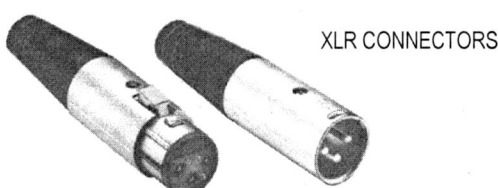 XLR CONNECTORS

**Rule #2 -** *"The male sends an Output signal, the female receives an Input signal."*

On **all** equipment, the males are the Outputs and the females are the Inputs - mixing consoles, crossovers, effects units, processors, from the biggest board down to your favourite Widgetron.

The microphone has a male output on it which plugs into the female end of a microphone lead. The other end of the lead has a male connector on it which plugs into the female connector on the stage box...and so on.

However, you may see on some equipment a Male connector next to the Input also marked as Input. This is not breaking the rule, but it enables a lead to be run from one Input to another when slaving up multiples of things.

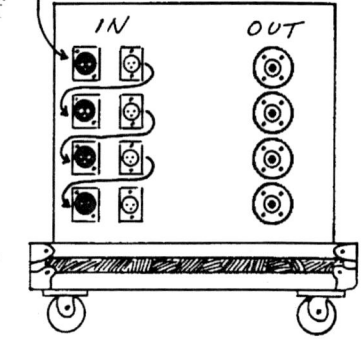

For Example: An amp rack may have 2 stereo amps in it, which is 4 separate amps. To get access to all 4 amps your rack needs 4 female Inputs. If you wanted to run the same signal to all of these amps you would have to make up a special splitter lead with 4 male Outputs wired together on it.

The easy way is to wire a male connector next to each female, so you can run an ordinary short microphone lead (a 'patch' lead) from one amp to the next. No special leads required that could get lost, and a very flexible set up.

### *Exception - Schools*

Someone who does a lot of school PA installations told me that many schools reverse this rule and the fixed microphone inputs up on the school stage are often male connectors. Why? Because it's easier to dig the chewing gum out of them! True!

### *Other Signal Connectors*

The common Mono ¼(6.5mm) Guitar/Phone jack plug (Tip +, Sleeve – and Ground) is also a common connectors, especially on signal processors and effects units.

The Stereo version (Tip +, Ring – and Sleeve Ground) is often used for insert points on mixers, but wired up as Tip In, Ring Out and Sleeve Ground. There is no standard for this so you will find on some mixers Tip is Out and Ring is In.

*From the biggest console down to your favourite Widgetron*

The Phono/RCA type connector is also common as a connector for external music sources - CD/DVD players, tape decks and similar items. These connectors work best on systems that are set up only once, like installations, as they are very fragile and will fail very quickly if they are continually pulled in and out each night.

The latest connector to make an appearance in Pro Audio is the ⅛" (3.5mm) stereo jack as found on MP3 players, Apple iPods, laptop computers and similar consumer units. This can be even more fragile than the RCA connector, but is a de facto standard on the above units, and a couple of sets of adapter leads to either XLR or Phone jacks will be a useful thing to have when someone brings their backing tracks up to you on one of these players.

## Speaker Connectors

In the past, 3 pin XLR connectors were a common choice for speaker cables as well as signal leads. But they weren't the best choice:

1. Speaker boxes and speaker cables in general don't get the pampered life of a microphone lead, and so they frequently worked loose, the latches broke, and they stoppped making a strong tight connection.

2. For safety. No matter which protocol you are using for leads, you always have the signal going from a male connector into a female one. At the low signal levels *before* the amplifier, this is quite safe. But at amplifier levels it can be dangerous, as anyone who's tried to connect up an amplifier in the dark while kneeling in a puddle of beer will agree. Any faults in the AC Safety Earth/Grounding and *ZP* - *you're* the Ground!

A multipin connector like the Cannon/Amphenol EP and AP series was the answer to #1. These look like an XLR on steroids, with larger bodies and fatter pins, and handle much more current.

But as far as #2 - safety, well they have the same problems as XLRs.

The answer is the Speakon connector, from Neutrik. These have been designed from the start to be used as a speaker connector, coming in 2, 4 pin and 8 pin models. They are made from Nylon/Plastic, with no bare terminals at all.

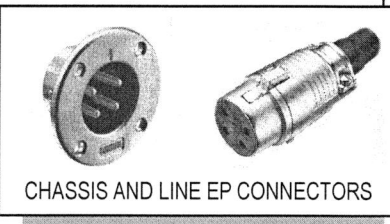

CHASSIS AND LINE EP CONNECTORS

You'll recognise them when you see them because when connected up they look like something off your garden hose! The only thing you have to remember when using them is to twist them to the right after you push it into the connector on the amplifier or speaker box.

The earlier versions had a locking ring which you also twisted to lock the connector in. The later versions have a push button lock similar to an XLR type connector. Luckily for us, the two versions are compatible.

More and more speaker cabinets are being fitted with Speakon connectors as standard, because they're cheap, strong and safe.

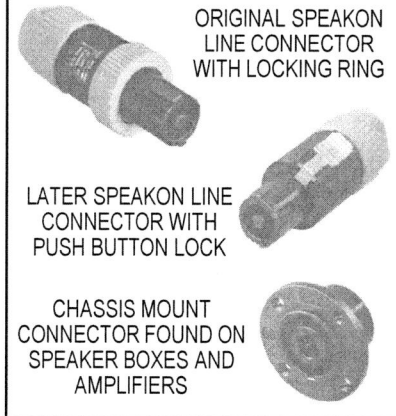

ORIGINAL SPEAKON LINE CONNECTOR WITH LOCKING RING

LATER SPEAKON LINE CONNECTOR WITH PUSH BUTTON LOCK

CHASSIS MOUNT CONNECTOR FOUND ON SPEAKER BOXES AND AMPLIFIERS

*See Chapter 15 – Appendix*, for popular pin connections on XLR, EP/AP and Speakon connectors

## Shielded cable and speaker cable

There are two different types of cable used in leads:

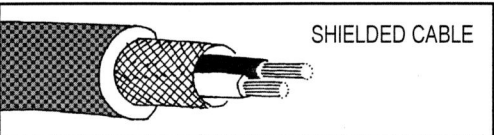

1. Shielded cable, which has wire braid around the outside, and one or two wires running down the inside; and

2. Speaker cable, which has two thick copper or steel wires side by side.

Both cables can look similar from the outside, since they are sheathed in heavy duty plastic or rubber. They are definitely *not* interchangeable.

**Rule #3:** (Burn this one into your mind, because it is really important)

> *"You can only use speaker cable between the amplifier outputs and the speakers. Nowhere else!"*

**Every** lead that comes *before* the amplifiers must be made from shielded cable, and preferably be Balanced (see next section). From the longest microphone lead to the shortest patch lead, you *must* use shielded cable.

This also applies to any leads that the band use to plug into their amplifiers. Keyboard racks, guitar racks, drum machine setups - check their wiring carefully.

If you don't use shielded cable, you will let all sorts of electrical noise get into the system, and also R.F.I. (Radio Frequency Interference). This will play havoc with any wireless microphones you may be using, and can also mix CB radio, TV and taxis in with the band!

Worse still, excessive RFI can severely damage amplifiers and High Frequency horn drivers.

### Balanced and Unbalanced Lines

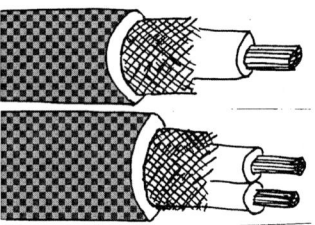

An **Unbalanced** lead has criss crossed woven wire braid around a **single** wire running down the centre.

A **Balanced** lead has criss crossed wire braid around **two wires** running down the centre.

In both cases the outside braid is shielding to protect the centre wire(s) from electrical noise and interference. For convenience we call the Positive (+) 'In Phase' signal HOT, and the Negative (–) 'Out-of-Phase' signal COLD. They are actually the same temperature!

The **Unbalanced** lead has the HOT (+) signal running down the centre wire, and both the COLD (–) and the audio Ground running down the outside braid together.

The **Balanced** lead has the HOT (+) and the COLD (–) signal running down each of the centre 2 wires, and ONLY the audio Ground running down the outside braid.

### Why Bother With All This?

The answer is NOISE. When we discussed the gain stages of mixers earlier on, the main concern was keeping the noise floor as low as possible, because from there onwards any noise that is present will be amplified throughout the whole system. Well, since the microphones and leads come *before* the channel, our aim is to keep these as quiet as possible for the same reason.

Microphone signals are measured in millivolts (thousandths of a volt), and the gain stage of the mixer amplifies this to around 1 volt. A long length of cable like a multicore snake, often

*You can only use speaker cable between the amplifier outputs and the speakers -NOWHERE ELSE!*

150 feet (50 metres) long or more, can act as a giant aerial, picking up all kinds of electrical noise, all of which will be amplified the same amount as the original signal running down the line.

An **Unbalanced** lead will drop all this unwanted noise into the circuit, since the COLD (–) and the audio Ground are the same.

The **Balanced** lead, with a separate audio Ground braid completely surrounding the HOT (+) and COLD (–) wires, will send all this noise straight to Ground. Also, since the HOT and COLD signals are 180 degrees out of phase with each other, any noise that does find its way on to the two centre wires will be cancelled out at the Balanced Input of the mixer.

If you want a noise free system, you must use balanced leads. Unbalanced are OK for instruments, since they're only about 10 to 15 feet long (5 metres), but for your 150 feet (50 metre) long snake, and *all the leads that plug into it*, only balanced will do.

### Mixing Unbalanced with Balanced

Sometimes you have to run from a 3 pin XLR output to a guitar jack input, or vice versa. No problem at this point. Just solder the HOT to the centre pin of the guitar jack, and solder both the audio Ground and the COLD to the outer leg of the guitar jack. This setup is often necessary when making up leads to go in and out of effects units, since they often come with just jack connectors on the rear panel.

### Older Equipment

In the past, just about the only thing that was in universal agreement on XLR connectors was that Pin #1 was the audio Ground. Debate raged over whether it should be Pin #2 Hot or Pin #3 Hot.

*The aim is to keep the noise floor as low as possible*

Mercifully, all that has changed. The AES (Audio Engineering Society, an organization that worries about these things on our behalf) campaigned long and hard to win international agreement, officially, for Pin #2 to be HOT.

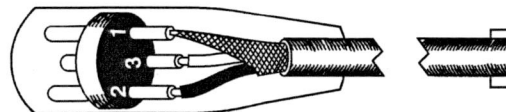 

BALANCED THIS END         UNBALANCED (SINGLE ENDED) THIS END:
COLD AND GROUND SOLDERED TOGETHER

Since 1991 all Manufacturers, TV, Radio, Sound Reinforcement, Studios, Installation Contractors, have at last all come around to a common way of thinking, and all currently sold products should be Pin #2 Hot.

However, you will *very* likely come across older equipment that has been wired Pin #3 Hot, and so it's wise to be aware that there is a difference.

### Why should it matter?

Well, as long as every lead is balanced, there is no problem. It's only when you have to interface Balanced with Unbalanced that problems occur.

Have a think about this situation:

> If you are using Pin #2 as HOT, and you wire #1 and #3 together for an unbalanced line, and you plug it into a piece of equipment that has Pin #3 HOT, then your HOT signal is going to run down the audio Ground braid, picking up so much noise that it will make you tear your hair out trying to track it down.
>
> And, it only takes ONE lead in the system to do it!

If you have to link up with some other equipment that isn't your own, then it's a good idea to have some Phase Change connectors handy, in the same 2 XLR package as the Plug In

Pad connector we mentioned earlier. You can use them anywhere, even on the microphone inputs of the mixer if it doesn't have phase change switches.

Always know how your equipment is wired, and always ask if you have to use other equipment with your own.

### Phase change adapter

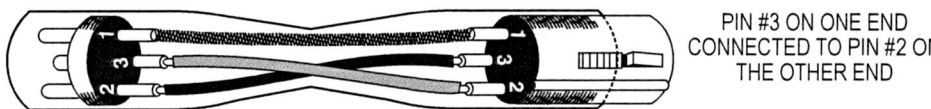

PIN #3 ON ONE END
CONNECTED TO PIN #2 ON
THE OTHER END

### Looms

It's a good idea to make up a set of leads especially for a typical drum kit, and tape them together to make a Drum Loom. Mark the leads KICK, SNARE, HATS, TOM 1, TOM 2, FLOOR, and maybe AUX 1 and AUX 2 to cover any extras, like extra Kick drum or extra Snare Bottom. Don't forget to mark the leads *before* you tape them together, otherwise the job will take 5 times as long as you carefully trace each lead!

Using a drum loom speeds up drum miking, looks much neater, and lessens the chance of any errors, especially during quick changeovers.

Any collection of leads that needs plugging up the same way every time is worth making into a loom. Monitor sends from console to equalizers, from equalizers to amps, all the effects rack Ins and Outs, etc.

They all speed up the system setup, leaving you more time for soundchecks... or sleeping!

*Mark the leads BEFORE you tape them together!*

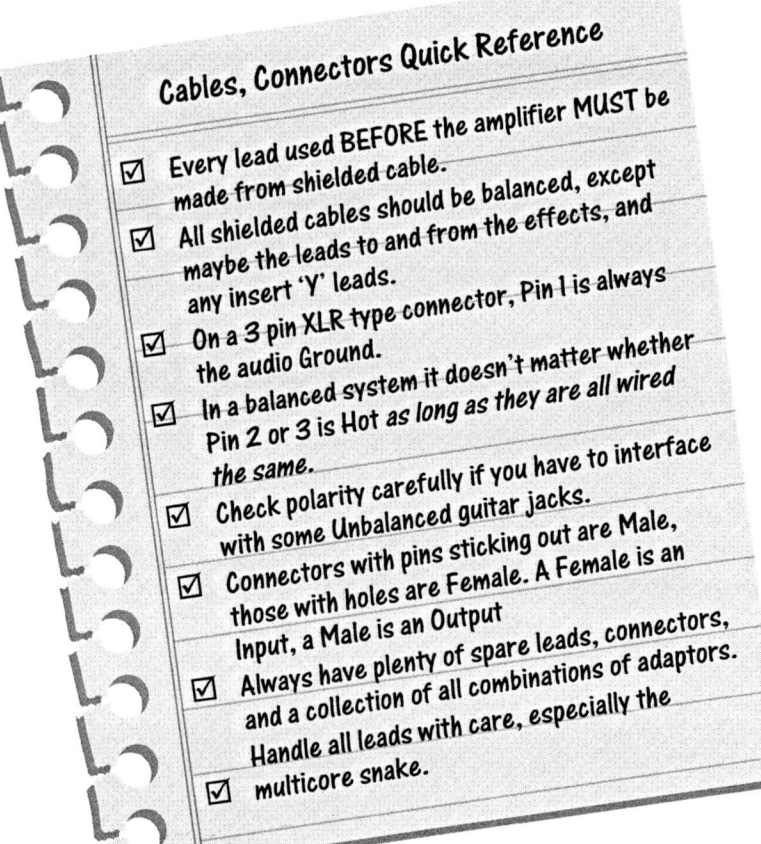

**Cables, Connectors Quick Reference**

☑ Every lead used BEFORE the amplifier MUST be made from shielded cable.

☑ All shielded cables should be balanced, except maybe the leads to and from the effects, and any insert 'Y' leads.

☑ On a 3 pin XLR type connector, Pin 1 is always the audio Ground.

☑ In a balanced system it doesn't matter whether Pin 2 or 3 is Hot as long as they are all wired the same.

☑ Check polarity carefully if you have to interface with some Unbalanced guitar jacks.

☑ Connectors with pins sticking out are Male, those with holes are Female. A Female is an Input, a Male is an Output

☑ Always have plenty of spare leads, connectors, and a collection of all combinations of adaptors.

☑ Handle all leads with care, especially the multicore snake.

## 5     *Microphones*

These days, a good microphone will pick up everything you want to hear. However, at the same time it can pick up everything you don't want to hear! Just about every piece of equipment between the microphones and the amplifiers is dedicated to removing what you don't want to hear and keeping the rest.

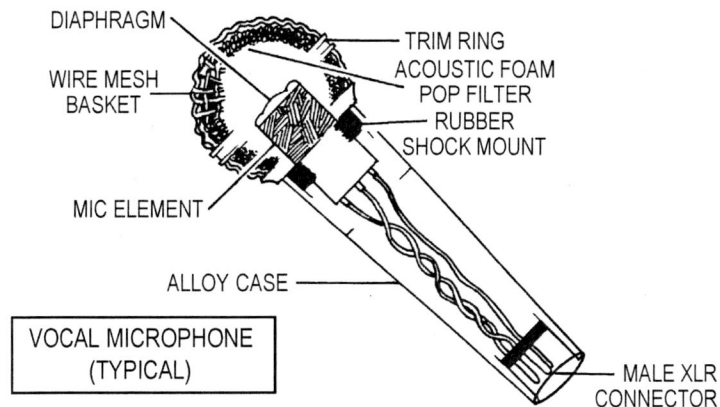

DIAPHRAGM — TRIM RING — ACOUSTIC FOAM POP FILTER — RUBBER SHOCK MOUNT — MALE XLR CONNECTOR — ALLOY CASE — MIC ELEMENT — WIRE MESH BASKET

VOCAL MICROPHONE (TYPICAL)

Not all microphones do the same job; some are good all-round microphones, some are specialized vocal or instrument microphones.

As soon as you start recommending one microphone over another, you're opening a real can of worms. There are as many ideas on sound as there are bubbles in a can of beer. No two people have the same ears, the way no two people have the same fingerprints, and when you start discussing what microphone for what purpose, then you find that everyone has their own preferences.

Still, we can establish a few ground rules:

- It must have excellent feedback rejection.
- It must sound good.
- It should only pick up the instrument or voice that it is supposed to, and disregard everything else.
- It must stand up to life on the road.

In practical terms, these prerequisites mean that for most purposes, we'll be using Dynamic microphones, needing no batteries or external power, with a 'Cardioid' or 'Super/Hypercardioid' response - meaning the microphone picks up sound from a heart shaped area exactly in front of it, and very little from anywhere else.

THE CARDIOID MICROPHONE PICKS UP MAINLY FROM THE FRONT

THE SUPER/HYPERCARDIOID HAS A TIGHTER FRONT PATTERN BUT ALSO PICKS UP A LITTLE FROM THE REAR OF THE MICROPHONE

AS YOU CAN SEE, NEITHER OF THEM LOOK THAT MUCH LIKE A HEART - MAYBE THOSE DESIGNERS OUGHT TO GET OUT A BIT MORE!

### Condenser Microphones on stage

In recent years a whole lot of condenser microphones have come on the market, aimed mainly at the booming home/project recording studio. Established manufacturers like Shure, EV, Neumann, plus newcomers like Rode all have well priced, high quality vocal and instrument condenser mics.

Should you use this type of microphone in a Live situation?

Provided you have:

- Good phantom power - they need 48V DC down the mic lead
- Enough budget - some of these mics can be fragile and won't survive many drops - then why not? Condenser mics have the ability to make a poor singer sound good, and a good singer sound great, and they have a high end sparkle that can pull individual instruments out of the mix

Make sure you can switch them to a Cardioid pattern, for good feedback rejection, and use them where their benefits can be heard. Small laid back trio or solo artist and instrument - yes; band with lots of vocal harmonies - yes; grunge/heavy metal - hmmm, I don't think so!

The increased sensitivity of condensers make them an ideal choice for miking up choirs, where the microphones are typically placed further away than they are with solo artists.

Let's have a look at what is happening on stage at a live gig, with the band on stage playing and singing.

1. There is a microphone in front of each singer, each instrument amplifier, and each drum.
2. The monitor system is blaring out across the stage and also up from the wedges.
3. We want to get this monitor sound into the musicians' ears, but we don't want it going into the microphone.
4. Ears are at the most only 5" (100mm) from the mouth, and the mouth is about 1/4" (5mm) from the microphone!

Once you look at it like this, it's amazing that microphones work at all, but they do, and most of them work very well.

### Vocal Microphones

You won't get far along the live audio trail without coming across the Shure SM 58. The typical vocal microphone, it looks like an ice-cream cone painted battleship grey. Much copied, it is still *the* industry standard in vocal microphones. Every engineer knows its sound - big bass boost up close (known as proximity effect), a kick up in the HIGH MIDs and excellent feedback rejection.

*For most purposes we'll be using mics that don't need batteries or external power*

SM58

BETA 58A (WITH A BLUE STRIPE)

If you are using a different system every night, with little or no soundcheck time, when the singer walks on stage with a 58 in their hand, you know exactly how the vocals will sound, so you can set up the desk EQ accordingly.

TMS 105

The SM 58 is also very robust. According to ads it will withstand 6' drops onto a hardwood floor; not something I would try with a Beyer M 88. I suspect that the popularity of the 88 as a kick drum microphone is that it doesn't have far to fall, and when it does it's usually onto a pillow!

The newer Beta 58a with Neodymium, a 'rare earth' super efficient magnet has a hotter signal, better feedback rejection, and is just as robust but more expensive.

However, luckily for other manufacturers there are a whole lot more vocal microphones to choose from. Here are some favourites that spring to mind, as well as some condenser mics designed especially for live vocal use.

RØDE S1

| | |
|---|---|
| Shure SM 58, Beta 58 | Shure SM87a condenser |
| Beyer M 88 | Neumann TMS 105 condenser |
| Sennheiser 421, 431 | Rode S1 Stage condenser |

## No Switches

Whatever vocal mic you use, it mustn't have an On/Off switch! Mics with switches are for real estate agents, bingo callers, bus tour operators and karaoke machines, not for pro audio. As a mixing engineer, you need to know that if a mic is on stage, you are the only one controlling it.

Singers have been known to fiddle endlessly with mic switches, ending up with a broken switch or one that is switched off when it should be on. They start to sing, there's nothing there, you pull your hair out trying to find out what is wrong, suddenly they switch it back on, and with a crackly bang half the audience get their fillings rattled!

The *only* exceptions to this rule are wireless mics, and we'll get to them later.

SM87A

As a final word before we leave vocal microphones, remember that if you are running one monitor send to all the front line of vocal monitors, your job is made so much easier if all the vocal microphones are the same. Trying to EQ for 4 different models or brands on the one send can be a nightmare, as they all have different responses.

There will be so much cut out on the Graphic EQ that you will end up with **reduced** level in the monitors, which is usually the opposite of what the band wants!

## Drum microphones

The choice of Kick drum and Snare microphones is very important, and the others probably less so. Kick and Snare appear in every beat in every song, so they've got to be right.

M88

A good Kick drum microphone must be able handle high SPL without its diaphragm breaking up and giving a distorted sound. Kick drum sound is very subjective. Some engineers will prefer lots of 'click', others want a 'thud' that will rattle your fillings, still others want a 'boomy' sound. It all depends on the sound of the band. Whichever sound you prefer, it must be clean to start with. From there, your preferences can be taken care of by the desk EQ. Here are some favourites:

| | |
|---|---|
| Beyer M 88 | Sennheiser 421 |
| Electro-Voice RE 20 | Audix D6 |
| AKG D 12 or D 112 | Shure SM 57 |

Snare drum microphones need a lot of the same properties as the Kick, but in a more compact form. They also need accurate transient response, to give the true snare drum 'crack'. Try these:

D12

| | | |
|---|---|---|
| Shure SM 57 or Beta 57 | Sennheiser 421 | Audix i5 |
| AKG 451 or 310 | Beyer M 201 | |

D112

421

SM57

BETA 57

RE20

The microphones on the toms are less critical, so if your budget is running tight, then virtually anything directional will do. If you do have a choice, though, try these favourites:

Shure SM 57 or Beta 57          Beyer M 201

Sennheiser 421

Also, a number of microphone manufacturers make small clip-on mics that can attach to the edge of the drum, well out of the way of the drummer's flying sticks, and these would be worthwhile checking out if stick damage is a problem. Otherwise keep a safety zone between the end on the microphone and the stick area!

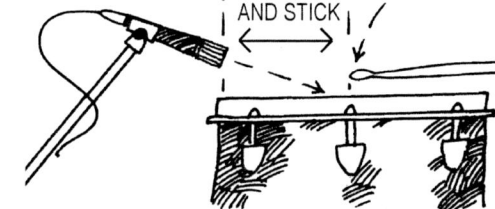

KEEP A SAFETY ZONE BETWEEN MIC END AND STICK

### Hi Hats and Overheads

The Hi Hat cymbal microphone needs shimmering top end, and a tight directional pattern to try to lose the snare drum. Here are some suggestions:

Beyer M 201                          Sennheiser 416

Shure SM 57, Beta 57, SM 81      AKG D140

The Overhead mics are there to pick up the wash from cymbals, tambourines and any other percussive elements on the drum kit. You'll usually only use them on larger stages where there is plenty of physical distance between the players; on smaller stages your vocal mics will pick up more than enough. If you have the budget some of the newer condenser mics would be great on overheads and hi hats.

### The 3 to 1 rule

When we discussed the Phase Reverse switch on mixers, we mentioned 'the 3 to 1 rule', which says: ***keep the microphones 3 times as far apart as each one is from its source.*** Having said that, though, my own practical testing has shown that in a live environment it is less of a problem when miking up drums, since they are not all hit at exactly the same time, except when miking up a snare drum top and bottom.

## Instrument Microphones

### Guitar and Keyboard amps

You can stick almost any microphone in front of a guitar amp, as long as it will handle a high SPL. Place the microphone in front of the speaker, but not in the exact centre where the dome is, unless you want it really bright. Place it between the dome and the edge of the speaker, but never in the space between two speakers (as on the Vox AC30 on right, for example) unless you're really after a hollow thin sound.

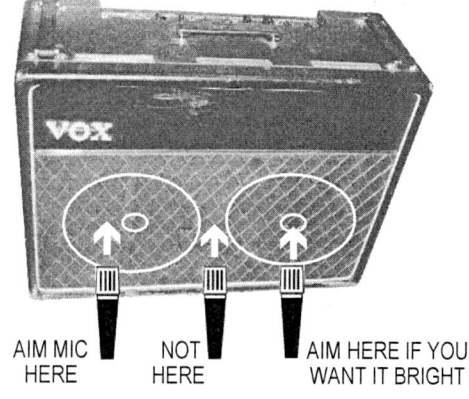

AIM MIC HERE          NOT HERE          AIM HERE IF YOU WANT IT BRIGHT

### Acoustic Guitar

Hopefully, most of the time the guitar will have a built-in pickup in the bridge, which you can run into the desk using a DI box. If you need plenty of level to allow an acoustic to compete with the rest of a band, then ***an on-board pickup is mandatory***. However, if you are working with a solo guitarist or singer/guitarist, and you have to mike it up, then point the microphone towards the bridge area or the pickguard area, and about 4" (100mm) away from it.

Then cross your fingers and hope that the guitarist will keep still! This will give the cleanest sound, but you will need the utmost concentration, as acoustic guitar sound tends to 'boom' very easily, and guitarists don't always stand still! Roll off quite a bit of LOW and LOW MID, and watch out for feedback. An alternative choice might be a small clip-on condenser out of the way of strumming fingers, aimed at the same area.

### Acoustic Bass

Once again this will hopefully have a built-in pickup installed, but otherwise the same rules apply as for acoustic guitar. Shure recommend wedging a microphone with its body wrapped in foam rubber (not the grille) behind the bridge or between the tailpiece and body. Watch out for LOW and LOW MID feedback.

### Piano

Well, we're not talking about classical accuracy here, so we want a fairly bright sound that won't get lost onstage. Hang a microphone over the strings, about two thirds the way from the bass end. If you don't like this sound, move the microphone more towards the centre. If you have a piano dominant solo artist, then use two microphones; one a third the way from the bass end, and one the same from the treble end. Keep it well up in the mix.

Some people swear by C-Ducers, which are microphone strips that you tape onto the soundboard of the piano!

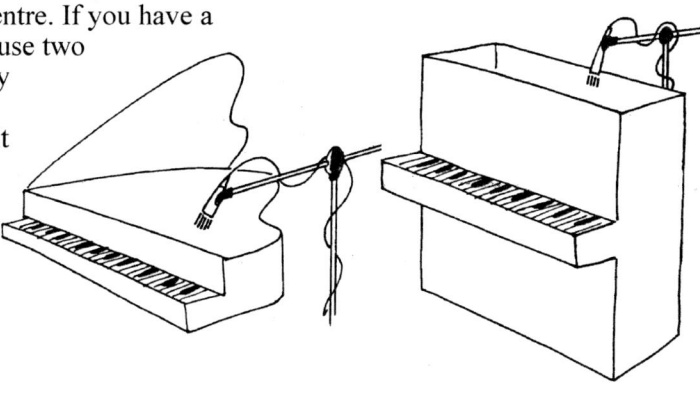

### Brass - Trumpet, Saxophone

For one trumpet, let it play straight into a vocal microphone setup; for more than one, group them around the microphone at equal distance. If they have their own monitor, most players can balance themselves as they play. Otherwise, if you have lots of spare microphones and channels, you could give them one each. Remember the 3 to 1 rule, though.

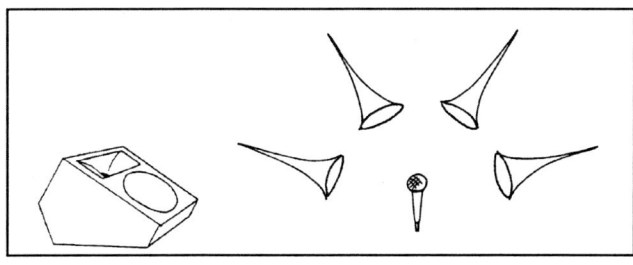

201

For saxophone, either clip a small microphone in the centre of the bell (the big hole in the end), or use a vocal microphone set up as if for a short person. It depends on whether the player likes to roam around while playing or stands still.

### Flute

Most players will use a vocal microphone, and position themselves so the flute sounds best in their monitor. This position will usually be in a direct line with the mouth across from the mouthpiece.

i-5

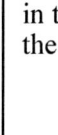

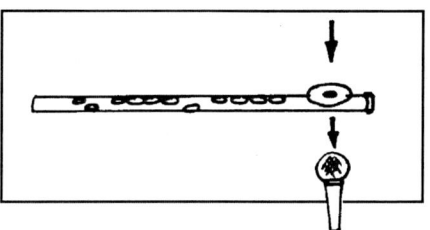

### Harmonica (Blues Harp)

This is a predominantly mid frequency instrument, and because players like to cup it in their hands along with the microphone, it's very prone to feeding back, especially in the monitors. So, be wary of any High Mid peaks, roll off the Low and maybe some Low Mid, because all you really want is that 'wail' to cut through. Maybe add some Highs, around 4 KHz, to give the sound some edge.

GREEN
BULLET

Since the player is usually holding the microphone, gain ride it if they get too close to monitors or main stacks. Favourite blues harp microphone of many players is the Shure Green Bullet, but experiment with what you have available; frequently the cheaper the better for that 'down home' sound.

For effects on brass and blues harp, definitely some reverb, maybe a small amount of chorus or slap echo, perhaps some exciter for sizzle.

Incidentally, if you ever have to mike up a real harp - you know, 7 foot tall with strings and Harpo Marx - mike it as you would a piano, only vertically!

### Leslie Cabinet

Loved by Hammond organ players and hated by those who have to carry them, this large and cumbersome piece of polished furniture has Highs coming out of the top slots and Lows coming out of the bottom slots. It will tie up a couple of channels, but put a mic on each one, and maybe pan one 10% Left and the other 10% Right.

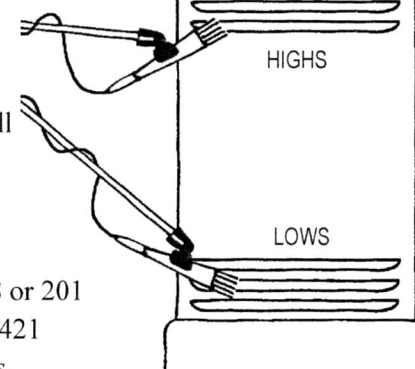

HIGHS

LOWS

### Suggested Instrument Microphones

| Shure SM 57 or Beta 57 | Beyer M 88 or 201 |
|---|---|
| Audix i5 | Sennheiser 421 |

Or try one of the better priced instrument condenser mics

As you can see the Shure SM 57 figures regularly on these lists. It is a truly versatile instrument microphone, and as its number suggests, is a close relative to the 58. However, with its plastic endpiece it is as fragile as the 58 is robust, so it must be treated well. If the endpiece comes off, don't stick it back on by winding some gaffer tape around it - you'll lose all the bottom end that way. You'll have to find the spring clip that holds it on and re-fit the endpiece. There must be fiddlier jobs than this, but I've yet to find one.

The Shure Beta 57 has an all metal end piece, so it might survive being hit by a drum stick for longer!

Keep in mind that the audience doesn't know a Shure from a Beyer from an AKG from a hole in the ground! If a mic sounds good to you, use it.

## Placement of drum microphones

Drums should always be set up on a good thick piece of carpet, preferably rubber backed, to stop them sliding around and to dampen any reflected sound off the stage. Using a carpeted drum riser will also help isolate them from the other instruments. This will make getting a good sound easier, both out front and in the drum monitor.

### Kick Drum

Put the microphone on a short boom stand, if possible with a shockproof mount, and point the microphone into the drum so that about 3/4 of the microphone length is inside the drum. If you want more 'click' on it, place it closer to the back skin. Put a pad of foam rubber under the stand, or you can just lie the microphone on a pillow in the drum if the front head is removed. If the drummer doesn't want the front head removed, then hopefully he has a hole cut in it so you can poke the microphone through. If there is no hole, and he doesn't want you to cut one, just point it at the centre of the front head and hope he plays like John Bonham.

*If the end piece of a 57 comes off, don't stick it back on with gaffer tape*

### Snare Drum

If you can't get a short stand in next to the snare drum because of the forest of cymbal stands, put a boom arm on the short stand and poke it through the cymbal stands towards the snare. Point the microphone towards the centre of the drum head (skin), with the front of the microphone about 2" above the edge of the drum. Don't put it any closer or the drummer may hit it.

Make sure the snare microphone points *away* from the drum monitor.

### Hi Hats

The microphone should be pointing down at about a 45 degree angle to the top edge of the Hi Hat cymbals. It should not be pointing into the air space between them, nor towards the centre (bell) of the cymbal. If your stand is not quite high enough to point down, you can put it underneath and point it up at the same angle. It won't sound too bad, but it will lose the 'ting' of the stick hitting the top cymbal.

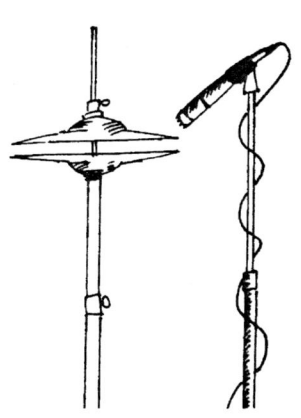

### Toms

What's good for the snare is good for the rack toms and floor toms - don't put the microphone in any closer than the edge of the drum. Providing it is pointing towards the centre of the skin it will pick up perfectly. And try out those new clip-on drum mics - they really work well

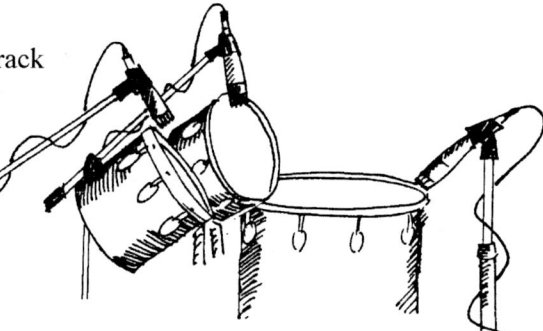

### Overheads

This can be 1 microphone, if mono, over the approximate centre of the kit; over each side if stereo, and about 18" above the cymbals. Use similar microphone choices as for Hi Hats.

If you are really enthusiastic you could try a couple of PZM (Pressure Zone Microphone) attached to squares of Perspex and mounted on stands over the kit. Just don't get carried away - at smaller gigs your vocal microphones will usually pick up more than enough cymbals!

There is nothing to stop you experimenting with drum microphone placement. For example, you may prefer the sound of the toms miked from underneath rather than on top; if you have enough channels you could try putting a microphone underneath the snare as well. This microphone will pick up a more 'rasping' sound that often sounds good mixed in with the sound of the top snare microphone (remember to flip the phase reverse switch on the snare bottom channel). If you have any new ideas, try them out.

## Wireless (Radio) Microphones

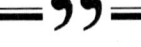

Every vocalist and lead singer wants a wireless microphone.  And if they like to prance around, run up and down the stage, jump up on the front of house boxes, dive into the audience, that sort of thing, well it's a lot safer than having them get tangled up in a microphone cable and break a leg!

Other people who want them include theatre performers, corporate presenters, comedians, and preachers, and we'll deal at length with these various groups in *Chapter 13, Mixing.*

> *==" "==*
> *Don't put the microphone any closer than the edge of the drum or the drummer may hit it!*
> *=="=*

Even though they're getting better all the time, wireless mics are not perfect. Their signal is compressed, expanded, filtered, gated, and more, before it even reaches the mixer! It's been said that the very best, most expensive wireless mic is almost as good as an ordinary wired one - and chances are that these *won't* be the ones you'll be using!

You should also be aware that there are extremely stringent regulations covering the use of wireless microphone frequencies, and in some areas a permit to use them may be required. Read the paperwork that comes with them very closely.

### VHF or UHF

Your choices are VHF (Very High Frequency) and UHF (Ultra High Frequency). The VHF ones are cheaper, but are prone to picking up radio operators, taxis, FM radio, TV or even other wireless microphones! Lower priced units are usually a fixed frequency system - the microphone with the transmitter and the receiver with the aerial are a matched pair, and can't individually be swapped with other units, even from the same manufacturer.

DIVERSITY RECEIVER

For pro audio purposes the UHF wireless systems are the ones to choose, and the True Diversity ones are best; these have two separate circuits inside the receiver, each with its own aerial, and automatically switches between them for the clearest and loudest signal. Why? Because as well as going in a straight line to the receiver, the signal from the microphone also spreads out in other directions. One signal path will have better reception than the other, and so the receiver will automatically switch to it.

On newer models there is a choice of channels so that:

 • Multiple units can be used, or
 • The best performing channel with the least interference can be used.

### How do they work?

A handheld wireless microphone is a standard wired mic with a radio transmitter inside, with a replaceable battery to supply the power. A receiver tuned to the frequency that the mic is transmitting on picks up this signal and sends it down a lead to the mixer, and it is mixed in with the rest of the audio just as with a regular microphone.

Singers who have to dance and move their arms a lot will need a headset wireless mic. This needs to be a cardioid type, with the capsule positioned directly in front of the mouth. The headset plugs into a beltpack, a small box about the size of a deck of cards, which contains the battery and transmitter. This either clips onto a belt or fits into a small pouch already on a belt.

HANDHELD
WIRELESS
MIC

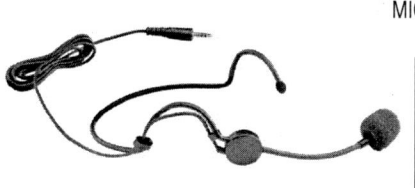

HEADSET WIRELESS
MIC

### Handheld and Beltpack controls

Depending on the type you have, it should have some or all of the following switches and controls:

### Mute switch

This mutes the signal coming from the microphone, without switching it off - it is still chewing through the battery's power.

Mute will stop the microphone from accepting any signal but will keep the channel open from transmitter to receiver open. Otherwise if the transmitter is turned *off* and the receiver is still *on*, the receiver will be susceptible to all kinds of signal and noise.

BELTPACK CONNECTIONS - NOTE
SPECIAL 'SCREWABLE' MINI JACK
SOCKET TO LOCK IN THE HEADSET
CONNECTION

### On/Off switch

This switches off the power to the microphone, and can send a 'Thump' through the system if the levels aren't pulled down at the mixer.

On a handheld this may be a three position switch controlling On, Mute and Off.

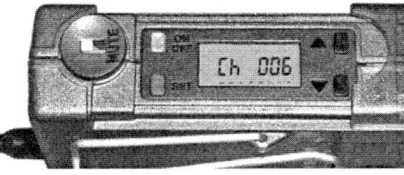

BELTPACK
CONTROLS

BELTPACK

### Channel readout

This shows you what channel the mic is transmitting on, and should be the same as on the receiver!

### Channel change buttons

These are often nudge buttons, and change the channel to the one required - Up is higher, Down is lower. On handheld models this function can be handled by a multi position switch.

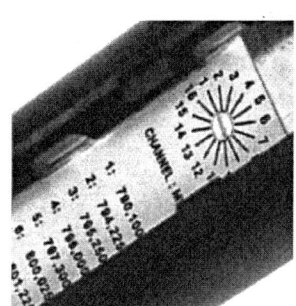

### Set or Lock switch

This locks the channel once it has been set, so it doesn't get accidentally changed.

On Handheld wireless microphones, these controls are usually recessed under a safety cover so that they don't get accidentally knocked and changed. You can access them by unscrewing or unclipping the lower end of the mic body.

### Aerial

Keep it as straight as possible, with no kinks.

### Autoscan

On many new wireless systems this button on the reciver will automatically scan for available frequencies, and synchronize the transmitter and the receiver to the best one available. If you are using more than one transmitter and receiver, then do this for the first, then leave it on before going to the second, leave them both on before going to the third.

*=** 66 **=*

*Always
have a
back-up
mic and
cable
plugged in
and ready
to go*

*=** 99 **=*

### How to get one to to work

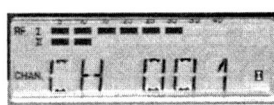

SIGNAL STRENGTH METER
ON DIVERSITY RECEIVER
SHOWS THAT RECEIVER **I** IS
PICKING UP A BETTER
SIGNAL THAN **II**

Switch the microphone on and the Mute off, and make sure the channel number on the microphone or beltpack is set the same as on the receiver, if there is a choice.

Plug the receiver into a channel on the mixer, and set the mixer channel Gain low to start with. Make sure the Output control on the receiver is turned down, then switch the receiver on.

With someone talking into the mic, the signal strength meter on the receiver should start to move.

Turn up the Output control on the receiver to maximum, and bring up the channel fader on the mixer. If the person is talking then you'll hear it through the system.

Here are some suggestions for keeping your wireless microphones running smoothly:

1. Keep the batteries fresh or freshly charged. *Always* have fresh spares ready to go.

2. Locate the receivers near the stage box, or the monitor mixing desk, rather than in the Front of House mix bunker. The distance from microphone to receiver is much shorter, and you can keep them in a line-of-sight with each other.

3. Wireless microphone receivers often put out a really LOUD signal. You may get better results plugging them into a LINE input on the channel, to avoid overloading the sensitive microphone input. When doing the soundcheck, set up the channel gain as you would for a wired mic

4. Check them out thoroughly before the show. Walk around with them, on the lookout for 'dead' spots, noisy areas, whatever. When you're satisfied, switch the microphone off and put it away safe until showtime. I once had a wireless microphone die on me because someone knocked it over before the show and dislodged the battery. The singer came on, picked up the microphone, yelled "Hello" and there was nothing. Which leads me on to the next point

5. Whenever you are using a wireless microphone for an important gig, you should *always* have a backup microphone and cable plugged into a mixer channel, tuned and waiting on stage ready to go, in case of emergency. Try and be prepared for anything.

## Other Microphones

### Lavalier

These are the small microphones you see clipped to the clothing of newsreaders and people being interviewed on TV. They are omni-directional (pick up sound from all directions) and are designed for sound that is being recorded or broadcast, and not usually for live sound.

Occasionally you'll have to amplify sound from these mics, perhaps to supply an audience feed, and then you'll need to do some swift EQ'ing. Because of the greater distance from mouth to micrphone, they pick up a lot of room sound. This usually means cutting the will need LO MIDs, so sweep around the frequency on the mixer EQ until you find the exact one. Start at 300 Hz. You'll probably also need to bring up the highs as well.

We'll look at mixing with omnidirectional mics in *Chapter 13: Mixing*, in the section on Theatre show sound.

### Shotgun

A very long, thin directional microphone commonly used for Stage productions. The principal performers will have individual headset mics, and shotgun mics will be pointed at the stage to pick up performers with occasional lines, and the chorus line. Their very tight pickup pattern enables them to pick up sound from the area they are pointed at only, and reject any other sound.

For Stage Productions they can be hung in front of the stage, pointing upstage (towards the back). Sometimes you see them on the floor on little stands, but not when there is a lot of feet noise onstage.

## D.I.Boxes (Direct Boxes)

DI stands for Direct Injection, a way of bypassing the use of microphones when amplifying many instruments. It converts a High Impedance (Hi Z instrument signal into a Balanced Low Impedance (Lo Z signal that the mixing desk can handle.

Instead of the instrument amp being miked up, the output of the instrument itself is plugged into the system directly through a DI box. By doing this you successfully eliminate all of the microphone hassles, unwanted stage noise, leaving just the sound of the instrument itself.

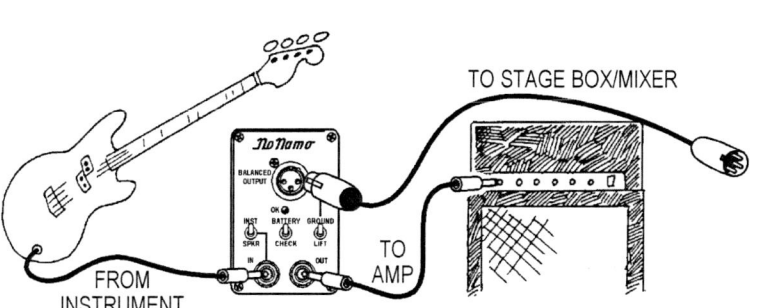

A lot of instrument amplifiers these days have a LINE OUT connector, which you can plug into if the artist wants the sound of the amplifier as well. Just make sure that it doesn't shut off the speakers when you plug into it! A HEADPHONE OUT will definitely shut off the speakers!

SM 89
SHOTGUN
MIC

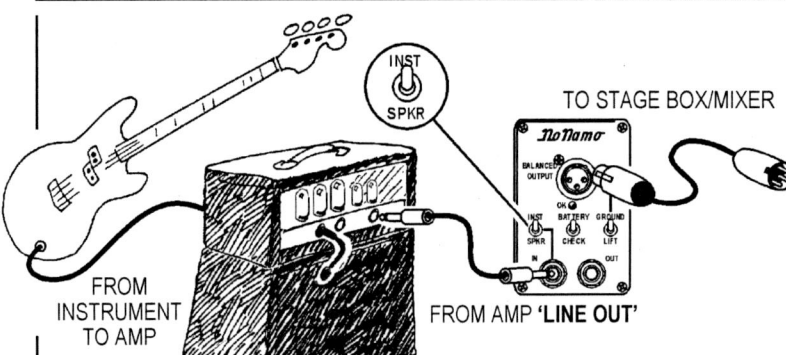

FROM
INSTRUMENT
TO AMP

TO STAGE BOX/MIXER

FROM AMP **'LINE OUT'**

A DI box is great with Bass, Keyboards, Drum machines, or anything electronic. They are not so good on guitars unless you can plug it into a LINE OUT or PRE AMP OUT socket on the back of the amp. In any case, guitars often rely on the interaction between the guitar and the amp/speaker combina-tion to get the correct sound, and for this reason DIs are not commonly used on guitars. They are great for getting a good fat signal out of an acoustic guitar piezo or 'bug' pickup.

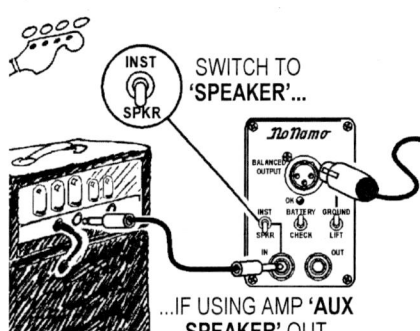

SWITCH TO
'SPEAKER'...

...IF USING AMP **'AUX SPEAKER'** OUT

If you do try one with a guitar amp, ***don't plug it into a speaker output socket unless there is a switch or jack socket on the Direct Box marked 'Speaker Level Input' or something similar!*** If you do, you run the risk of frying the expensive transformer or electronic circuit inside the DI box. *See Page 168 for a circuit diagram of a speaker level pad.*

Note: Never disconnect the speakers on a valve/tube amp, either, or it will cook itself.

### Passive DI boxes

Passive DI's consist of a High Impedance to Low Impedance audio balancing transformer, IN/OUT guitar jack sockets, an Audio Earth/ Ground lift switch, and a balanced XLR type output, all inside a shielded metal case

There are no batteries, nothing really to go wrong. It will work all day, every day unless you plug it in wrongly (see above warning). However, ***it is only as good as the transformer inside it***. A cheap passive DI will mean a cheap transformer, often prone to humming and easily distorting when a percussive signal like some 'slap' bass is sent through it. It can also be noisy, since the signal sent down the multicore snake can be weak, making you increase the channel Gain at the mixer and resulting in a poor signal-to noise-ratio.

### Active DI boxes

Active DI's need power to run them, usually in the form of one or two 9 volt batteries, or they can run off the mixer's Phantom Power supply, if it has one. An electronic circuit inside the DI converts the Hi Impedance instrument signal into a Balanced Low Impedance signal. It will have the same INs and OUTs as the passive unit, plus Battery LOW or OK warning LEDs with Battery Check switch, and either a Gain control or switches for Speaker, Line or Instrument Inputs.

Active DI's are popular because the active circuit does not overload as easily as a passive, the signal to noise ratio is better, and they can send a good 'fat' signal down the long multicore snake to the desk. They are unpopular because the batteries can go flat when you least

PASSIVE DI BOX

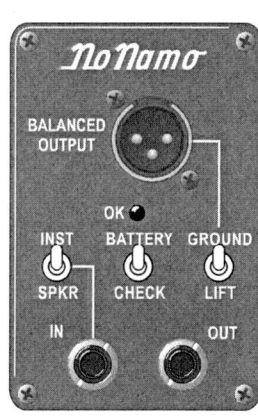

ACTIVE DI BOX

expect it. If possible, make sure it can run off Phantom power as well as batteries.

If you are short on available microphone channels, you could bring an active DI signal back into the desk via an Auxiliary return. An active DI runs at LINE rather than microphone level, and the Aux returns are set up for LINE level signals from tape decks or effects units.

### External Music Sources

Sooner or later someone will come up to your mixer with an Apple iPod, an MP3 player or some other similar piece of consumer audio, and say "Can you play this while I sing ?"

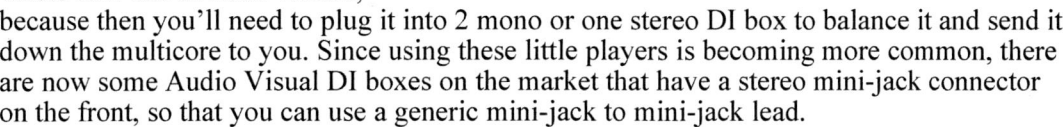

As I mentioned in the previous chapter, these units typically have a stereo 3.5mm ($^1/_8$") Mini Jack connector on them, so you will need to make up a stereo minijack lead to 2 male XLR connectors (or mono jack plugs if you want to use the line inputs).

However, if they want it up on stage with them, that opens up a whole new can of noise worms, because then you'll need to plug it into 2 mono or one stereo DI box to balance it and send it down the multicore to you. Since using these little players is becoming more common, there are now some Audio Visual DI boxes on the market that have a stereo mini-jack connector on the front, so that you can use a generic mini-jack to mini-jack lead.

If you're doing a corporate meeting or product launch, then as sure as eggs is eggs you'll have a steady stream of people coming up to you with their laptops wanting to put some sound through the system for their PowerPoint presentation.

We'll look at this in more detail in *Chapter 13: Mixing,* but for the moment set it up the same as an MP3 player with a stereo DI.

### Microphones Quick Reference

- ☑ Keep wireless receivers well away from anything digital
- ☑ If all the vocals are on the same monitor send, make sure they all use the same model of microphone.
- ☑ Keep a safety zone between the end of the microphone and the drumsticks
- ☑ Always have a backup microphone, lead and channel plugged in and ready if you're using wireless microphones.
- ☑ Always have spare batteries for wireless microphones and active DI's.
- ☑ Wash out and disinfect the vocal microphone baskets regularly. A quick spray with Glen 20 during a band changeover is a good precaution. There are some very nasty things floating around these days!

# 6    *Effects*

Effects are the devices that let us add echo, chorus, reverberation, pitch change to the original signal. In the majority of cases effects are run from the Auxiliary sends of the mixer.

Let's say we want to add some reverb to the lead vocal, and Aux 1 and 2 are being used for monitors.

Firstly run a lead from the Aux 3 Output on the rear of the mixer into the Input of the reverb unit. Then from the Output of the reverb you run a lead back into the mixer, into either an Aux return or a spare channel. We'll use Channel 16 for this example. Push up the fader on the lead vocal channel so you can hear some vocals, then turn up the Aux 3 send on the lead vocal channel to about 10 o'clock, and bring up the fader on Channel 16 until you hear a reverb effect adding to the vocal.

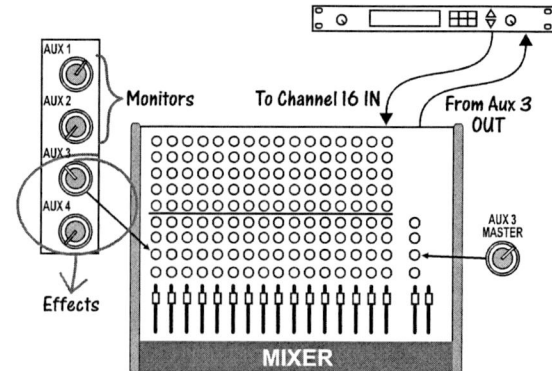

So the process is as follows: The signal goes out to the effect unit, is modified, and is then brought back into the mixer and mixed in (sometimes in very small amounts) with the original signal.

Some things to check:

1. The Aux 3 Master control, somewhere over in the master section, is turned up - around the 2 o'clock position for a start

2. The Input Level control on the reverb unit is also turned up. If the Input meter or Signal

Present LED is lighting up or bouncing, then you know a signal is getting out of the mixer

3. If there is an Output level control on the reverb, make sure it is turned up and a reverb program is selected.

That's all there is to it. You can fine tune the levels and the effect, but this basic process applies to all effects units and mixers.

There are just so many models of effects units that a book like this can't go through them all, so we'll stick to models that have all the typical characteristics and controls of a particular type of effect.

We'll split delay units into four categories: Tape, Analog, Digital with knobs and Digital without knobs. Reverbs will be covered by three sections: a short one on the Spring type, and then Digital Reverbs with knobs, and Digital Reverbs without knobs. In this way we'll cover just about every type of effects unit you're likely to come across.

### Tape Delays (Tape Echo units)

Tape delays have been around for a long time, and although superseded by the digital delay, they do have a 'feel' to their sound that many digitals don't have. They are also a cheap way of getting a very long delay.

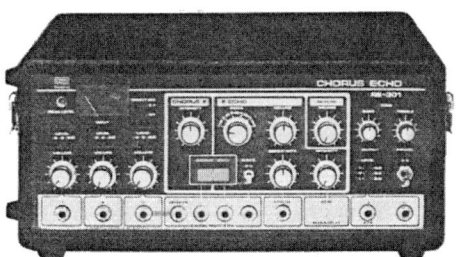

ROLAND 301 SPACE ECHO

### How to get one to work

Use any input unless there is one marked "PA In". Set the LEVEL switch at the number closest to 0 dB, and the Input Volume control at about 2 o'clock. Set the Output Level the same if it's adjustable. The Mode switch sets up the type of echo (short, medium, long), and the Repeat Rate fine tunes the echo speed by speeding up or slowing down the tape.

Some Space Echo models have built in electronic Chorus effect, like a guitar pedal, and this whole family of delays has one of the twangiest reverbs ever!

A shorted out guitar jack plugged into the Remote or Foot Switch socket will shut off the motor during the band's breaks to avoid wearing out the tape. Don't forget to pull it out when the band goes back on stage again, though.

One final thing on Tape Delays. If the tape chews itself up, you'll have no delay. Keep a spare tape in the drawer of your effects rack for emergencies. Don't use ordinary recording tape or it will chew up in about 2 songs. The tape is special graphite lubricated tape; if you can't get any you could gut an old 8 track cartridge (remember them?) or the professional cart version that radio stations used.

### Analog Delays

Analog Delays were an interim model between Tape and Digital. Even the good ones suffered from a lack of HIGH end on any delay over 300 milliseconds (ms), but they usually worked reliably enough, having no tape to wear out.

YAMAHA E1010

### How to get it to work

Set the Input at about 2 o'clock, and the Output the same if there is one. Set the Mixing control at all Delay, as we only want the delayed signal; set up the delay you want in milliseconds (usually switches for Short through Long and a knob to fine tune the delay), the amount of repeats on the Feedback control, and bring up the return on the mixing desk.

*This whole family of delays has one of the twangiest reverbs ever!*

---

## Digital Delays

Digital delays offered far more flexibility, and can be split into two basic groups; those with knobs, and those without.

### Digital Delays with knobs

These were the first, and are still commonly found in a lot of systems. As a typical example, here's a look at the Delta Lab Effectron II, one of the first and a very popular unit. The company is no longer around, but their effects are.

EFFECTRON 2

### How to get it to work

Set the Input Level at about 2 o'clock - less if the Limit LED lights up. Set the Delay Mix control at +100%, and set up the delay time you want in milliseconds (marked above each switch) by pressing the appropriate switch and fine tuning it with the Delay Factor control. Next, set the amount of repeats on the Feedback control, and bring up the return on the mixing desk.

Note two important features: both the Delay Mix and the Feedback controls are off at the 12 o'clock position. Turning them to the right gives you the Delay Mix and Feedback repeats In Phase (+), while to the left gives you them Out of Phase (–).

Stay away from the modulation controls (Width and Speed) unless you are using the first 3 (Flange) switches. To get an idea of their effect, set them both to 12 o'clock, and press the second Flange switch in. You should hear a sweeping, chorus type effect. Move each control and listen to the difference.

SDE 2000

Another very popular delay with knobs was the Roland SDE 2000 (and others from the same family). You get it to work in a very similar manner to the Effectron, except you adjust the delay time by pressing the Up (for shorter) or Down (for longer) nudge buttons, and the delay time shows up on the screen.

### Digital Delays without knobs

Instead of a row of knobs and switches, these delays have banks of 'nudge' buttons and a readout screen on the front panel. The concept is the same as setting the time on your digital watch or clock radio. Here's the front panel of a typical one, the Yamaha D 1500.

D 1500

### How to get it to work

The D 1500 has 15 memory banks, 0 through 9, and A through F. Start off with your Input and Output levels at about 2 o'clock.

Press the UP or DOWN arrow buttons to scroll through the factory presets, and have a listen to each one. If you find one that comes close to what you want, use the bank of square buttons on the right to modify each parameter until it is what you want. Pressing either the UP or DOWN button and the STORE button simultaneously will store your new settings in that memory bank until you change them, even when you disconnect the power from the unit.

To clear all the memories, hold down the Data Entry Up and Down buttons while turning the power on. To reload the factory presets, hold down the Copy button while turning the power on.

Holding down buttons while turning on the power will work for most Yamaha products, but you'll have to work out which buttons they are (or look through all the Service manuals!).

### Use care when Racking

These older digital delays are *very* deep - 16" for the Yamaha, 15" for the Roland. They need support at the back of them or they will twist and tear the front rack mount ears.

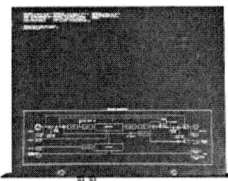 

By present day standards, these early digital delays are noisy, and if they go wrong, their memory chips are impossible to replace. But, apart from specialised installation models there are hardly any stand alone delays being made new today, as the trend is to multi-effects processors that do everything. So the only way you may get to use any of these delays is on someone else's rig, or via the second hand market.

## Reverb

Reverberation (to use its complete name) is a different effect to echo or straight delay. It's a whole series of short and long delays that combine randomly together to give an effect of space and depth.

The same technological revolution that brought us digital mixers, equalizers, crossovers, affordable digital delays also brought with it affordable digital reverbs. Because good reverb is such an awkward thing to achieve in an analog manner, digital has taken over completely for live use.

They are available with programs that recreate digitally what would be totally impractical in a mechanical form; Studio Plate reverb, Huge auditorium reverb, falling-down-a-well reverb, anything you can imagine, in a little box 1¾" high!

### Spring Reverb

However, you still may come across a Spring unit now and then. AKG made a couple of them, so did Roland, there was the Great British Spring (mounted in a piece of plastic drainpipe), and probably many others. They worked exactly along the same lines as the one in your good old Twin Reverb guitar amp.

Basically a long coil spring(s) is excited at one end, and its random vibrations are picked up and amplified at the other. The spring keeps vibrating long after the original signal has stopped, giving the reverberation effect. The gain in the pickup stage is enormous, so these units have to be well shielded as they are very susceptible to hum.

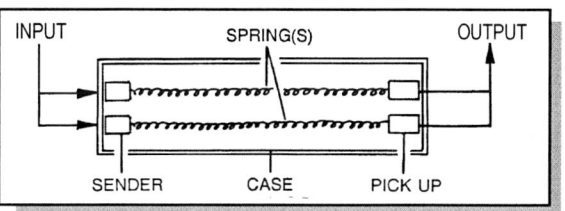

Spring Reverbs are very MID efficient devices, and should have some EQ controls on the front to try to lessen the Mid response and boost the HIGH end. A good one should also have a limiter on its Input, as signals with lots of transients like drums will make the spring physically Twang on each beat. If you do come across one it's best to keep it for vocals.

They are also popular with guitarists, and that's why you still find them in guitar amplifiers.

Also, if a drunk bangs into your effects rack while you have a spring reverb wound up (no pun intended!), the resulting CRASH sound from the PA system has to be heard to be believed!

## Digital Reverb

Digital reverb units can give you the sound of any place you like, from that of your favourite bathroom to the digital equivalent of Notre Dame cathedral, or any combination in between.

Like Digital Delays, they fall into 2 categories; those with knobs and those without.

*If a drunk bangs into your spring reverb the sound has to be heard to be believed!*

### Digital Reverbs With Knobs

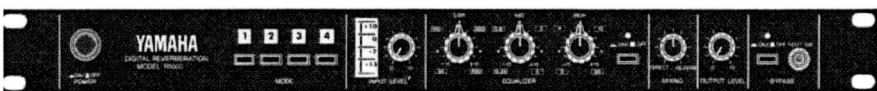

R 1000

One of the first of these was the Yamaha R 1000, with 4 different reverb programs. This was extremely popular and easy to use.

### How to get it to work

Set the Input and Output controls to 2 o'clock, press one of the 4 reverb program switches (1 - short, through to 4 - long), set the Mix control to Reverb (hard Right), and bring up the return level on the mixer. If there is no reverb, then the Bypass switch is on. Switch it off and the reverb will appear.

PCM 60

We're starting to see less knobs with the Lexicon PCM 60 and 70. The 60 has knobs for Input level, Mix and Reverb level, but switches for the rest. There are 2 types of program, Plate (simulating Large mechanical Reverb plates, from studios) and Room. These programs can be modified with 4 switches for Small through Large, and 4 more switches for Short through Long. EQ is limited to Bass boost and Treble boost switches.

### How to get it to work

*The sound of your favourite bathroom or the digital equivalent of Notre Dame*

Basically, as long as the Input and Reverb levels are up, the Mix control is on Reverb (hard Right) and some switches are pressed, then this unit will work. Try all the switch combinations until you find some that you like, then make a note of them.

Later Lexicon models  (PCM 71/81/91) are also popular and had refinements on this layout.

A product from the Alesis company broke the cost barrier on digital reverbs and effects - the original Midiverb. This was a small plastic box looking like a remote control, affectionately nicknamed the 'soapdish', with 69 various reverbs and a few delay effects.

ORIGINAL MIDIVERB

### How to get it to work

By pressing the Up or Down buttons you can scroll through all these programs until you find one you like, and although you can't adjust them, there are plenty to choose from.

The Midiverb 2 had the same package as the original, but the Midiverb 3 and 4 went 'up-market' into a 1 RU (Rack Unit) package.

1 RU MICROVERB (ABOVE) AND 1/3 OF 1 RU NANOVERB (RIGHT)

## Digital Reverbs Without Knobs

This is the current design concept for nearly all reverbs on the market today, and since as well as reverb they also handle digital delay effects, compression, gating, and pitch transposing, there's a new name for them - Digital Effects Processors.

One of the first, and perhaps the best known, was the Yamaha SPX 90. You'll see a lot of these around, and nearly every other Digital Effects Processor follows the same operating protocols.

SPX 90

### How to get it to work

The only knob is on the left hand side, the Input level, so as usual start with it at about 2 o'clock. Next to that is a LED level meter, then Red program memory numbers from 1 to 90, and then 2 lines of green words.

There are 2 sets of UP and DOWN arrow buttons. Pressing either of the RIGHT ones changes the red memory numbers up or down. When the program you want flashes up, press the Recall button and it stops flashing and the effect starts working audibly. Now you can use the LEFT set of arrow buttons to adjust the parameters of the program you have chosen. For example, if the reverb time shown was 3 seconds, pushing the UP arrow would make it longer, and the DOWN arrow make it shorter.

Press the Balance button, and you can adjust the Left/Right output levels; press it again and you can adjust the ratio of the Original Signal to the Effect Signal. Leave it on 100% Effect for mixing purposes, as you'll be doing all this at the desk.

Now this unit has 30 preset memories, and another 60 you can store yourself. Let's say you have #3, Rev 3 Vocal, and you've increased the reverb time to 5 seconds. If you want to keep this, press the arrow buttons next to the Store button until say #31 comes up. Press the Store button and your customized #3 program is now #31, until you decide to change it.

The later SPX 500, 900 and 1000 have a modified front panel design that groups the control buttons together in a slightly more 'intuitive' layout, more preset programs, and the ability to string up to 4 different effects together.

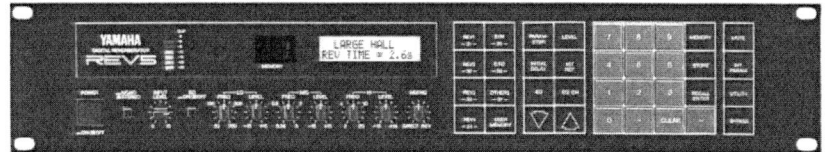

REV 5

The Rev 5 and Rev 7 models from Yamaha had a slightly different layout in a 2 rack unit package, with the ability to have hot keys for your favourite settings. The sweepable EQ on the front panel is very useful when you need to return them via an Effects return rather than a channel.

Other models are Multi Effects Processors, like the SPX 1000, Alesis Quadraverb and a whole lot more, which can handle Compression, Gating, Delay, Reverb all at the same time. So if you want a compressed Chorus effect on your reverse gated Reverb, with a couple of repeats thrown in, you can have it!

SPX 2000 - STILL RECOGNISABLE AS COMING FROM THE SAME FAMILY!

Recently, though, a new reverb from Eventide has reversed the trend towards multi-effects nudge button layouts. The Princeton Digital Reverb 2016 is a pure reverb unit, with instant access knobs and no menus! There is a choice of 99 user-definable presets, including ten spare blank ones, and any factory preset can be overwritten and saved with your own.

### How to get it to work
As long as the inputs and outputs are connected up properly and you have a program selected, something will come out of it!

### Pitch transposers/Harmony machines
For a long time these have been effects looking for an application. Apart from special 'one off' guitar or vocal special effects, or adding in an extra low octave to drums, they haven't been too useful. A great sounding gimmick, but one that was hard to find any real world applications for.

The problem was that they weren't 'smart' enough. Real vocal harmonies are not always a fixed percentage higher or lower than the original - they can vary with the particular note or mode of harmony.

However, with the advent of better digital

MXR PITCH TRANSPOSER - OLD, CHEAP, NOISY

technology, all that has changed. Today's harmony machines will recreate soaring 3, 4, or 5 part harmonies in real time, from a single instrument or voice. You can use existing presets, or you can make up your own.

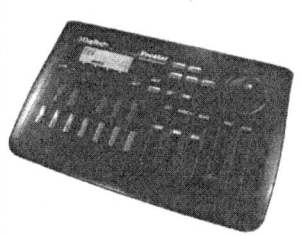

DIGITECH VOCALIST - SMARTER, MULTI HARMONY, QUIETER

Set them up either as a standard effect, from one of the Aux sends, or as an 'effect in place' *(see page 58)* on a single voice, although if you try the latter I'd recommend a fairly 'believable' setting most of the time.

### How to get one to work

Set the Input control to three quarters up as a start point, and scroll through the presets until you find one you like. Unless you have a super good ear for harmonies I'd leave it right there. Harmonies are not a good thing to experiment with at the gig because bad ones leap right out at you and make you cringe!

EVENTIDE HARMONIZER - STATE OF THE ART

I'd also recommend that you gate the send to its input, otherwise the it tries to add the effect on to all the background noise the microphone picks up, and usually not very successfully. By gating it you make sure the effect only works when there is some signal going into it.

A popular trick to fatten up a vocal with an Eventide Harmonizer - try a few milliseconds delay combined with a few cents (one octave = 100 cents) detuning. Pan the original (dry) signal Left and the harmonized (wet) signal hard right. It's a great real-time double tracking effect.

### Unfamiliar effects units

When you are faced with an effects processor that you haven't seen before, don't panic. They are all there to do a similar job, so take it easy and just try it out. Learning by actually doing it for yourself is by far the best way, because then it sticks with you for a long time. If you get really stuck, don't be afraid to ask whoever is running the system. There is nothing people like talking about more than their new toys, and if you explain the effect you are after, most will be happy to show you.

### Onboard effects

Given that digital effects are so common nowadays, a lot of small and even medium size mixers have a basic effects unit with Delay, Reverb, Chorus presets built in to them.

These will be driven by a dedicated Auxiliary Send, usually marked Effects, and there will be a multi-position switch or nudge buttons over in the Master section that steps through the various effects available. A separate control may also modify the effect.

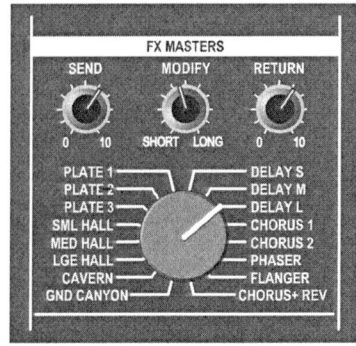

TYPICAL ONBOARD EFFECTS MODULE

### How do you use them?

You use them in the same way you would an outboard effect, except that as it is already returned into the mix so it can't be plugged into a channel and have its own fader. Instead you'll have to use the rotary return knob to control the blend of wet (the effect) and dry (the original signal. Some manufacturers who actually use the stuff they make give you a return control on a fader, which makes life a lot easier.

Digital mixers take onboard effects a few steps further, and have complete multiple effects units built-in, with all the controls that are on standalone outboard versions. These can be routed to any input, auxiliary, group or output. If the effects suit your needs this can remove the need for any outboard effects at all.

### Summing up

Well, that's about as straightforward as I can make it. It's beyond the scope of this book to list all of the various effects available, since they are continually evolving, but whatever the brand or model, the same process applies to nearly all of these 'knobless' digital effects processors: scrolling through the presets, choosing the one you want, adjusting the parameters, then storing them.

Since basically they all work along the same lines, I've tried to stick to representative models that are available worldwide, stuff that you're likely to use when you walk up to a mixer. It doesn't matter whether they come from Alesis, Korg, Lexicon, Roland, Yamaha, or anybody. If you can master one, you can master any of them. They may have different names for the controls, but they'll all work the same way, and, unless they're built in, they'll all plug in and out of the mixer in the same way.

Yes, setting up some digital units can be time consuming, but it is the only way to have complete control over the effect sound without a front panel about 8 rack units high! My advice is to start with the factory presets until you get the hang of manipulating the parameter options.

And you thought you were just going to sit there and wait for the band to come on!

## What do we do with all this stuff?

These effects are just that - effects. They help you to enhance the sound of the various instruments to bring life into the mix. They can add a feeling of space and depth, as we mentioned before, plus change the sound of instruments and vocals, and add excitement. How you use them is up to you - that's what the band pays you for.

### Delay Effects

Here are some typical uses of different delay settings.

- 1 ms (millisecond) through to 16 ms, with a little modulation, will give you a gentle chorus type effect to a hard metallic flanging effect, by adding in more feedback or regeneration.

- 16 ms to 25 ms delays give a double tracking effect, which may be made more realistic by a very small amount of modulation. This simulates the inevitable differences that occur in real double tracking, due to things never being played or sung exactly the same way twice.

- Delays up to about 50 ms are not perceived by the ear as 'echoes' but as a gradual 'thickening' effect, and are very effective in making instruments or voices appear 'fatter' without actually being louder.

- At 80 ms to 100 ms, depending on the person, the ear starts hearing definite separate echoes, similar to the 'slap' echoes from the rear wall of a large room.

From 200 ms onwards the discrete echoes can be used as special effects; in time with the beats of the music, for example.

If you're using long delays, one or two repeats dialled up is plenty - any more will muddy up the sound of the vocals, with the echo of the previous words over-running the sound of the next words.

*Listen to what other sound engineers do with their effects - you can always learn*

### Reverb Effects

Reverb programs often have names like 'Small Room' 'Large Hall' 'Warm Plate' 'Auditorium' and so on, in order to try to convey some of the various textures in the sound. Don't worry what they're called, just find the ones that sound 'right' to you. You can usually save and rename them to whatever you like, anyway.

With the proliferation of reasonably priced digital effects units now, you can have live sounds that were just wishful thinking a few years ago.

You can have a Compressed and Gated Reverb on the Snare Drum, and a wide Stereo Large Room on the rest of the drums, plus a little Chorus for some 'sizzle'; a short compressed 'double tracking' type delay on the Lead vocals, with a longer one slightly in the background, and maybe a Bright Hall Reverb as well; a slight Chorus on the backing vocals plus a short warm Reverb; the list is endless, the choice is yours.

Listen to as much music as you can, work out what effects are being used on them, then try them out at your next gig. Listen to what other sound engineers do with their effects - one of the first things you learn in this industry is that you can always learn!

### Practical PreSets

Let's say you've got four effects units in the rack. Set the first one up with a short delay (50 - 100ms, the second with a longer 'slap' type delay 300 - 500ms), the third with a reverb that suits drums, and the fourth with a nice lush hall setting for vocals.

Now you're set for anything that might come up. If you have the time, you could set up some presets on each unit - say a range of short delays, a range of longer ones, and 3 or four reverbs that sound good.

*The effects are there to enhance the sound and bring life into the mix*

It never ceases to amaze me how many unusable reverb presets there are on some units (usually the cheaper ones!). But persevere until you find the ones that *are* usable. If you can't save your settings, make a note of the presets you like on a sheet of paper, or on some masking tape stuck to the side of the rack (not on the unit itself unless it's yours!).

Unless you have a special requirement for a particular hard flange or specific gated reverb, these presets will be more than enough to get you through the night.

### Effect in Place

At the start of this chapter I explained how to run effects from the Aux sends of the mixer.

However, if you are short on available sends for all these, you can always insert the effect on the actual channel using the insert points on the mixer, or inserted into the groups. Just bear in mind that by doing this, only *that* particular channel or group can access the effect. With the affordably priced effects units available today, you can economically put together a very useful set of discrete effects units to cover just about everything.

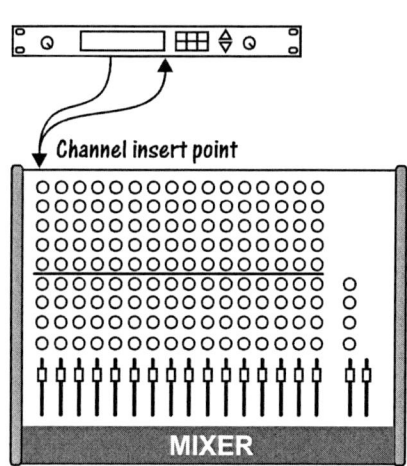

Channel insert point

MIXER

If you decide to use this method on some effects, you will have to mix the original signal and effect on the actual unit, rather than on the mixer as previously discussed.

This means that instead of having the Mix control on the unit set on 100% effect, as you would if you were using the mixer sends and returns, you have it set on maybe 70% original, 30% effect. Listen and use your judgment.

Less is probably better than more, as you may run out of hands to pull these things down in between songs. If the effect is subtle you can probably leave it up in between songs. See *'Midi Control of Effects'* next in this chapter.

Some typical choices for this 'Effect in Place' technique would be Harmonizer/Delay/

Reverb on Lead vocal, and Backing vocals (on a sub group), and Reverb on Kick drum, Harmonizer/Delay/Reverb on Snare drum.

All of these have specific effects requirements that are not always possible when using, say, a general reverb setting for all the drums. The snare may have just the sound you've been looking for with a reverse gated reverb, but the other drums probably won't.

## Midi control of effects

Midi stands for Musical Instrument Digital Interface, and no, it's not just for keyboard players! Most digital effects units have Midi ins and out on the back of them - those little 5 pin DIN connectors like you used to see on your grandfather's Grundig tape recorder.

DIN
CONNECTOR

By using a Midi patch changer built into some larger mixers, or a laptop computer and linking up all these midi effects, you can control them by typing a single 2 digit number code.

### *Why bother?*

Speed and convenience, mainly. You can modify all the parameters on each effect to sound the way you want, then assign a number to those settings. Each time you punch in that number each effect instantly reverts to the original parameters that you assigned to that number.

Have a think about this situation, for example. For simplicity, let's stick to the four effects units mentioned before, although this method will control more than just four.

*Ist song:*

    Effect #1 Gated Reverb on Snare drum

    Effect #2 Long decay small room reverb on Toms

    Effect #3 Chorus type delay on all vocals

    Effect #4 Longer delay on lead vocal

All is going well, and the song finishes. Straightaway the band launches into its big hit, which needs some very different effects:

*Second song:*

    Effect #1 Gated Reverse Reverb on snare, but with 200 ms pre-delay

    Effect #2 Short decay big room reverb on Toms

    Effect #3 Large concert hall reverb with long decay on lead vocal

    Effect #4 Double tracking delay/pitch change on lead vocal

That's a lot of knobs to twiddle or buttons to nudge in just a couple of seconds! And in the 3rd song, the settings need to change again. Somewhere you need to find time to mix, as well!

Now with Midi control of all this, you could call the settings for the first song 01, the second 02, the third 03, and so on. Just by pressing 2 buttons, or 'Next' on your computer screen you can control *all* these settings on *all* these effects, virtually instantly.

Sure, all this takes time to set up and program, but digital effects without knobs do anyway. By using Midi control you can make that time work for you, by saving you time during the gig because you only have to do it once.

This type of setup is ideal when you're working with the same band all the time, but what if you're a freelance engineer working with a different band each night?

Well, if you have your own small rack of effects you can still keep your favourite settings, linked up ready to go. You don't necessarily have to have all the effects return faders pushed up in all the songs, so you can still vary things as necessary.

Plus, you can modify parameters 'on the fly' using the manual controls, then saving them - as a different patch number, or overwriting an existing one; or maybe defaulting back to your original settings at the end of the song.

And if everything goes horribly wrong, you can always revert to your Practical PreSets. Don't overwrite them, so they're always there when you need them.

Sounds complicated? Of course it does, because it's new, and anything new sounds complicated at first. But it's not really. The more you use something, no matter what it is, the more used to it you become, until using it becomes second nature.

The first time you use a digital reverb without knobs you think that you'll never get used to it, but you do, because the end result justifies the learning curve. Once you do it a few times you realize it's no harder than setting your digital clock radio, and probably a lot easier than setting the VCR or DVD recorder! So don't think that Midi control of effects is just for big concert systems. It can be used successfully on smaller systems too, and economically, because prices are getting more affordable every year.

### Computers and Software Effects

Small, compact laptop/notebook computers are becoming so well priced that it makes great sense to get one. Instead of a Midi patch changer, you can use your PC or Mac to control these effects, and have the various assigns and their parameters print up on the screen, which can sure beat trying to read them in the dark on the little liquid crystal display on the front panel. Popular programs for doing this include Logic (for Macs only), Cubase, Sonar, Cakewalk, and many others, plus there is a staggering amount of advice and information on the Internet from many user groups.

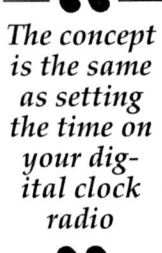

*The concept is the same as setting the time on your digital clock radio*

But why stop there? Inside every modern computer is more processing power than you can poke a stick at. Now that most audio recording is done by hard disk based Digital Audio Workstations, there are a huge amount of software effects available, and many of them free! Connect up a Firewire or USB2 in/out box to your laptop, open up an audio editing program, and you can have world class digital effects available to run into your mix. Connect an Aux Out to the inputs of the box, and connect the Outputs of the box to an Effects return channel, then choose from the effects you've got. OK, I've simplified things, but play around with the idea when you have some spare time and you'll see what I mean.

### Delay Stacks

Sound travels at approximately 1130 feet per second. If you want to set up some extra speaker stacks halfway down a long auditorium, or outside, you must run them on a delay. Here's how you do it:

Pace out the distance from the main stacks to the delayed stacks. As a general rule of thumb (or foot) you can use 1 foot (300mm) per millisecond as the basis of your delay calculations. It's not exactly accurate but it's probably as close as your foot is to 12", and it will give you a ballpark figure to start from.

The sound from the delay stacks must be delayed by the time it takes for the sound from the main system to reach them, so the audience hears the main system's sound reinforced by the delay stacks.

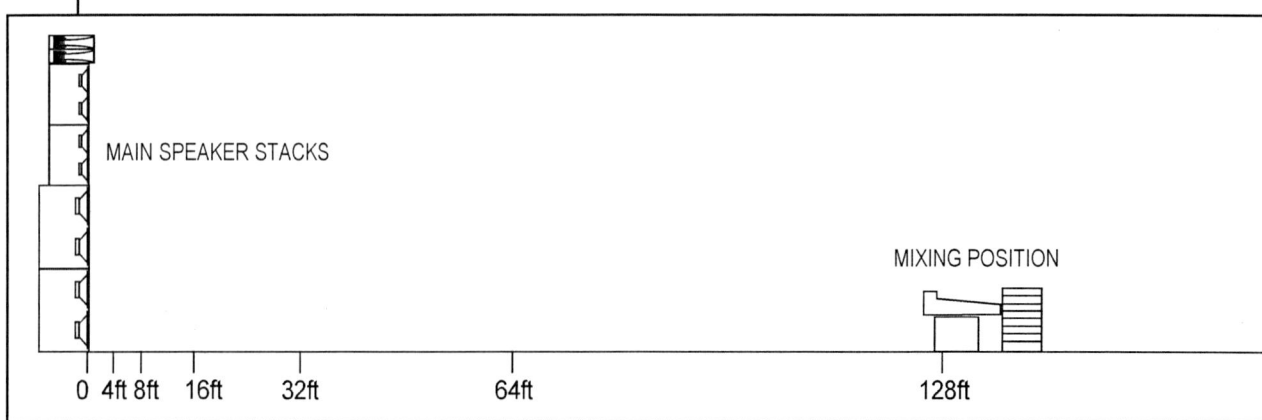

MAIN SPEAKER STACKS

MIXING POSITION

0  4ft 8ft   16ft   32ft              64ft                              128ft

Work out the approximate millisecond setting on your delay, then fine tune it using the Delay Time control, until the delay stack's sound is just a couple of milliseconds **behind** the main sound. This will preserve the feeling of distance in the sound, and keep the focus on the main stacks. Spend a little time on this process - if you are going to do it at all, it must be right, otherwise it will sound like a bad train station PA system!

Just a final note on this: recheck this delay after the audience is in and the place has warmed up. Sound travels differently in warm air, wet air, or thin air.

If you're looking for an all-round Live Pro Audio website, it's worthwhile checking  out: www.ProSoundWeb.com, which is chock full of product use and mixing advice from engineers around the world.

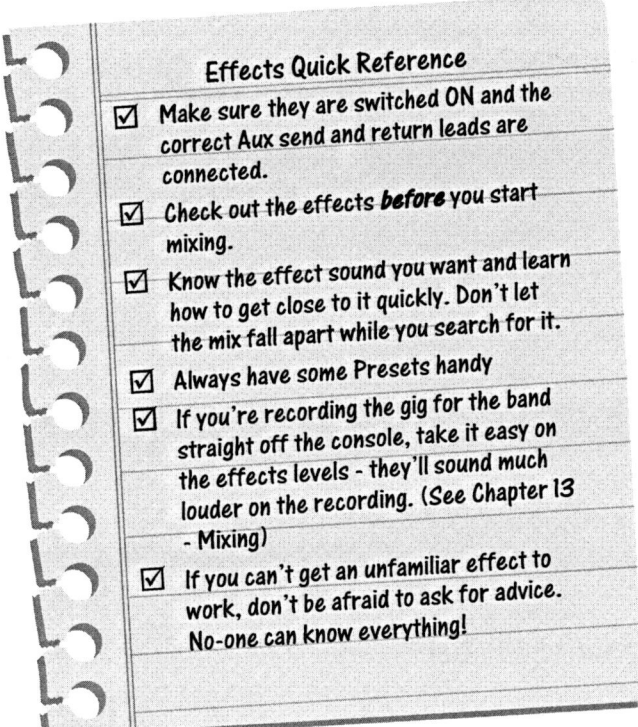

### Effects Quick Reference

- ☑ Make sure they are switched ON and the correct Aux send and return leads are connected.
- ☑ Check out the effects **before** you start mixing.
- ☑ Know the effect sound you want and learn how to get close to it quickly. Don't let the mix fall apart while you search for it.
- ☑ Always have some Presets handy
- ☑ If you're recording the gig for the band straight off the console, take it easy on the effects levels - they'll sound much louder on the recording. (See Chapter 13 - Mixing)
- ☑ If you can't get an unfamiliar effect to work, don't be afraid to ask for advice. No-one can know everything!

*=66=*
*Sound travels differently in warm air, wet air or thin air*
*=99=*

DELAY STACK

256ft                                                              384ft

## 7  Signal Processors

'Signal processor' is the generic name given to devices that modify the dynamics of the original audio signal, unlike an effect, which is an external signal mixed in with the original. The most common signal processors are compressors, limiters, noise gates, and other devices like an Aural exciter.

### Compressors and Limiters

Here's a couple of technical definitions first.

- A compressor is a variable gain amplifier whose output voltage compared to its input voltage decreases as its input level increases past a set threshold.

- A limiter is essentially a compressor with a high compression ratio, thus maintaining a constant output level despite any increase in input level above the threshold.

So, let's look at this is non-technical terms. Basically what these do is keep an eye (or should that be ear?) on signal levels, stopping them from getting any louder than the level you set (the Threshold). A compressor puts a gentle 'squeeze' on excess level, whereas a limiter hits it on the head with a hammer!

### Compressor Controls

The basic 3 controls that are common to all compressor/ limiters are these:

### Threshold

This control varies the level at which the compressor will start to modify the signal dynamics. As soon as the signal reaches this Threshold, it is prevented from going further. The extra level that the signal would have reached is 'squeezed' up until the signal level drops again.

Live Sound Mixing 4th Edition ©2005 D.R.Fry

### Ratio

This determines how much the signal is squeezed up once the Threshold is reached. It is usually variable from no compression (1:1), soft compression (2:1 or 3:1), medium compression (3:1 to 6:1), heavy compression (6:1 to 8:1) hard limiting (10 :1 to oo:1).

### Output

This controls the output gain of the compressor. For example, with a low threshold and a 10:1 ratio, a lot of overall volume can be lost. The output control is a gain recovery stage, and enables you to bring back the lost volume safely (*in theory - read* 'Using the Output Control' *further on in this chapter*) without having to worry about any peaks that may cause distortion.

Other controls can include:

### Attack and Release

These control how fast the compressor reacts to the signal increase (Attack) and how quickly it returns to normal (Release). If there are no controls for these, then the Attack and Release are either fixed, or else they vary automatically with the type of program material.

### Separate Compressor and Peak Limiter

The first lets you set up a soft compression ratio to pull the mix together, and the second lets you set an absolute peak level control.

### Master/Slave configuration, or Stereo Link

When running stereo, both channels (or both units, if using 2 mono units) can be controlled by the one channel or unit. Thus if the Left channel squeezes up, the Right will as well. This keeps the stereo image centred and not jumping from side to side, as it could if the two were not linked.

### Noise Gate

Some compressor/limiters have a Noise Gate included on each channel. The Threshold of this can be set at just above the system noise level, to keep buzzes, hiss etc out of the system when nothing is playing.

### Input level control

This allows the unit to accept a wider range of signals, from guitar pickup to professional console levels. If the control is calibrated in dB, then 0dB would be a good place to start. Set the Output the same. If the control is just calibrated 0 to 10, then set it at about 2 o'clock to start with. Set the Threshold at 0dB. Play a CD and adjust the Input level until the first LED of the Gain Reduction/ Compression lights up. Now you're close to 0dB Input level.

### Bypass switch

This switch enables you to compare compressed and non-compressed signal levels.

### Hard Knee/Soft Knee

This phrase refers to the action of the compressor at the threshold point. Hard knee means that the compressor waits until the signal actually reaches the threshold point before any squeezing occurs. Soft knee means that the compressor starts to come in just a few dB before the Threshold and rolls over into compression gently. The idea is that the 'soft' start to the compression makes it less audible.

This is fine when using the compressor as a desk insert on vocals, instruments etc, but when you are

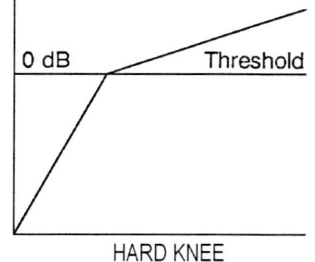

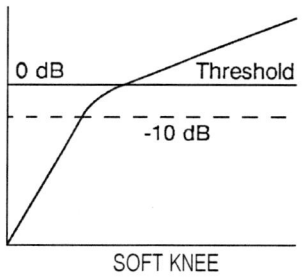

using one as an overall system protector you want the maximum power output before any compression or limiting takes place. For this application choose Hard knee.

It's not surprising that a lot of engineers call the soft knee setting 'the support band switch!'

### Where do you use them?

Compressor/limiters can be placed almost anywhere in the signal chain from microphone preamp to before the amplifier. Big touring systems have lots of them, because the bigger the system is, the easier it is to overdrive it.

Where a small system will probably just have one over the main outputs, as system protection, a larger system may have one on each output of the crossover, one on each monitor send, one on the Drum group, individual vocals, Bass, and a stereo pair on the main Left/ Right outputs from the desk.

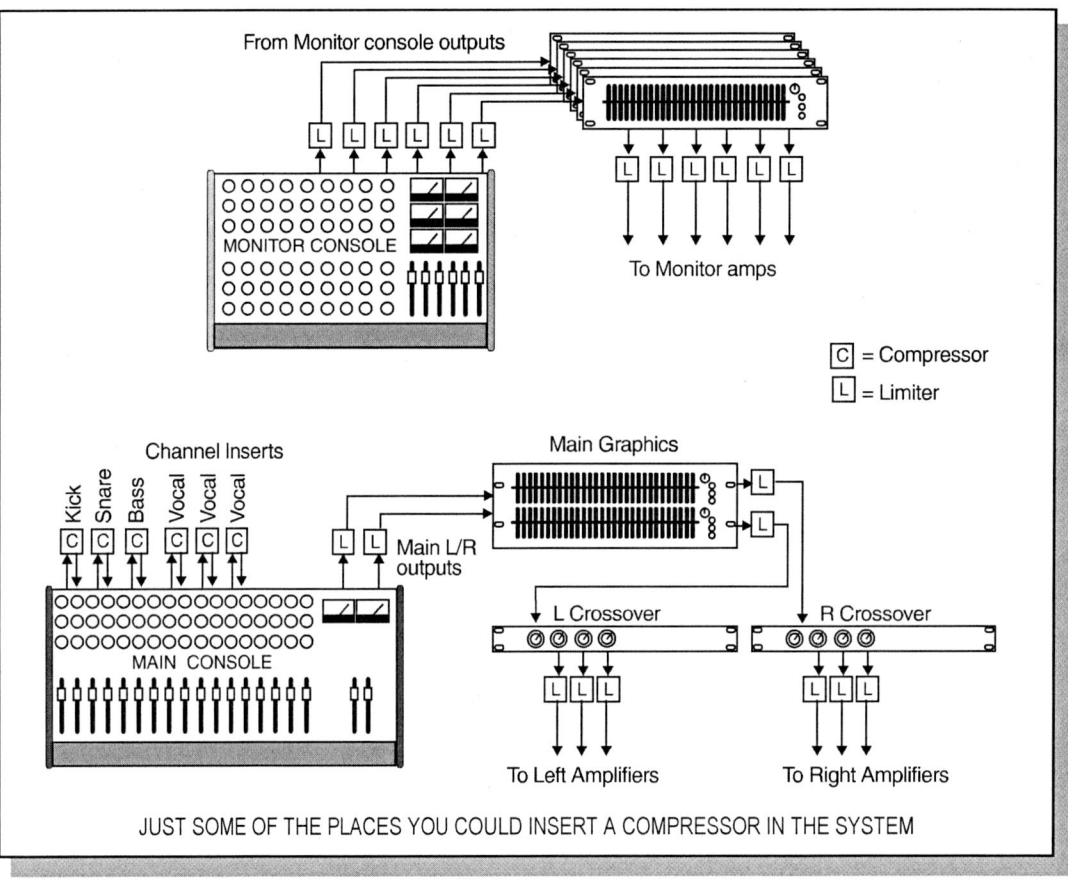

JUST SOME OF THE PLACES YOU COULD INSERT A COMPRESSOR IN THE SYSTEM

> *A lot of engineers call the soft knee setting 'the support band switch!'*

You can insert a compressor wherever you need to control levels without having to gain ride the faders all the time. To experiment with them, set the main system compressor on 0dB Threshold, a Ratio of 3:1, and 0 dB output, and play a tape through the system, pushing up the level until the compressor's metering tells you it's compressing. Now vary the Ratio, from 3:1 up to 10:1, and listen to the difference. Try varying the other controls until you are familiar with what each one does. In the use of compressors especially, the more you know about how they work, the better you can use them to keep the mix under control but still loud and up front.

### Compressor applications

When you feel comfortable using compressors in the mix, you can let them look after the housekeeping while you look after the window dressing - setting up delays, reverb, stereo panning, solos, looking cool, that type of thing.

There's an old saying from recording engineers: "Everything sounds better with a little compression." And it's true for Live sound as well, as long as you remember that adjective 'little'!

If you've only got one compressor, try using it over the whole mix at about 3:1 ratio. The improvement on no compressor is amazing - the whole mix improves because any sudden loud parts are pulled back before they get too loud - automatically. If you're running stereo, it's the same thing times 2, but make sure they track together (see Stereo Link switch above).

Tracking together means one channel usually controls the dynamics of the other. In real terms it fattens up the bottom end and keeps your stereo image centred.

If your system is too small for the venue you can still keep some impression of big and loud by increasing the compression ratio to about 10:1. Now it's a limiter. This is going to soak up any peaks, so you can push things harder, raise the compressor output a couple of dB (more on this later), and keep the whole mix a lot louder. However, only one thing at a time is going to be up front.

Why is this so? Well, one thing you have to remember is that compressors are not infallible. With Live music being what it is - Live - most compressors make a pretty good job of keeping a constantly changing, unpredictable signal under control. But they can be easily fooled. Whatever is loudest in the mix will trigger them, and attempt to push out the rest.

So, when there's vocals, they take over, and when there's not, the band shifts up front. Instantly. You just couldn't move enough faders manually that fast. You are compromising the sound, sure, but you are getting the gig done. Just make sure the whole thing is not being modulated by the kick and snare drums. Otherwise, everything but those drums will drop out momentarily on each beat.

If you have more compressors, say four, then you can put one on the kick drum, one on the lead vocal, and one each on Left and Right.

That way you can have a big kick sound that's really up front but not overpowering, and vocals that can be loud but not so loud that they push everything else down on a loud scream. Start at about 3:1 and experiment; too little compression and the levels will be too uneven; too much and the sound will be strangled.

### Using the Output control

Be careful. Don't increase the output gain any more than 2 or 3 dB above 0 dB (unity) unless you are *positive* that your room EQ is perfect.

What happens is simple; when the music is happily bopping away, there's no problem. When it stops, there's nothing to compress, so all that extra gain is just sitting there waiting to feed back. And it usually doesn't wait very long!

If you're just using one compressor over the console main output, well, you can usually catch things in time. Four or more, though, and they will demand constant attention to stop them feeding back. Kick drum and Bass guitar are particular culprits.

Since most people's EQ'ing (mine included!) is not always perfect, you have to 'gain ride' the outputs. At the end of the song, just ease the master faders down a few dB, to compensate for that extra gain you've dialled into the compressors. You can pull the instruments down a bit more, perhaps, as there will usually be a little bit of inter-song chat from the band to the audience, and if you've pulled the levels down then you won't get any stray drum beats or guitar chords interrupting it.

The instant (or preferably the instant before) the band launches into the next number, push those masters back up where they were.

If your compressor has controls for attack and release, I'd set them on medium to start with! Compressors that don't have attack and release controls have those kind of decisions made internally, automatically, depending on the signal characteristics. Personally I prefer to let the machine make those decisions, because, on a constantly changing signal like Live music, frankly, most of them do it better. More importantly, they do it faster!

Most compressors can function as limiters as well, on ratios of 10:1 up to infinity:1. Apart from special applications like the 'too small' system, the most common use is as overall system protection. In its most basic form, this consists of a single limiter placed before the system crossover, or, if the system is passive, before the amplifier.

A more sophisticated form is to put limiters on each output of the crossover. This works well, because each frequency band is limited separately and doesn't interact with any others, making any limiting less noticeable. On the downside, though, you'll need a lot of limiters on, say, a stereo 4 way rig!

A more musical, less expensive idea is to use a multi band compressor over your main mix. This splits the signal into Low and High frequencies, compresses them separately, then recombines them into one and sends it off to the rest of the system. A unit like this gives you the opportunity to make creative compression changes to either Low or High frequencies, for more perceived bottom end, perhaps, or as a unique sound creator when used as a channel insert.

Let's look at a typical budget rock and roll set up; say a 24 channel console, a couple of 4 channel quad compressors, and a dual band stereo compressor like an ARX Afterburner or Aphex Dominator on the main outputs.

Where are we going to use 8 compressors? A minute ago we were lucky to have just one!

Well, I'd insert them on:

    Kick drum

    Snare drum

    Bass guitar

    Lead guitar

    Lead vocal channels for a start.

If there are keyboards, then I'd put one on each keyboard channel.

The problem with keyboards is that the volume levels of different synth patches can vary enormously. Where one just sits happily in your mix, a sudden switch to another can really bend the needles, usually just when you're busy reprogramming a digital delay! Plus, if the keyboard player has his own volume pedal, he can effectively take control of the sound away from you. Not good! So, counteract this with a harder compression ratio, say 8:1, so that sudden volume changes are taken care of until you have a chance to reduce the level.

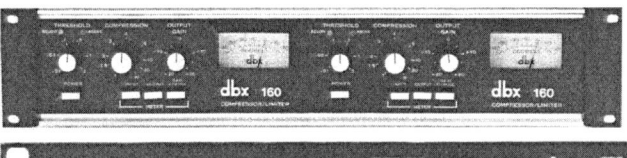

ORIGINALLY THE LIVE MUSIC INDUSTRY'S STANDARD WORKHORSE WAS THE DBX 160 AND 160X SINGLE CHANNEL COMPRESSOR.

DUE TO THE DEMAND FOR MORE COMPRESSORS FOR MORE SYSTEM CONTROL, FOUR CHANNEL COMPRESSORS IN A SINGLE RACK UNIT PACKAGE ARE AVAILABLE FROM ARX, APHEX, BSS, DRAWMER, KLARK TEKNIK AND MANY OTHERS.

You don't have to use compressors just on individual channels. If the console has submix groups, or busses, you can insert the compressors there as well, depending on what you have assigned to them.

We've used maybe seven compressors so far, so maybe I'd use the remaining one on percussion, or any other instrument - sax, trumpet, other guitar. However, if I had a band with a few backing vocalists, I would ***definitely*** use it on a vocal submix group.

Harmonies are an important part of the vocal sound. To really pull them together, assign all the vocals to their own group and insert a compressor on it. Set the ratio on about 3 or 4:1, judiciously increase the level, and it will grab those soaring harmonies together and push them up front. Gate that group as well for maximum clarity.

If you're running a stereo drum submix, you could insert 2 compressors there rather than on individual drum channels, which you may prefer to gate. You've got slightly less control, but compressing the group will pull all the drums together. Just be careful of that output gain.

## Noise Gates

First, a technical description.

> A Noise Gate is an audio signal processing device that shuts off a signal when the level drops below a user adjustable threshold.

> When the signal is below this threshold the gate will close and the signal won't be heard; when it is above it the gate will open and let the signal pass through unaffected by the gate.

Not too technical, is it? You can see that a gate can be set up to discriminate between the audio signals you want, and unwanted sounds such as hiss, buzz, background noise and leakage from other instruments. All that is necessary is a level difference of a few dB for the gate to distinguish between wanted (louder) and unwanted (softer) sounds. By careful adjustment of the threshold control, you can let through what you want to hear and shut out what you don't.

Noise gates are very useful for controlling drums in live sound. For example, inserting a gate on each drum microphone means that when each drum is not actually being played, no sound will come out of that drum microphone.

On Kick drum, you can set the gate to open (turn on) the instant the beater hits the skin, and to close (turn off) a few milliseconds later. No ringing or 'boing', just a solid thud. The same goes for the Snare, and gates are just great for those toms that hardly ever seem to get hit, but just sit there feeding back. You can't pull down their level in case the drummer hits them, and drastic EQ can suck out all their punch.

With a set of gates, you have the freedom to use the desk EQ to give the drums the sound you want, rather that the sound you have to put up with to stop them feeding back.

### Gate Controls

Most gates have some or all of the following controls:

### Attack

This controls how fast the gate opens when the signal reaches the threshold. On many gates it is an automatic function, varying between fast and very fast depending on the program material.

### Release

This controls how fast the gate swings back closed after the signal has passed through. It is usually user variable from fast (a few milliseconds) to slow (a few seconds).

### Depth (or Range or Attenuation)

This determines how much signal and/or noise is let through by the gate when it is in the closed position. There are times when you don't want the gate to be totally shut, but left slightly ajar. Vocals, for example, can sound very choppy if they suddenly go from completely off to on to completely off to on...and so on. Setting this control so there is less of a jump when the vocals turn on gives a smoother, more natural sound.

### Threshold

This control varies the level that the signal has to reach before the gate opens and lets the signal through. When the signal drops back below the threshold the gate then closes. How fast it closes depends on your Release setting.

### Key Input

You'll find this on a lot of gates, so here's what it is.

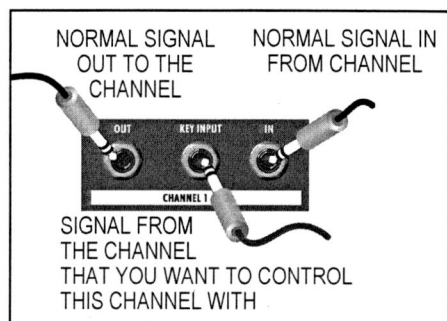

When you plug a signal into the Key Input of a gate, the gate is no longer controlled by the signal plugged into the normal IN socket, but by the signal you have plugged into the Key Input. In other words, you can control one signal with another. Controlling the Bass guitar with the Kick drum signal, for a funky sound, is a popular application, but there are plenty of others.

For example, if the brass section of a band is a bit ragged, you could assign them all to a subgroup, gate it, and key that gate with a line from the lead brass player's channel. Now when he or she plays, they all play!

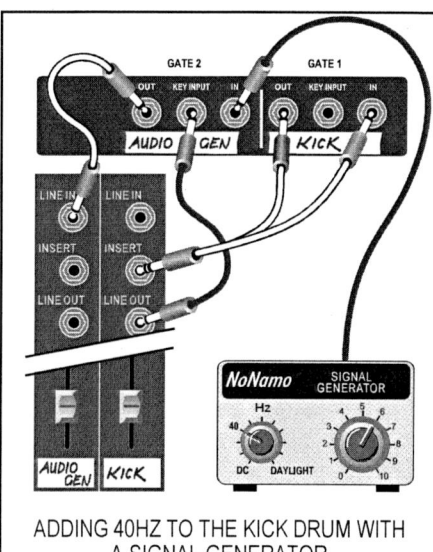

If you have access to a signal generator you could run a 40 Hz signal into a gate and key it with the Kick drum signal for a really fat sound that no amount of EQ boost could give you. You could also try the same thing with a white noise generator keyed by the Snare drum (or pink noise for a deeper sound).

ADDING 40HZ TO THE KICK DRUM WITH A SIGNAL GENERATOR

Using Key inputs can be fun. Just be careful you don't get so involved that the mix falls apart while you work on them!

### Tunable filters

Some gates have tunable Low Pass and High Pass filters, to make the gate not just level sensitive but 'frequency sensitive'. The Drawmer company pioneered this concept with their DS 201 Dual Gate, and now a lot of gates feature it. By using this method you can tune the gate to be 'deaf' to certain frequencies.

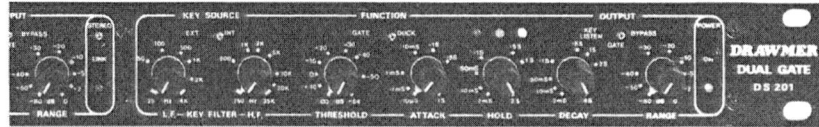

For example, on a drum kit, the gate on the Snare drum microphone can often be falsely triggered by the sound of the Hi Hats, which are right next door and can be very loud. On the DS 201 you can adjust the two filters so that the gate rejects the high frequency sound of the Hi Hats and only opens with the lower frequencies present in the Snare drum. If you have a gate on the Hi Hat cymbals you can tune it to do the opposite.

SNARE DRUM

HI HATS

## Using Gates

Let's look at a typical gate application - drums.

1. Insert a gate on the Kick drum channel

2. Set the Threshold as low as it will go

3. Set the Attack (if there is one) to Fast

4. Set the Release at Medium

5. Set the Depth (or Range, Attenuation) at Medium

6. As the drummer hits the drum, slowly turn the Threshold control up until the sound of the drum gets progressively 'drier' as the gate starts to open on the beats of the drum, and close in between. Don't go too far or the drum sound will shut off completely.

That's all there is to it.

Now you've got it going you can fine tune the gate action. If you still have too much 'boing' coming off the drum, shorten the Release time. If there is too much background noise coming through, increase the Depth control.

Now you've got the gate on one drum happening, you can go on to do the rest.

When you're gating Vocals, you will need less Depth that you will with drums, so that there is less of a jump from Closed to Open. As I mentioned before, set it at just enough attenuation to lose the background noise, or the sound can be unnatural and 'choppy'. Your release time should be longer, too, so the end of words can fade away more naturally.

A buzzing Bass can be cured by inserting a Gate on its channel, and so can a hissing guitar amp or a keyboard set up. The sound of the instrument will mask the buzz when it is playing, and the gate will shut off the signal when the instrument isn't playing.

Backing vocals can be cleaned up very simply by assigning them all to one subgroup on the desk, and inserting a gate on that subgroup. Now those microphones will only turn on when someone sings into them. This stops them picking up all the onstage noise when they're not being used, and muddying up your mix.

Gates are a very popular signal processing device, and can clean up the sound from any system. Like compressors, manufacturers are starting to put multiples of them in 1 rack unit. Klark Teknik, dbx, Drawmer and many more make Four channel gates, and ARX makes a Six channel gate in a one rack space unit!

> **"**
> *Gating backing vocals can really clean up a stereo mix*
> **"**

## Aural Exciters

The Aphex Aural Exciter is a very different type of signal processor for PA systems. It's a system 'enhancer.' They are easy to use, and also very easy to abuse. For this reason you'll find that engineers either love them or hate them. When used well, they can put life into a dull sounding system, pull vocals and solos out of the mix, and also give you more apparent level in the monitors. Used badly, they can make the sound harsh and tiring.

## How does it work?

The exciter principle is patented by Aphex, and works along these lines:

Let's say you play two exactly similar guitar solos, both at the same volume, but one is distorted and the other is clean. The one with the distortion sounds louder, because the distortion in the higher frequencies aggravate, or 'excite' the ear mechanism.

So the Aural Exciter generates a very small amount of harmonic distortion and mixes just a tiny bit of it back into the original signal. While doing this it delays the signal very slightly, and combined with the extra harmonics generated, produces a unique effect.

Tests have shown that a tiny amount of the right kind of harmonic distortion actually makes things sound 'better' to our ears. The even order (1st and 2nd) harmonic distortion generated by the tubes/valves of a guitar amp, for example.

In a live sound system, you can use the exciter as an effect, on one of the auxiliary sends from the desk; on a subgroup, to cover all the vocals or instruments on that group; or on the Left/Right master outputs of the desk, to brighten up the whole mix. It can also make a big difference on monitors *(see Chapter 14 - Problems)*.

Like many effects, a little is a lot. Adding a bit of exciter to the mix will produce a sparkling clarity; adding too much can tire out the audience's ears very quickly. The 'Big Bottom' effect available on the type C exciter is a low frequency delay that gives the impression of more bottom end.

Other 'psychoacoustic' devices available include the BBE 'Sonic Maximizer' which uses another patented process to split the signal 3 ways, then delay parts of it, EQ other parts and recombine the whole lot back into one signal. It also has a control to affect the LOW end.

## Sub Harmonic Processors

These are units that will create extra sub bass one octave below the regular bass notes, giving you an enormous fat sub rumble, ***as long as your speakers can handle it!*** Sub bass as generated by these units create large speaker cone movement, and can damage any bass drivers not designed for this type of signal. Use them with care! Typical units include the Peavey Kosmos and the dbx 120A.

## Meters

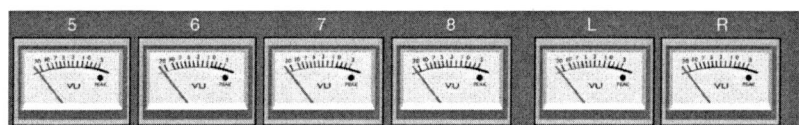

Meters are there to give you an idea of relative levels. They come in 2 main types, the analogue VU (Volume Units) meter type, with the familiar bouncing needle, and the ramp of multi coloured LEDs which flash on and off as the levels change. This type is usually known as a PPM (Peak Program Meter).

Both have their good points. The VU meter is excellent at giving you an average level reading, much the same as our ears hear things. On the other hand, the needle won't move fast enough to catch sudden peaks.

LED PPM meters can respond to peaks instantly, and so have a fast attack time, but usually a slower release time. This is because the LED can turn on or off the instant the signal changes, often too fast for the eye to see. The slower release gives you time for your eyes to register the peak. However these meters can make your mix levels too low if you interpret them as average levels.

To compensate for the VU meter's deficiencies, many of them now have a built-in 'peak' LED, that flashes independently of the needle; the better LED meters are now switchable between VU meter and PPM characteristics.

Either way, they are there to tell you what's going on.

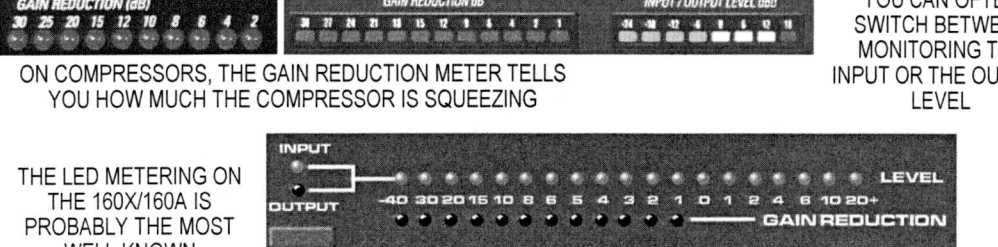

ON COMPRESSORS, THE GAIN REDUCTION METER TELLS
YOU HOW MUCH THE COMPRESSOR IS SQUEEZING

YOU CAN OFTEN
SWITCH BETWEEN
MONITORING THE
INPUT OR THE OUTPUT
LEVEL

THE LED METERING ON
THE 160X/160A IS
PROBABLY THE MOST
WELL KNOWN

I promised that there would be no complicated audio theory, so without getting into technicalities, let's just say that on a piece of professional equipment, a constant level of more than +3 dB above 0 dB is probably too much, and less than –20 dB is not enough. This is a complicated area, so use this just as a general rule of thumb.

Unless you are absolutely sure what the meter is telling you, don't rely on it too much; use your ears to tell you if something doesn't sound right.

## 0 dB

0 dB is not nothing. 0 dB is a standard reference point/operating level for sound equipment. Consumer items like your home stereo have a nominal operating level of –10 dB, while pro audio equipment has a nominal level of +4 dB. Your mixing desk can handle peak levels of +10 dB or more quite happily; your cassette deck can't.

A lot of equipment available these days is also used for the home studio market, and has a –10 dB or +4 dB switch on the back. Use the +4 dB setting for all PA system use. Be especially careful with equalizers with these switches. If there are two switches, one for the input and one for the output, make sure they are both switched to +4 dB, otherwise you can run out of headroom and get a very distorted signal.

See *Chapter 16 - Technical Stuff*, for more information on the Decibel.

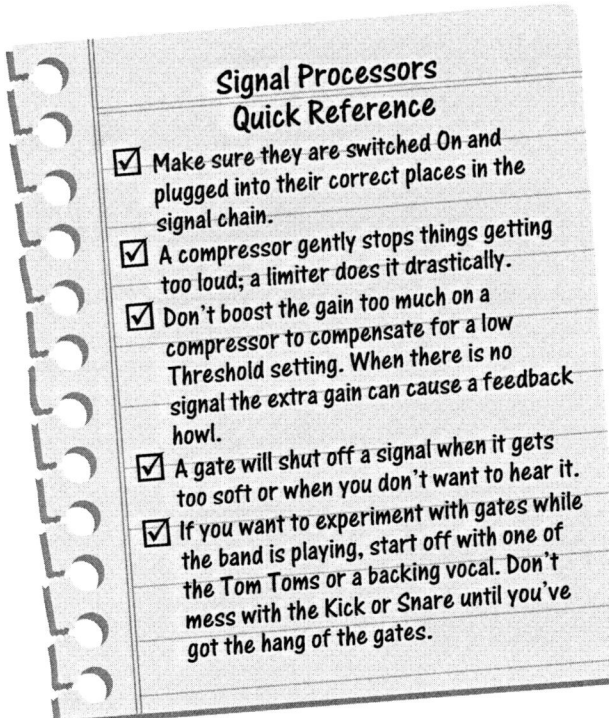

### Signal Processors
### Quick Reference

☑ Make sure they are switched On and plugged into their correct places in the signal chain.

☑ A compressor gently stops things getting too loud; a limiter does it drastically.

☑ Don't boost the gain too much on a compressor to compensate for a low Threshold setting. When there is no signal the extra gain can cause a feedback howl.

☑ A gate will shut off a signal when it gets too soft or when you don't want to hear it.

☑ If you want to experiment with gates while the band is playing, start off with one of the Tom Toms or a backing vocal. Don't mess with the Kick or Snare until you've got the hang of the gates.

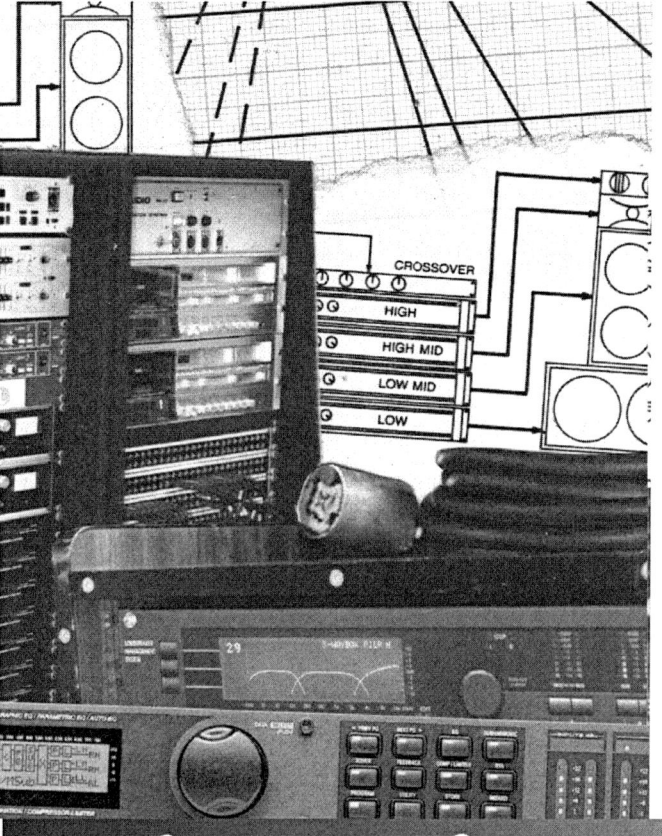

# 8     *Crossovers*

A crossover splits up the Audio signal into different frequency bands for different speakers, and is known as a 2, 3 or 4 way depending on the type of system.

LOW and HIGH is a 2 way

LOW, MID and HIGH is a 3 way

LOW, LOW MID, HIGH MID, and HIGH is a 4 way

Let's take a look at our famous *NoNamo* brand equalizer and see where these crossover points would typically occur.

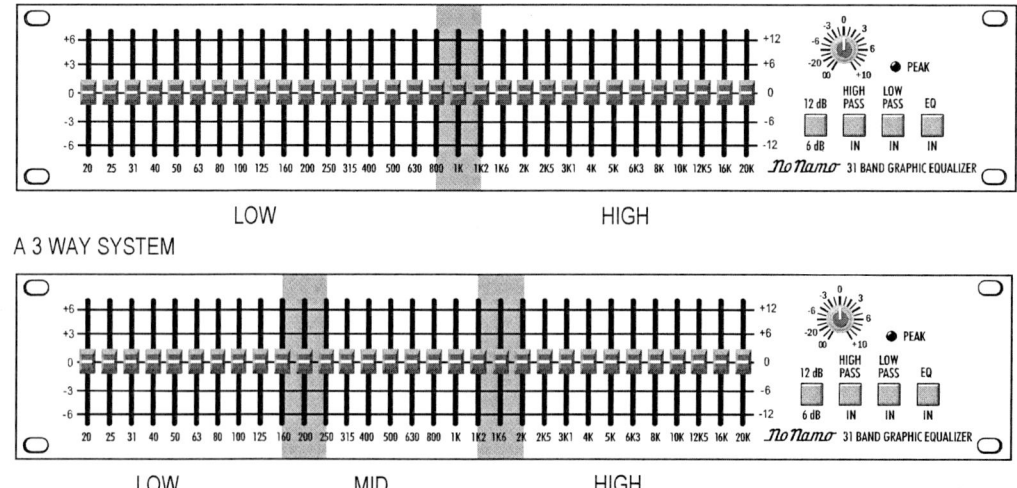

Live Sound Mixing 4th Edition ©2005 D.R.Fry

A 4 WAY SYSTEM

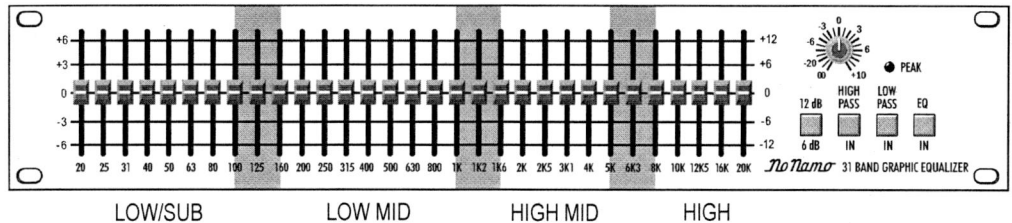

LOW/SUB          LOW MID          HIGH MID          HIGH

There are two types of crossovers: Active and Passive

### Active Crossover

An active crossover needs mains power and splits up the signal before the amplifier, needing a separate amplifier for each frequency band.

### Passive Crossover

A passive crossover is similar to the type found in your music speakers at home. This crossover is placed *after* the amplifier, usually inside the speaker box, and consists of a network of coils, capacitors and resistors.

## Active or Passive?

An Active crossover should have at least Unity gain; 100% in, 100% out. Most of them will also have a degree of cut or boost available on each output, at least + or – 6 dB, to allow matching up with amplifiers of different sensitivity.

This degree of control is not available with a Passive crossover, and you will get less than unity gain out of it; perhaps 100% in, 80% out. This is unavoidable as the coils and capacitors in the network tend to soak up a bit of the energy.

As a general rule, for high power sound use an Active crossover. If you don't have the amps, or where you don't need high power, a Passive crossover will do fine.

Passive crossovers are rarely found in Front of House speaker systems, except maybe Mid to High in smaller systems, but can often be found in the Monitor system, where the extra amps are either not available or not an economic proposition.

### Crossover Points and Slopes

This is a little bit technical, but don't worry, I won't go into it too deeply. But please stick with it as the more you understand about how a crossover works, the better you'll be able to make a system do what you want it to do. Knowing the crossover point of the system can make your room EQ'ing a lot easier, as you will know where to start looking for peaks

When we talk of a crossover point of, say, 1 KHz (1,000 Hertz, or Cycles per second), the signal just doesn't stop there. The Low frequency rolls off (drops away) there, and the High frequency rolls up there. How fast it rolls off depends on the Crossover Slope, and these are talked about in terms of dB per octave. e.g. 12 dB, 18 dB, 24 db per octave and so on. Crossover slopes are also sometimes talked about in 'orders', each order being 6 dB. Thus a 24 dB per octave crossover would be a 'Fourth Order' crossover.

Why we consider this important is to avoid, as much as we can, the same frequencies being handled by more than one driver. This causes audible distortion in the system, and also sudden peaks and dips in the response that your equalizer will find hard to fix.

As a general rule, the faster the signal rolls off after the crossover point, the cleaner the sound. A 24 dB per octave crossover would have hardly any MID going into the HIGH section after the crossover point; a 12 dB per octave crossover would have twice as much.

Have a look at the graphs on the following pages to see what I mean. It's a simple 2 way

= " =
*A passive crossover is similar to the one in your home music speakers*
= " =

### 6 dB per octave filter.

In this graph you can see that there is overlapping signal right off the scale - from 100 Hz through to 16 KHz. With a crossover like this your horns would be unlikely to last the night!

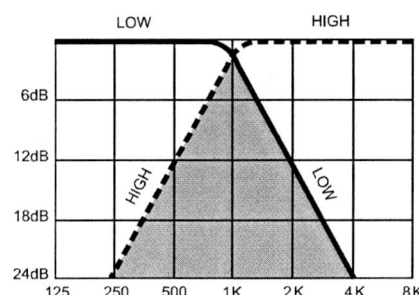

### 12 dB per octave filter

With a 12 dB crossover things are starting to get better. This is a common type for passive crossovers as it has a low parts count; it works tolerably well, and it's cheap!

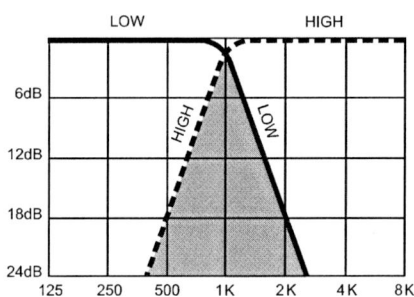

### 18 dB per octave filter

It's getting better all the time. 18 dB was a common active crossover filter about 20 years ago. It's pretty good, and it works. The most popular version was designed in the 30's by Stephen Butterworth *(handy information for Pro Audio Trivia quizzes!)*

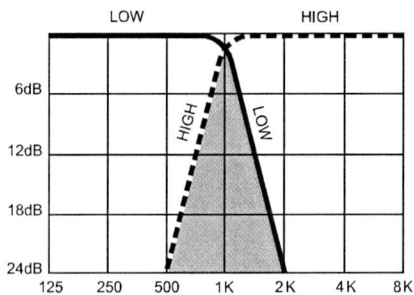

### 24 dB per octave filter

This is the best; the analog equivalent of a brick wall. Each frequency band has minimal interaction with the one next to it. Designed by Linkwitz and Riley, this is the one to pick if you have a choice

> ❝ Not all speakers are designed to handle all frequencies ❞

system with a crossover point of 1 KHz, but the same concept applies to 3 way and 4 way systems as well. The solid line is the Low frequency signal, the dotted line is High, and the triangular shape they form represents the amount that the two frequencies overlap.

Like everything else audio, crossovers can be digital. True digital crossovers (not digitally controlled analog ones) can have 48 dB slopes for a true 'brick wall' filter, where one frequency literally does stop and another starts.

### Why bother with a crossover?

Why not run the signal from the console straight into the amplifiers and then straight into all the speakers?

The answer is that not **all** speakers are designed to handle **all** frequencies, but are designed to handle specific frequency ranges only.

A heavy duty 18" or 15" speaker for LOW

A lighter duty 15", 12" or 10" speaker for LOW MIDS or MIDS

A Compression Driver and Horn for HIGH MIDS and/or HIGH

If the signal going into a speaker can be as close as possible to the frequency range that the speaker is designed to handle, the better the sound and the longer it will last.

## A Golden Rule

> *"Never send a speaker a signal that is a lower frequency than the speaker is designed to handle"*

Let's take an extreme example. If you ran your LOW signal into your HIGH horns and wound up the volume, those HIGH horns would have a life of between 1 to 5 seconds before they failed. Not because they were badly made or badly designed, but because they were just not designed to handle LOW frequencies.

For this reason, great care should be taken when wiring up crossovers, amps and speakers, as this kind of mistake can cost you a lot of money, and make the system unusable.

To sum up crossover functions, we can say that the crossover filters out the unwanted frequencies, and ensures that the LOW speakers only get the LOW frequencies in the music, the MID speakers only get the MID frequencies, and the HIGH speakers get the HIGH frequencies.

## Active Crossover Features

### Variable Crossover Point

With active crossovers, one size doesn't fit all. The crossover point needs to be adjusted to suit the particular type of system and speakers that you are using. As we've seen in the start of this chapter, 2, 3 and 4 way systems all need different crossover points.

So virtually every one of them has some way of adjusting the crossover frequency. It can be a knob on the front, with graduations marking each frequency or maybe a digital readout of the frequency. It could be a rotary switch, with a click at each frequency, or it may have plug in cards, or it could be a digital crossover with presets for many different systems, with parameters changed by nudge buttons or a scroll wheel, just like digital effects units

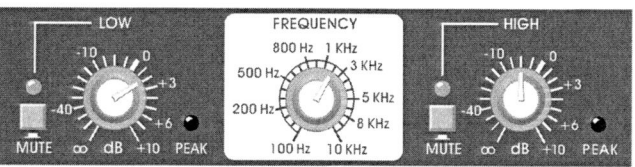

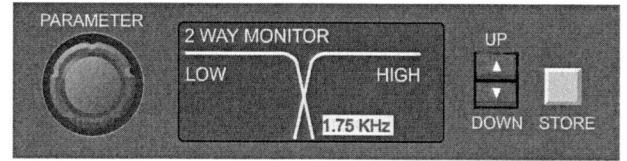

### Delay

Because LOW speakers may be large folded horns, with a throat length of 8' (over 2 metres) or more, the is a time delay between them and the MIDs if they are placed on top of each other. Instead of putting the LOW speakers 8' out into the audience, many crossovers have time delay circuits built in to bring the apparent acoustic start point back to the same place. Likewise for the MIDs to HIGHs; the Mid speaker could be a front loaded 12" (300mm) driver and the High compression driver might be on a horn a foot (300mm) long.

### Limiters

Many crossovers have built in limiters on each output to prevent the power going to each amp reaching speaker destroying levels. These limiters have been set up for particular amplifier/speaker combinations, and should not be changed casually. For this reason their controls are deliberately not easily accessible, and many digital crossovers can be password protected or locked to stop anyone but the system engineer from changing settings.

### Phase Reverse

Some speaker designs deliberately require that a particular frequency band be out of phase to the bands adjacent to it for the smoothest frequency response. For this reason some crossovers have either a phase reverse switch or a control that can vary it from 0 to 180°.

### Mute switches

These are switches on the front panel next to each of the Low, Mid or High level controls. Pressing it will mute or un-mute the output of that frequency band. There should be a big LED to let you know that the output is muted.

## How do you set a crossover up?

### Active

Well, there are an enormous amount of active crossovers out there, but some things remain constant with all of them, whether analog or digital. You've got a Level control for each frequency band which corresponds to an output for that frequency.

For simplicity let's deal with a 2 way system again, and we'll have to assume that the crossover frequency is correctly set for the speakers we are using.

**Active crossover connections**

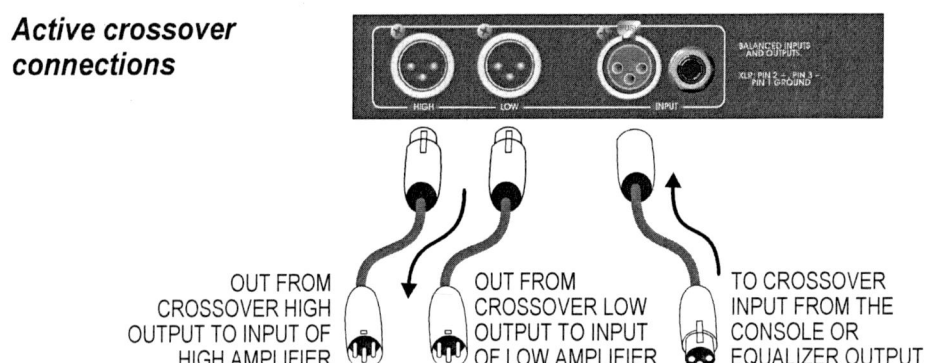

OUT FROM CROSSOVER HIGH OUTPUT TO INPUT OF HIGH AMPLIFIER

OUT FROM CROSSOVER LOW OUTPUT TO INPUT OF LOW AMPLIFIER

TO CROSSOVER INPUT FROM THE CONSOLE OR EQUALIZER OUTPUT

1. Initially set up all the outputs at the 0dB point.
2. Bring up the system level and have a listen to the sound.
3. If there's not enough bass, increase the low frequency control slightly; likewise for high frequencies
4. Listen and repeat the process until you're happy
5. Plug in a microphone and bring up the level some more until feedback rings start to appear.
6. From here on in it's back to our methods for EQ'ing a room in Chapter 3.
7. If there are 3 or more adjacent bands on the EQ cut or boosted by 3 dB or more, then the Crossover should adjusted to even up those frequencies.

For a 3 or 4 way system the process is the same, but with more frequency bands, of course.

What we are trying to do is make sure that an equal amount of energy at all frequencies comes out of the speaker system. Once you have achieved this then you can start to tweak individual sounds and frequencies to deliver the sound you're after.

A spectrum analyzer with a pink noise generator will help you set a crossover up fast, but if you don't have one your ears can do just as good a job.

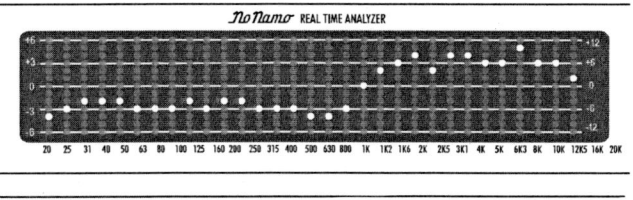

THE HF IS A LOT LOUDER THAN THE BOTTOM END. THE LF NEEDS BOOSTING AND THE HF NEEDS CUTTING

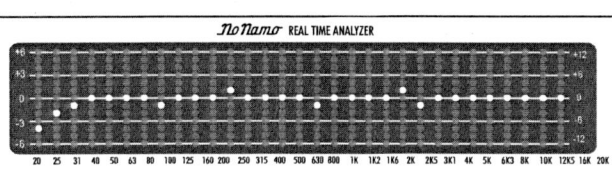

THAT ELUSIVE FLAT RESPONSE - ALL LEDS WITHIN 1 OR 2 DB OF THE CENTRE (0 DB) LINE

## Passive

Since a passive crossover is usually built into the speaker box, there isn't much you can do about relative Low and High output levels at the crossover level. If the passive crossover is built right, then your mixing job will be relatively easy. If it's not, then pulling a good sound out of it will require some wrestling with the equalizer. See *Chapter 14 - Problems*, for some suggested solutions.

## Speaker Processors, Control Units

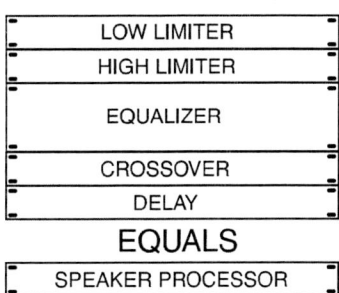

Around the middle of the 80's there was a growing trend towards dedicated crossover/ delay/ equalizer/ limiter units designed to run particular speaker systems only. These units were called Speaker Processors, Control Units, System Controllers or similar

The controls for these units are recessed behind a security cover, with some status LEDs being the only things visible on the anonymous front panel. Behind the security cover are level controls, and various trim and mode switches that set up the unit for the particular speaker system. All this added to the 'black box' mystery of these devices, but not for us! We're here to cut through all that and leave their marketing/hype/ black magic to the guys with Porsches and pony tails!

*...leave the black magic associated with them to the guys with Porsches and pony tails!*

## What are they?

Athough there are differences between speaker processors, the concepts behind them are very similar. Consider these two points:

1. Every speaker, no matter what brand, has a point at which it won't take any more power. A point at which it either jumps out of the voice coil gap, burns out, and/or grinds through the windings and stops working. Hopefully (ho ho!) the more expensive the speaker, the more power it will take before this happens.

2. As well as this, every speaker is more efficient at some frequencies and less efficient at others. Although a speaker may have a rated response from 50 Hz through to 2 KHz it won't have an even response at all points in between. Once it's put in a box then the response can become even more ragged.

So, if you made a little black box that knew the speaker would stop working when it was hit with 40 volts, and you set it up so that it could never get more than 39 volts, that would be a pretty neat idea. And if you also knew that the speaker had a 3 dB peak at, say, 80 Hz, 400 Hz and 800 Hz, you could design that black box to cut each of those frequencies by 3 dB, to flatten the response. Well, that's what a speaker processor, or controller, does.

While you're sticking all this into the black box you can build in an active crossover, for a start, with the exact crossover frequency, and anything else that the speaker might require to

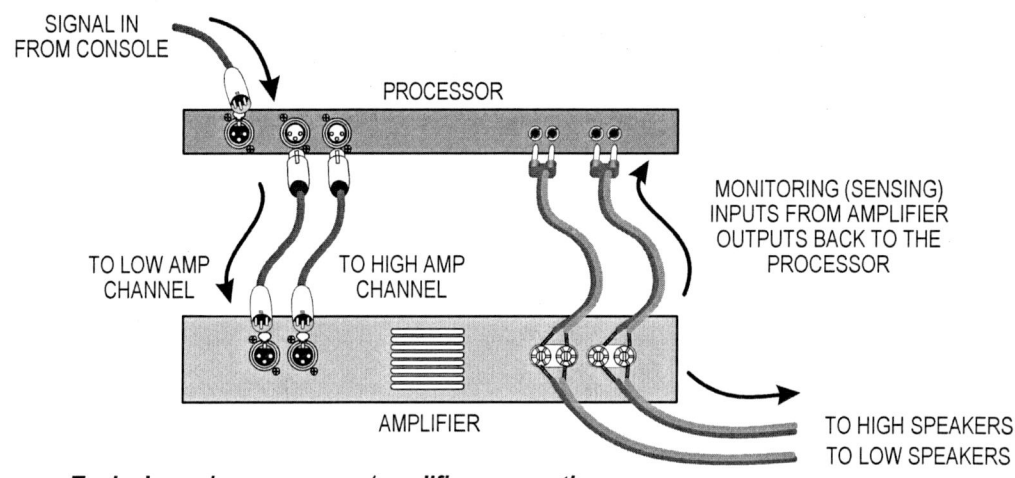

CROSSOVER POINT SHIFTS
UPWARDS ON PEAKS...

...AND BACK DOWN AGAIN
WHEN PEAK HAS PASSED

let it deliver 100% every time.

Some processors have sliding filters, which are crossover points that shift upwards at peak signals, thus reducing the power going into a particular frequency band, and shifting back down immediately afterwards.

Others can have 2 stage limiting, with a gentle 'squeeze' applied if the level is only slightly too high, and a hard clamp down if the signal reaches speaker destroying levels.

There is usually some Equalization built in, to make sure that the speaker box has as 'flat' a response as possible, and any time delay, phase correction required is also built in.

*A hard clamp down if the signal reaches system destroying levels*

SIGNAL IN
FROM CONSOLE

PROCESSOR

TO LOW AMP
CHANNEL

TO HIGH AMP
CHANNEL

MONITORING (SENSING)
INPUTS FROM AMPLIFIER
OUTPUTS BACK TO THE
PROCESSOR

AMPLIFIER

TO HIGH SPEAKERS
TO LOW SPEAKERS

*Typical speaker processor /amplifier connections*

A common feature is an extra set of leads that run back into the processor from the speaker outputs of the amplifier. This is a foolproof way that the processor can monitor the output level of the amplifier at all times, and trigger the speaker protection limiters if that level gets too high.

So basically they are automatically self correcting devices for getting maximum output from the system, with minimum risk of destroying it.

### How does all this work?

When you connect up a signal from the outputs of the amplifier back to the processor, the amplifier, speaker and processor are now operating as a feedback loop (electronic feedback, not acoustic!)

Whatever the processor does, the amplifier follows.

Whatever the amplifier does, the processor follows.

Since the processor is calibrated to know exactly how much power a particular speaker will handle before it rolls on its back and plays dead, then it can automatically (and instantly) reduce the amount of signal going to the amplifier by the exact amount required to keep the power output to a level the speaker can handle.

This process is different to putting a compressor on the input to the amplifier, because the compressor has no way of knowing how much power the amplifier is delivering. It can make a guess, but without monitoring the actual amplifier outputs it can never know for sure. And its guess would usually be on the safe side, so you may never be getting the full amount out of your amplifier/speaker combination.

And if you change your amplifier your compressor will probably need re-setting for a different amplifier sensitivity and power output. A speaker processor is not bothered by any of that; all it wants to know is that there is enough power available for it to do its job.

The downside is that they are usually dedicated systems; that is, the processor is calibrated for a particular brand and model of speaker box *only*.

## Digital Crossovers

However, the latest digital controllers mean that one unit can have multiple program settings that can be recalled, used and modified depending upon the model of speaker to which it's connected. These are available from quite a few manufacturers, but one of the most typical and popular would be the BSS Omnidrive Compact Plus (FDS 366), a one rack unit product with three inputs and six outputs that can be configured as required - three two way channels for use with active monitors, through to two stereo 3 way channels for use with an active 3 way system.

### *How do you get it to work*

Like digital consoles, you're not totally on your own when you turn it on. There are standard configuration presets you can call up, such as a stereo three way system, with crossover points, compressors, limiters etc all ready to go.

After you've turned it on press the RECALL button (bottom left) to pull up a list of presets. Turn the rotary encoder knob (right of screen) to scroll through the list. Programs that have a diamond shape next to them are factory presets, and programs with a key symbol have been locked and may not allow any editing of the parameters. Press RECALL again to select the preset you want.

Just like digital effects units, these crossovers can take a fair bit of time to set up and modify, since you can change and save anything - crossover slope, type, points, limiters, levels and more. Changing parameters is a process requiring much use of the Navipad, a circular pad to the left of the screen with up, down, left or right arrows. Up or down will scroll through the available parameters, and left or right will modify them. The Enter/Store button will save them.

You may find that the unit is in Safe mode, which means it has been preset by the owner/installer and you won't get any access to any functions, no matter what you do.

If nothing comes out when you you run a test signal through the system, check that the Mute buttons are not active. These are red when active, and are located at the bottom of each LED ramp, next to the Level trim controls. Push to turn them on or off.

You could also check that the gain is not turned down on the input or output channels.

And if all three Input LEDs on a channel light up at once, it means that the unit is clipping internally, so reduce the gain or the amount of EQ on that channel.

There is a whole lot more to this flexible unit, but this should get you started.

## Loudspeaker Management Systems

These are the new generation of processors that digitally control every aspect of the speaker system, and nearly everything that you might have had in your rack is now integrated into the one unit. Manufacturers include dbx, XTA, Community, and several generic models.

One of the most popular is the dbx DriveRack, which has two inputs and up to six outputs, and functions that include: Feedback suppressor, multi-way crossover, compressor, Sub synthesizer, speaker alignment delay, output limiters, parametric EQ, pink noise generator,

Real Time Analyzer with automatic room tuning, the ability to load presets for a wide range of systems, and also to store your own custom/modified ones. And, just in case that isn't enough, you get a built-in stereo graphic equalizer!

DRIVERACK PA - 2 INPUTS, SIX OUTPUTS

### *How to get it to work*

When you turn it on you are in program mode (if you're not, press the Program button, which is bottom Left on the keypad). Use the DATA wheel to scroll through the factory programs until you find one that suits your configuration. There are generic programs for standard configurations - a stereo 3 way, for example, is #1 - and there are also brand specific programs, which are understandably biased in favour of JBL speaker systems! (JBL and dbx are both Harman companies). Press the DATA wheel to see a block diagram of what the preset is. Use the NEXT PAGE and PREV PAGE buttons to scroll through the settings to confirm or change them.

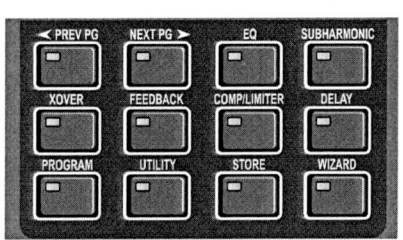

Once you have gone through all the settings, you can keep them by pressing the STORE button, in which case a screen will appear so that you can name your own preset.

You can't over-write the factory programs, so if you want to save your changes you have to re-name the program. Naming it can be a fiddley job, but it only has to be done once.

Access to functions like the Feedback suppressor, compressor/limiters, Sub synthesizer, speaker alignment delay, EQ, and auto room EQing is done via the buttons on the keypad.

Particularly important is the Wizard button, which brings up the DriveRack PA Wizard setup menu to guide you through the System Setup, Auto EQ setup and Auto Feedback Suppression Wizard.

Once you have your own system configuration named and saved, you can call up the Wizard each night to run through the auto room tuning. This will also involve plugging a microphone into the XLR connector on the front panel so that the RTA (real time analyzer) can hear what is happening in the room and make changes accordingly.

Despite the fact that a 28 band stereo EQ is included in the DriveRack's programs, it has to be said that it's not something you'd want to adjust in a hurry, given that it all happens on a very small LCD screen.

In fact, despite the enormous amount of EQ flexibility and control available in all of the current crop of digital speaker controllers, nearly every system will have a stereo analog graphic EQ in the rack for instant access to the right fader at any time during the show. Even though the auto feedback suppression should take care of any sudden feedback squeals, most engineers like to have the security of a good graphic EQ handy...just in case!

Both these two digital crossovers/controllers have many more functions on board - all I have tried to do is show you how you can get one to work if you're suddenly confronted with one. Just like digital effects units, setting them up is a matter of scrolling through parameters, modifying them, moving on to the next one, modifying, and eventually saving them so you don't have to go through the whole tortuous process again!

Many digital devices let you save your settings on a removable card or drive; the BSS for example will save your settings to a PCMCIA (or PC for short) card, which you can keep with you and use next time. Others will save to a USB (Universal Serial Bus) Flash RAM key which you can keep on your keyring. In an all-digital system you could save your console settings, your mix settings, your EQ settings, your favourite effects settings, song cues, your crossover settings and anything else you can think of, on a little thing the size of your thumb!

The ultimate aim of all speaker processors is to provide a single package, with all control functions taking place automatically, according to preset internal controls. Assuming that the quality of the Analog-to-Digital (and Digital-to-Analog) converters is up to scratch, the end result is a very high degree of reliability, and accurate, predictable sound quality from one venue to the next.

The whole business of crossover design may sound extremely complicated, and indeed it is. This small amount of very generalised information has only scratched the surface to give you an idea of where crossovers fit into PA systems, and how to get one working. Complete books are written on the subject of crossover filters alone, and there is continuous research into better designs, since crossover circuitry is a major factor in creating good live sound.

### Crossovers Quick Reference

- ☑ A Passive crossover is in the speaker box, an Active one is a separate unit before the amplifiers
- ☑ Check your wiring carefully - make sure the correct crossover outputs go to the correct amplifiers and speakers
- ☑ 18 dB good, 24 dB better, (48 dB best?)
- ☑ Set the levels initially at the 0 dB point, and adjust them as you equalize
- ☑ Don't change the crossover points. They are not a matter of taste or preference, but design; fiddling with them can destroy parts of the system!
- ☑ If the crossover has built in limiters, don't play with them either, for the same reason (unless it belongs to you!)
- ☑ Allow plenty of time for a first-time setup

# 9    *Amplifiers*

Out of all the electronics in a sound system, an amplifier works the hardest. It takes the small signal from the mixing console and turns it into a large signal that will drive the speakers to high volume levels.

For professional sound systems, an amplifier must be powerful, reliable, abuse proof with the ability to work and work, night after night. In the past this ruggedness has usually translated into big and heavy pieces of equipment that need 4 crew to pick up each rack.

Today, however, in the never ending search for 'more for less', amplifier technology has given us smaller, lighter and more powerful designs, with 'smart' power supplies and built-in failsafe protection circuitry.

The old racks of heavyweight units weighing 70 lbs (30 kilos) or more **each** and taking up 4 rack units are giving way to 2 rack unit (3½" or 89 mm) models, weighing 30 lbs (14 kilos) or less. As truck and crew costs climb higher and higher, so the 'system shrinking' process accelerates.

### Amplifier controls

Most amplifiers commonly in use for live sound equipment are 2 channel units, although 4, 6 and even 8 channel amplifiers are used in installation work.

There is an enormous range of amplifiers out there, so we'll put together a *NoNamo* typical amplifier to look at. Once again as with equalizers, not **all** amplifiers will have **all** these functions, but they will all have some of them.

The front panel will have:

❶ Handles. To pick up the amplifier with, and to slide it in and out of racks

❷ Level controls for each channel. These can either be marked as 0 to 10, where 0 indicates no volume, or in dB increments.

❸ Power Switch. This may light up itself to show that the amplifier is on, or it may switch on one of the

❹ LED indicators. These indicate the various functions of the amplifier, and its current status. For example, Green Signal Present LEDs to show that there is signal coming into the amplifier, Orange ones perhaps to show that any internal limiting is active. Red LEDs often show that AC power is On, the amplifier is Clipping or Overloading, or that there is a fault and the amplifier has shut down to protect itself.

❺ Many amplifiers use an array of LEDs to operate as a meter, so that as long as you can see them bouncing away from the console you know that all is well. Some amplifiers even have analog VU type meters on the front panel.

❻ Air inlets for the fans. Amplifiers get hot when they work hard, so most of them have inbuilt fans to blow cool air over the output transistors or mosfets, and through the heatsinks. These may also be on the back.

For amplifiers that blow the air out of the sides of the chassis, there will be air exit holes. Don't block them - the air **must** have somewhere to go. Also, if there are any filters, clean them on a regular basis - at least once a month.

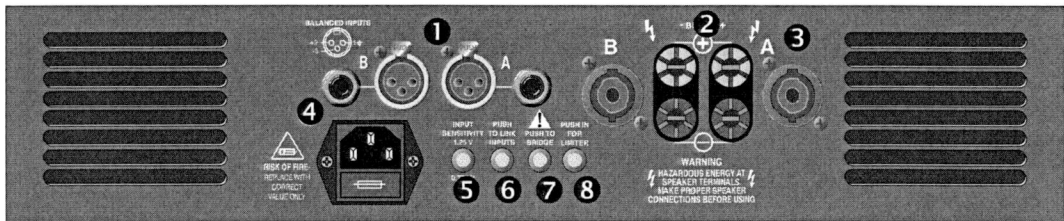

The rear panel will have:

❶ Input Connectors. On budget amplifiers these are often unbalanced jack sockets; on more professional models they are always balanced 3 pin XLR type.

❷ Output Connectors. Lower power amplifiers can have jack connectors as outputs, too, but for high current, high power applications the standard used to be the 5 way binding post. For safety reasons the European Community (EU) has outlawed binding posts like these that have holes for banana plugs in the end of them, and this is an interim step towards banning them completely.

❸ The connector that will supersede binding posts is the Speakon connector, from Neutrik, which we looked at back in *Chapter 4 - Cables and Connectors*. This is a totally safe connector that has no bare terminals. It is the de facto standard for speaker connections, and most new amplifiers have Speakons on the back of them.

❹ AC Power connector. On lower powered amplifiers this will often be a removable 3 pin IEC connector sometimes known as a 'jug plug'. On higher powered amplifiers the power lead will be hard wired into the amplifier chassis.

❺ Sensitivity switch. Sensitivity is a measure of how much input level an amplifier needs to deliver its rated output. For high power amplifiers, about 1.25 volts is normal. But many consoles have a hard time delivering this much at their Left and Right Outputs, especially if there is no crossover or equalizer to bump up the level. So this switch will let the amplifier run up to full power on say 0.775 volts. Switching this in will *not* give you more power out of the amplifier! It just means the amplifier will get to its maximum power with less input.

**❻** Input Link switch. If you want the same signal to go to both channels of the amplifier, normally you'd have to make up a Y lead. This switch saves you the trouble. Switch it in and whatever goes into Channel A goes into Channel B too.

**❼** Bridged Mono mode switch. Many amplifiers can be bridged to run as a mono unit delivering twice the power, into a single load. Usually one of the inputs is designated as the one to use in bridged mode, and the + speaker cable is connected to the Red binding post of one channel, and the - cable is connected to the Red binding post of the other channel. With Speakons there is often a separate bridged mono output Speakon connector. *Always* power down the amplifier before changing this switch and connecting the cables. Check the wiring very carefully before powering up the amplifier.

**❽** Limiter Switch (sometimes with a Threshold control as well). This switch stops the amplifier from clipping and trying to put out more power than it can. However it won't stop the amplifier putting out a distorted signal if you feed a distorted signal *into* it.

### What is Clipping?

Once an amplifier reaches its maximum power output, you can't get any more out of it. If you keep pushing more Input into it, the amplifier will give up trying to accurately reproduce the signal, and start chopping off, or squaring off, the top and bottom of the signal. This is called clipping. You can see it on an oscilloscope, and you can hear it as distortion. You want to avoid this as much as possible.

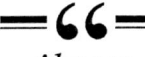
*Always power down the system before switching to bridged mono mode*

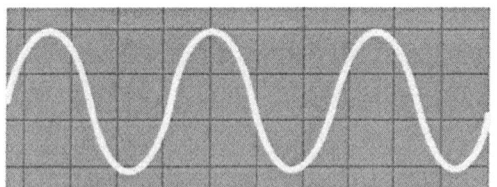
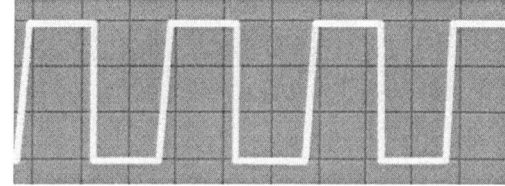

CLEAN SIGNAL SHOWN ON AN OSCILLOSCOPE          A SIGNAL THAT IS CLIPPING

Professional speakers will usually handle momentary peaks far in excess of the their rated power, provided that the peak is a clean signal and not distorted. Once the signal to the speaker becomes distorted, though, failure is not far away.

### Last On, First Off

This is how you power up the system.

1. Make sure the amplifiers are turned down and switched off
2. Switch on the AC power to the Mixing consoles and the effects racks
3. Wait 10 seconds then switch on the AC power to the amplifier racks
4. Turn on the amplifiers one after the other, with 5 seconds in between each one
5. Check that all the fans are turning, then turn the amplifiers up one after the other; just a little at first, then if everything sounds OK, turn them up all the way

In live sound systems it is usual for the amplifiers to be turned up to maximum, as the level going to each one is controlled firstly by the mixing console, and secondly by the crossover.

By powering up this way you avoid putting any clicks and thumps through the system, and you give each amplifier a chance to charge up its power supply before you turn on the next one. This will help to avoid blowing any power fuses or circuit breakers in the venue, which can happen when you turn them all on at once.

Turning off the system is the reverse of the above procedure, except that you may want to disconnect the speakers before you turn off the amplifiers. Not all amplifiers have internal relay muting to disconnect their outputs when the power is shut off, and so can send a gigantic THUMP through the system when turned off.

If you drive an amplifier hard it will usually get hot, especially into low impedance loads, so you must give them every chance to keep cool. They need LOTS of air. Don't obstruct the airflow into the amplifier rack by placing them hard up against a wall or each other, or by letting the stage drapes get sucked into the inlets. If the amplifiers have thermal cutouts, when they overheat they will shut down until they get cool again. The audience may not like this!

At open air gigs, keep direct sunlight off the amplifiers and never let them get wet. Water is an excellent conductor of electricity, and so are you!

*Amps are always LAST ON, FIRST OFF*

## What to do when an amplifier doesn't work

1. Switch it off and disconnect the power and the speakers. ***Don't touch anything unless the power is off!*** Large amplifiers have DC voltages of 120v or more inside.

2. Don't stick your fingers inside the amplifier, ***even if the power is off.*** The capacitors inside can store the power for a LONG time, and give you a ***very*** nasty shock even when the amplifier has been turned off for a while. Leave this sort of thing to a qualified technician. Really!

3. Reset the amplifier's circuit breaker, if it has one (it's often the power switch as well). If it still keeps shutting down, then find another amplifier as there is no quick fix.

4. If the amplifier has fuses, then ***with the help of a technician***, check them all. Lots of amplifier problems are caused by blown fuses. They get tired and fragile, and then one night you turn them on and the fuse pops. There should be a separate fuse for each DC rail of each side of the amplifier, and a main AC power fuse or circuit breaker. Pull them out and check them all.

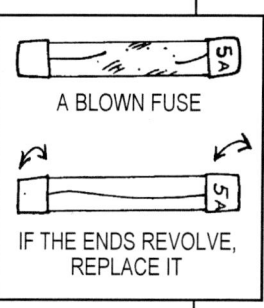

A BLOWN FUSE

IF THE ENDS REVOLVE, REPLACE IT

5. If they look OK and the amplifier still doesn't work, wiggle the fuse ends - quite often one of them may have come loose and not be connected inside. A multimeter set to OHMS (or resistance or continuity) will help you to check this.

6. If your replacement fuses keep blowing, ***don't put in a 35 amp one from the truck headlight circuit!*** Try one a couple of grades up, say from 5 amps up to 7 amps. If this one still blows, there isn't much more you can do. Fuses are there to protect the insides of the amplifier from being destroyed in the event of a component breakdown, and this one is only doing its job. Leave the amplifier for a technician to check out, and go looking for a spare one.

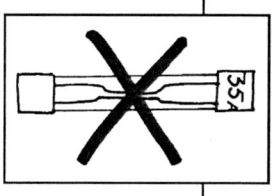

7. If you have no spare fuses, ***don't*** wrap the old fuse in silver paper and jam it back in - it's dangerous and will only make the amplifier damage repair much more expensive.

8. If the dead amplifier is from the Main speaker system, and you haven't got a spare, steal one from the monitor system. Two less wedges is better than no MIDs out the front.

9. Run through the following troubleshooting checklist:

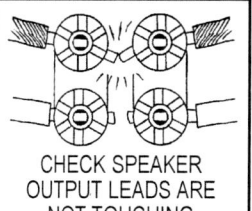

CHECK SPEAKER OUTPUT LEADS ARE NOT TOUCHING

☑ Check all the connections to the amplifier are correct

☑ Is the AC power lead OK?

☑ Are the wires connected inside the AC plug?

☑ Check the Input leads, especially if they are guitar jacks - they can vibrate out

☑ Check that a signal is actually getting into the amplifier. Plug the input into an amplifier that you know is working OK

☑ Check the speaker leads - vibration can loosen the binding post terminals, and the leads fall out of them

☑ If you are using binding post type outputs, make sure the bare ends of the speaker leads are not touching each other

☑ Is the fan turning? Check that no wires are poking into it and stopping it

☑ Check that the air filter isn't clogged up. Blocked filters don't let any air through, and the amp may have overheated and tripped a thermal switch

If all these things seem to be OK, then go back to #5 above, and start looking for that spare amplifier.

### How much power does an amplifier need?

As much as you can afford! You won't use all of it all the time, but extra power is not wasted power - it's headroom. Headroom gives the speaker the ability to handle sudden peaks without clipping or distorting. Most of the time a more powerful amplifier isn't working too hard, which makes it likely to survive for much longer.

Modern music is loud, ragged, jolting, with a huge dynamic range. To cope with this, we need lots of power, so let's look at it on a per speaker basis.

*RMS is the true power rating of an amplifier*

- For a smaller system with one 12" and horn cabinet per side, you need at least 300 watts per channel into 8 ohms, and for a small sub to go with them, about the same, although more would be better.

- For a bigger system bottom end, about 500 watts or more into 8 ohms. So if your bass cabinets have 2 speakers in each one, the amplifier will need to deliver 1,000 watts per channel into 4 ohms in order to have 500 watts available to each one.

- For good midrange, about the same. Midrange is the key to a good vocal sound, especially in rock music with its predominance of mid range instruments (guitars, keyboards, voice). Having this sort of power available gives us a lot of headroom to cover transient peaks without distortion.

- For good top end, at least 200 watts, for the same reason - we want plenty of clean, undistorted power to put the sparkle and snap into the system. Also, many compression drivers are 16 ohms, which effectively halves your 8 ohm output power from the amplifier. If you don't believe me - keep reading!

### How many watts into how many ohms?

Amplifier specifications should refer to "XXX watts **RMS** into Y ohms." RMS stands for Root Mean Square, and is a very conservative average power rating. ***This is the only power rating to consider***. See *Chapter 16 - Technical Stuff* if you'd like to know more

So disregard Peak power, Music power, Instantaneous power, or even Instantaneous Peak Music power! They are interesting to know, but only in relation to the true RMS power.

In the USA the FTC sets strict guidelines for amplifier power specifications, so on some brochures you may see FTC after the measurements, which indicates the maximum RMS power at 0.1% distortion over a minimum length of time.

The ohms figure refers to the resistance of the speaker to the signal coming from the amplifier. The higher the resistance, the less power the amplifier can put into the speaker. The figures usually quoted are 8 ohms and 4 ohms.

4 ohms is seen as less resistance to the signal than 8 ohms, so the amplifier power figures should usually be higher at 4 ohms than the 8 ohms rating. In theory an amplifier should deliver twice as much power into 4 ohms as into 8 ohms, but in practice it's a bit less. An

amplifier that delivers 300 watts into 8 ohms would probably deliver 500 into 4 ohms.

The problem is heat. Put your hand on an amplifier that is running hard and you'll find it's hot. Sometimes it's very hot! Our amplifier has to get rid of twice as much heat at 4 ohms as it does at 8 ohms, and four times as much heat at 2 ohms! Fan cooling, sophisticated heatsinks, temperature sensors, compact toroidal transformers, 'smart' power supplies; there are as many answers to these problems as there are amplifier manufacturers.

From a mixing point of view, your only concern is how well the amplifier works.

The following diagrams show you how the impedance that the amplifier has to drive into changes when the number of speakers changes. It's not too technical, but illustrates how impedance can change, and how series or parallel wiring makes a big difference.

### How do you know what the impedance is?

Let's say a typical speaker is rated at 8 ohms.

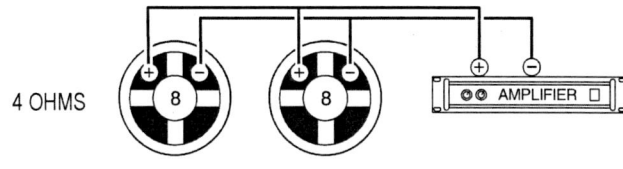

Wire 2 together in **parallel** and their combined resistance will be 4 ohms. Parallel means that the + and – on the amplifier go to the + and – on the first speaker, then to the + and – on the next speaker, and so on.

That's a pretty safe load. As we mentioned before, most amps are pretty happy putting out maximum power into a 4 ohm load.

But what happens when you wire 4 of these speakers together in parallel and their combined resistance will be 2 ohms?

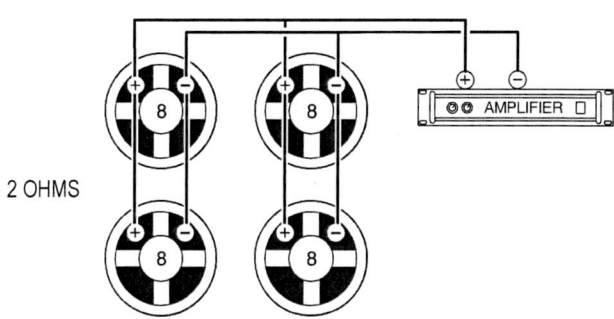

Unless the manufacturer specifically recommends it, it's not a good idea to run an amplifier hard into a 2 ohm load. At full power it generates a lot of heat and can outstrip the capacity of the amplifiers internal heatsinks and fans to dissipate it. If you do have to do this, don't get them even close to clipping, as this will increase the heat output considerably

At best you'll blow a fuse or it will shut down temporarily, at worst it will shut down permanently. But if that elusive spare amplifier is nowhere to be found, you will need to do something to get through the night.

So let's try **series** wiring with our 8 ohm speakers: Series wiring means that when wiring up 2 speakers, the + and – terminals on the amplifier are wired to the + on the first speaker, and the – on the second speaker respectively. Then the – on the first speaker is wired to the + on the secondspeaker. If you trace it on the diagram you can see that it forms a big loop back to the amplifier

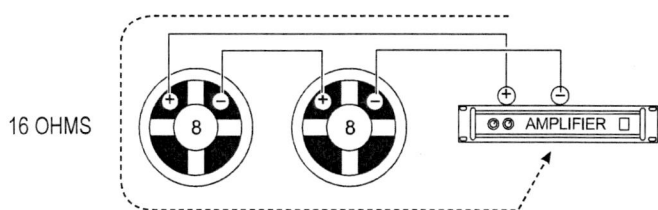

Wire 2 together in series and their combined resistance will be 16 ohms.

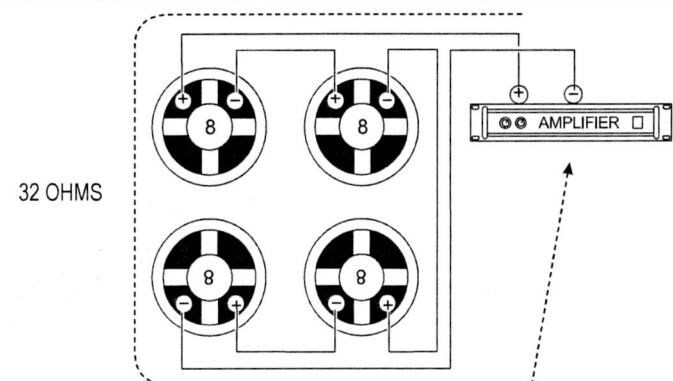

32 OHMS

Wire 4 together in series and their combined resistance will be 32 ohms!

Crikey - with a 32 ohm load the amplifier won't pull the skin off a rice pudding! Our 300 watt into 8 ohms amplifier will only deliver 75 watts into 32 ohms, and that's on a good day with the wind in the right direction!

Clearly we'll have to do something to get through the night.

So, if you ever need to run 4 speakers off the one side of an amplifier that won't run a 2 ohm load, this is what you have to do:

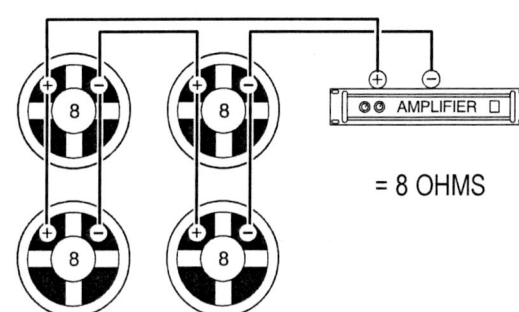

= 8 OHMS

Hook up each 2 together in Parallel (4 ohms per pair), and then wire these 2 pairs together in Series.

This will give you the four 8 ohm speakers wired together to give a combined resistance (or load) of 8 ohms.

*At 32 ohms load the amplifier won't pull the skin off a rice pudding!*

Note: This is something that you'd normally have to do only in an emergency; in practice, speakers in sound systems are *always* wired in parallel.

For a simple way to work out impedances, remember this:

In *parallel*, divide the impedance of the speaker by the number of speakers.

In *series*, multiply the impedance of the speaker by the number of speakers.

### Very Low Impedance amplifiers

There are amplifiers that will run into a 1 ohm load, but there is no guarantee that they will sound good while doing so, and the power they deliver at that kind of load is severely reduced. For example, while they might deliver double the output power into a 4 ohm load, in practice they deliver that same amount into a very low impedance load, too, so every speaker gets much less power, and that equals less volume out front.

But they do work well as a warmer for your coffee cup!

## Digital Amplifiers

The latest Digital amplifiers using Pulse Width Modulation or similar digital power stages convert 80 - 90% of the energy they use into output power, and so generate much less heat. Their internal power supply delivers exactly the right amount of voltage on demand, tracking the waveform of the signal and varying the power by the millisecond.

Like the Crown below, many will handle a digital input signal as well as an analog one. This is useful for installations running a digital audio distribution network, or large touring systems with a digital mixing console and digital snake.

With this comes optional computer control, and menu driven options. In many case output power can be set to the nearest Watt, and also power consumption and current.

However, assuming that they sound OK, their main benefit from your point of view is they usually weigh a lot less per Watt than standard amplifiers, so you and the lighting guy have less to carry!

4000 W PER
CHANNEL IN 2 RU

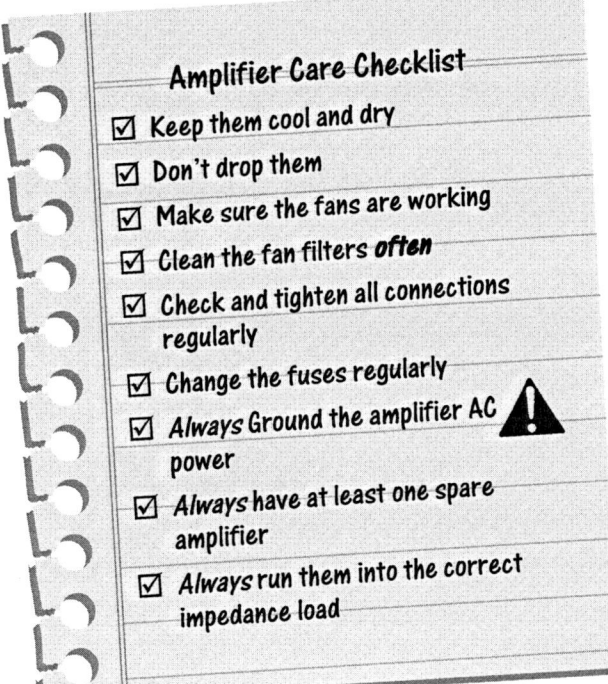

Amplifier Care Checklist

☑ Keep them cool and dry

☑ Don't drop them

☑ Make sure the fans are working

☑ Clean the fan filters *often*

☑ Check and tighten all connections regularly

☑ Change the fuses regularly

☑ *Always* Ground the amplifier AC power

☑ *Always* have at least one spare amplifier

☑ *Always* run them into the correct impedance load

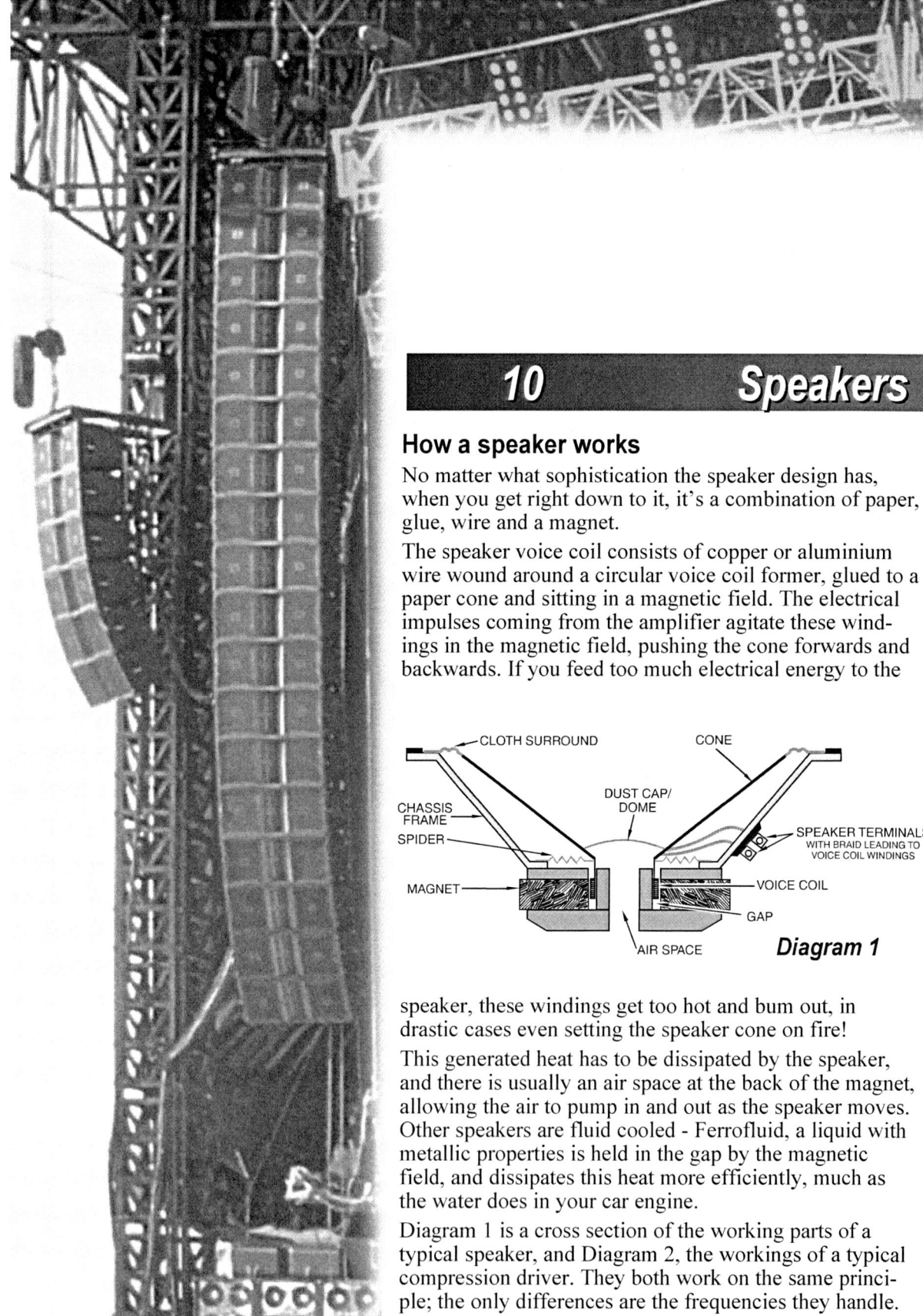

## 10  Speakers

### How a speaker works

No matter what sophistication the speaker design has, when you get right down to it, it's a combination of paper, glue, wire and a magnet.

The speaker voice coil consists of copper or aluminium wire wound around a circular voice coil former, glued to a paper cone and sitting in a magnetic field. The electrical impulses coming from the amplifier agitate these windings in the magnetic field, pushing the cone forwards and backwards. If you feed too much electrical energy to the

*Diagram 1*

speaker, these windings get too hot and burn out, in drastic cases even setting the speaker cone on fire!

This generated heat has to be dissipated by the speaker, and there is usually an air space at the back of the magnet, allowing the air to pump in and out as the speaker moves. Other speakers are fluid cooled - Ferrofluid, a liquid with metallic properties is held in the gap by the magnetic field, and dissipates this heat more efficiently, much as the water does in your car engine.

Diagram 1 is a cross section of the working parts of a typical speaker, and Diagram 2, the workings of a typical compression driver. They both work on the same principle; the only differences are the frequencies they handle.

In the compression driver the speaker cone has been replaced by the Diaphragm, a thin curved skin made of phenolic resin coated cloth, or aluminium, or even titanium. This sits up next to a phase plug, which compresses the sound waves and squeezes them out of a smaller throat. Hence the name compression driver.

Looking at diagrams, though, no matter how good, is not the best way to learn how speakers work. To truly grasp the concept you have to see one pulled apart.

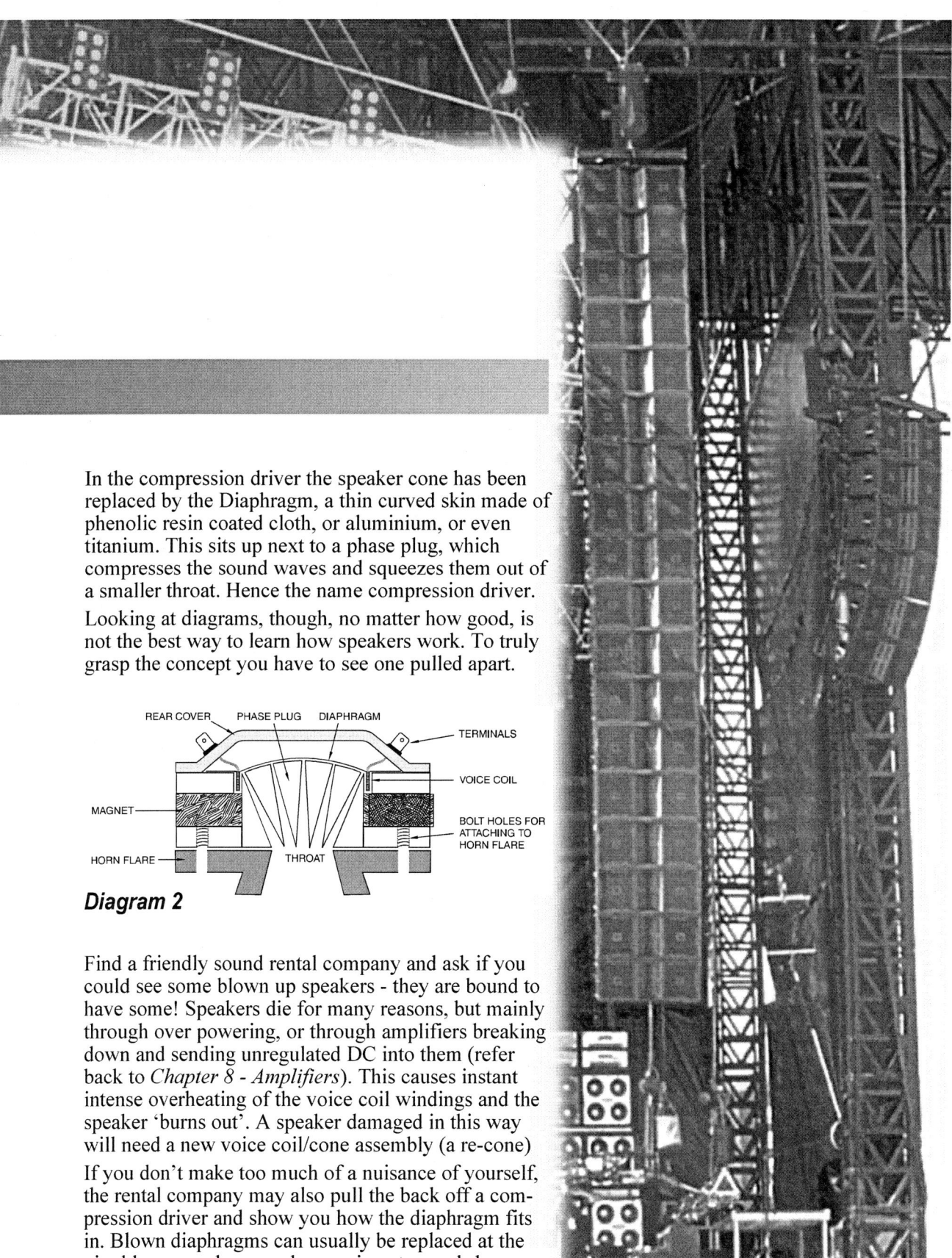

**Diagram 2**

Find a friendly sound rental company and ask if you could see some blown up speakers - they are bound to have some! Speakers die for many reasons, but mainly through over powering, or through amplifiers breaking down and sending unregulated DC into them (refer back to *Chapter 8 - Amplifiers*). This causes instant intense overheating of the voice coil windings and the speaker 'burns out'. A speaker damaged in this way will need a new voice coil/cone assembly (a re-cone)

If you don't make too much of a nuisance of yourself, the rental company may also pull the back off a compression driver and show you how the diaphragm fits in. Blown diaphragms can usually be replaced at the gig; blown speakers need re-coning at a workshop.

### What actually happens when a speaker 'burns out?'

The speaker coil is just that - a coil of very fine wire wound around a cylindrical former. This winding wire has an enamel coating around it which acts as an insulator. When too much current is pushed through this coil it gets very hot; sometimes so hot that the enamel insulation melts and the coil windings short out to each other, causing the wire itself to melt and warping or burning the cylindrical former the coil is built on!

In a compression driver the wire is even finer, so it takes much less current to cause the same problem.

It's a good idea to familiarise yourself with the technique of changing diaphragms, and also re-coning speakers. Most major speaker manufacturers run courses in speaker repairs, and PA rental companies usually have someone who does their repairs in house.

### How the speaker sees Power

This is a diagram of a 200 watt signal going into a speaker rated at 200 watts. It shouldn't cause any problems - it's nice and clean with smoothly rounded tops and bottoms to the wave forms. The technical name is a Sine wave.

This is a distorted 200 watt signal going to the same speaker. It's still 200 watts, but it's squared off (and it's called a Square wave!). This is not how the speaker sees the signal, though. It sees it like this -

The speaker sees the squared off signal as really being part of a MUCH larger signal, and tries hard to reproduce that larger signal. It may do it for a short time, but beware - the day of the speaker repair is at hand.

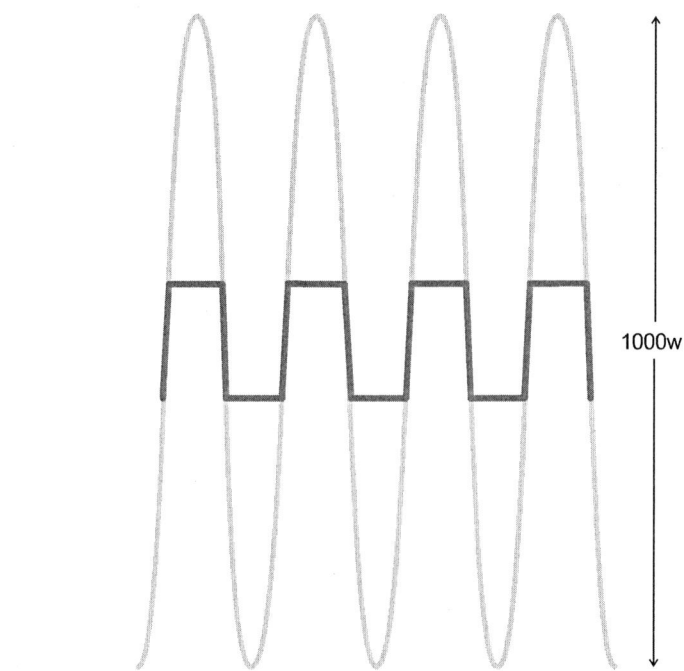

To use a motoring analogy, it's rather like driving your car over the gutter and curbs all the time. It may handle such treatment for a while, but sooner or later the front end will drop off!

### Want a more technical explanation?

The squared off waveform is effectively dumping DC voltage straight from the amplifier into the speaker for the amount of time that the signal is squared off. And if it's totally square, as in our previous example then that's most of the time. DC is **really** bad for the speaker.

## Horns

PA systems of all shapes and sizes invariably use horn loading in the HIGH section, and often in the MIDs and LOWs as well.

### What do horns do, and how do they work?

Get a friend to stand opposite you and say "Check ONE TWO". Listen to it and note how loud it is.

Now get them to cup their hands around their mouth and say it again, at exactly the level they did before. This time it's louder and clearer. There has been no increase in the Input, but the Output level has increased.

> *It's rather like driving your car over the gutters and kerbs - sooner or later the front end will drop off!*

This is the basic principle of how horns work.

When you open your mouth and say "Check ONE TWO", the sound comes out of your mouth and dribbles off in all directions. When you cup your hands around your mouth, you force all the sound into a small tunnel, and it squirts out of the end of that tunnel in a controlled beam at a higher volume.

Well designed horns can do the same thing for sound in a PA system.

The ear is most sensitive to frequencies in the vocal midrange, and the basis of a good sounding system is a good midrange sound. If you look back to the 2, 3 or 4 way layouts in the crossover section, you will see that traditionally the vocal midrange is split at around I KHz, a point that most LOW MIDs can run up to, and one that the compression drivers can safely run down to. This can present problems with having a crossover point right in the middle of the critical vocal range, making it difficult to pull a natural vocal sound.

Recently the trend has been towards using an 'extended range' mid range cone driver and horn combination, which allows the crossover point to be shifted up from 1 KHz to 2.5 KHz or higher, so you don't have a crossover point right in the middle of the vocal range. Further developments have also been made in 'phase plugs', diffusers and wave guides that provide more control over the dispersion pattern of the mid range drivers, as well as increasing their efficiency.

Improvements in the technology of compression driver diaphragms have also virtually removed the need to run separate HIGH drivers from 8 KHz upwards, in all but the biggest systems. The use of materials such as titanium for diaphragms has pushed the frequency response of the HIGH MID compression drivers to the audible limit.

Just as the ear is sensitive to the midrange frequencies, it is also a bit deaf to the LOW end frequencies, which is a bit of a problem if you want a solid gut thumping bass sound. If you'd like to read some technical information on this phenomenon, refer to the *Fletcher-Munson curves on Page 175.*

If you want a lot of bottom end, you have to move a lot of air. This means big speakers and lots of them. ***You can't get a quart out of a pint pot!*** (But you can make sure you get a pint!) Bass speaker boxes can be either horn loaded, bandpass or straight reflex boxes. There are no set rules as long as they deliver the sound you want.

One school of thought says that bass horns are best, where you make one speaker work to its optimum, whereas another says that you can get the same output by fitting as many speakers as possible into the one box.

In touring situations it's a question of economics. How many speakers delivering how much SPL (Sound Pressure Level - the true measure of loudness) can you fit in the truck? Some studies claim that direct radiating bass boxes have an advantage over horn loaded boxes in output vs. bulk volume, and others claim that bandpass or manifold technology delivers greater output for size. However, at the entry level of the mixing business bass horns offer good value for maximum output with the minimum number of speakers, so you'll probably be using quite a few of them.

### Bass Horns

Bass horns are big. The wavelength of a 60 Hz sound wave is 16 feet, and a true exponential bass horn can be 16 feet long! A bit big to carry or to take into most gigs, let alone pack into the truck!

*If you want a lot of bottom end, you have to move a lot of air*

Most of the work on bass horns was done in the early 1930's, when the advent of sound for movies meant that an economical way had to be found to fill movie theatres with sound. Harry Olson at RCA folded a 60 Hz exponential horn with a 3½ x 7 foot mouth into a box that was only 30" deep. This early work on bass horn design was so good that for a long time horn loaded bass cabinets hardly changed from those early designs. The only difference is that instead of putting only 30 watts into each box we started to put in 600 or more, and

4'W, 20"H, 30"D

With 2 x 18" speakers - 5'W, 40"H, 30"D
With 2 x 15" speakers - 5'W, 36"H, 30"D

Original design. Dotted lines indicate original size - 7'W, 40"H, 30"D
Now usually 5'W, 36"H, 30"D

20:W, 4'H, 24"D
Larger version 30"D

GOT THE URGE TO BUILD SOME BASS HORNS YOURSELF? THEN CHECK OUT THESE DESIGNS TO GET YOU STARTED

Arrows indicate speaker access

Smaller version of original design - 5'W, 36"H, 24"D

4'W, 24"H, 34"D

what was suitable for cinemas with no live microphones often turned into a nightmare with live microphones on a drum kit!

Recent advances in computer modelling have introduced many refinements to bass horn design, alleviating a lot of the peaks and dips in an effort to flatten out the response. The basic physical rules still apply, though - you can bend the rules, but it is very hard to break them.

## Other Bass Systems

The simplest Bass system is the speaker mounted on the front baffle of a sealed box, and it is an efficient way to pack a lot of speakers in a small space.

The basics are simple: choose the speaker, find out the optimum size cabinet for the lowest frequency you need, and build it around the speaker.

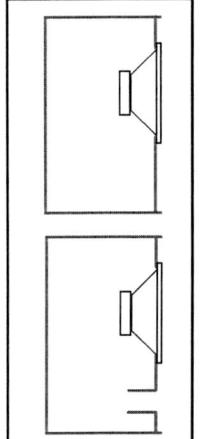

A more common design for greater Low Frequency output is one where the rear chamber opens to the outside air through a vent, or port. The idea is that this port enables the frequencies that the speaker radiates from the back of the cone to meet up with the frequencies coming off the front of the cone, for increased volume and more bottom end.

However, the size of this port is extremely critical to the success of the cabinet. Get it wrong and the speaker will either tear itself apart or just not deliver the goods. So if you feel like making your own, obtain some reliable plans and follow them *exactly*.

### Bandpass and Manifold design

Bandpass design loads a speaker into a ported chamber, firing into another ported chamber. The relative tuning of the ports is usually an octave apart. It is a very efficient sub design, delivering a large amount of output in a relatively narrow frequency band.

The Manifold system from EV wasa variation on bandpass design, and shoe horned four 18" bass drivers firing into a common centre chamber, into a box 36" x 36" x 30". For maximum power the box is run off one amplifier, as 2 x 4 ohm loads. Both the Mid/High and the Bass cabinets have the same external dimensions: 36" x 36" x 30" deep.

## Magic Numbers

If you have the urge to design and build your own cabinets (and who doesn't?), you should remember that there are some magic numbers in speaker box design: 30 inches and 22½ inches. These relate to the width of the truck.

A standard 8 foot wide truck pan is 96 inches externally. Allowing 6 inches for the walls, that leaves you with 90 inches across. Divide that by 3 and you have 30 inches, by 4 and you have 22½ inches. For systems to pack in economically, these are the figures that matter.

Why do you think the rack mount standard is 19 inches? Because the Bell telephone company worked out that with equipment 19 inches wide in a rack they could fit 4 exchanges across the width of a truck, when they were sending them out around the countryout in the early days of the telephone system.

Telephone research led to amplified sound, and eventually led on to Pro Audio - all still using the same rack mount size. Some standards go on forever!

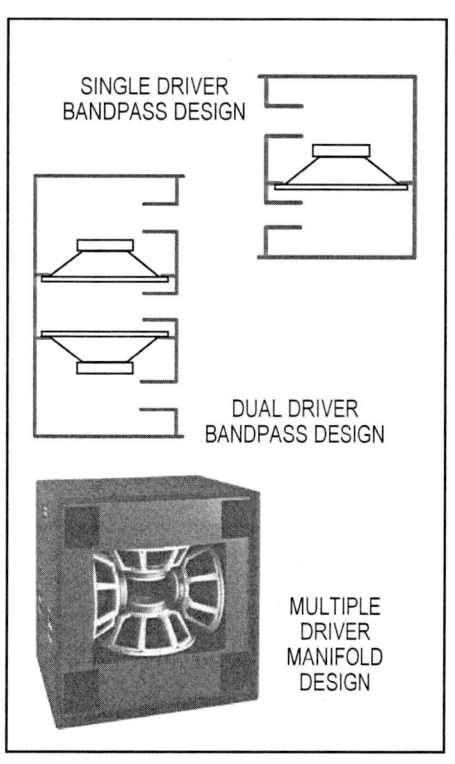

SINGLE DRIVER
BANDPASS DESIGN

DUAL DRIVER
BANDPASS DESIGN

MULTIPLE
DRIVER
MANIFOLD
DESIGN

*Instead of 30 watts into each bass horn we started to put in 600!*

## *Speaker Positioning*

We want to position the speakers so that as much of the audience as possible can hear the music, so depending on how many boxes we have, we aim them towards the audience.

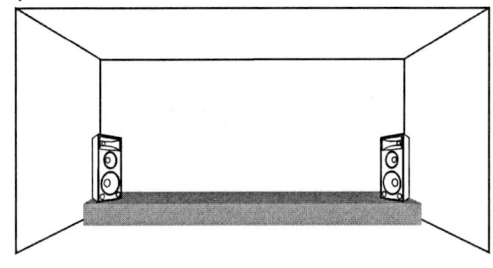

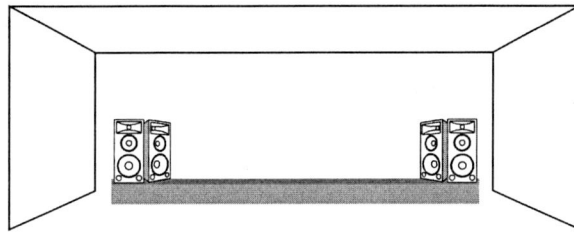

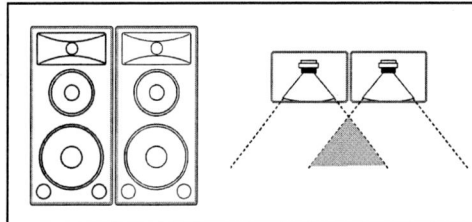

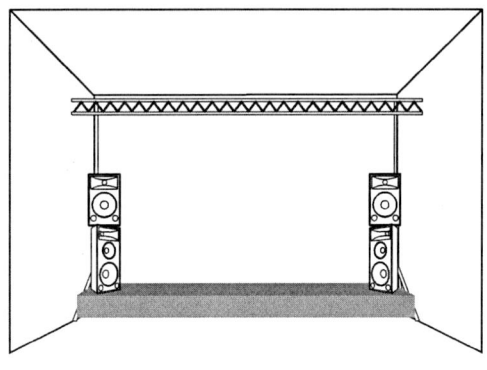

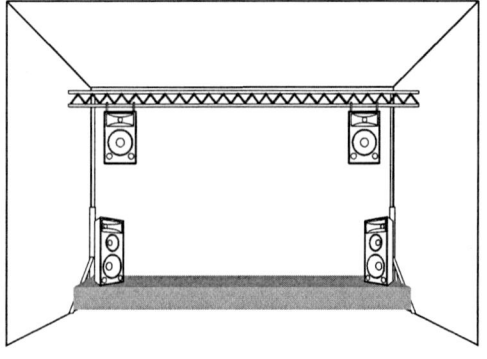

If you're just using a one box system, with say a 15", 12" and a horn, aim them towards an imaginary point in the middle of the audience. Position the speakers so that the bulk of the audience in front of the stage (presumably the most interested) will be adequately covered. Those at the very front will

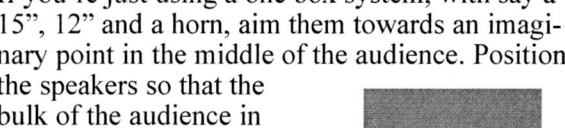
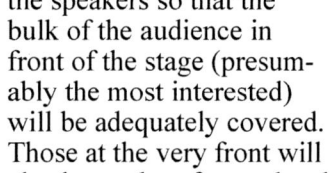
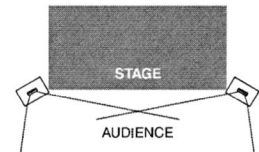

also hear a lot of stage level plus monitor spill, but less of the main system.

*See Chapter 12: Setting Up/Small Systems*

If you have more speaker boxes, then spread them to cover more of the audience. With two or more boxes per side you can have a broader coverage pattern and

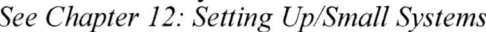
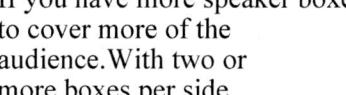
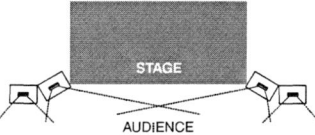

keep more of the audience happy! In a wide room, splay the speakers horizontally to get a wider coverage.

Putting the boxes side by side parallel to each other will give you a hot spot where the two coverage patterns (especially the HF horn outputs) overlap each other. This will create excessive peaks and dips where the waves move in and out of phase with each other.

If you're down one end of a long narrow room, the system needs vertical height to reach down the end.

You *could* stand the boxes on top of each other, or even flip the top one upside down. Since the HIGHs find it hardest to go long distances, this can couple up the horns for greater output.

*However* this can also create severe phase cancellations at longer distances, with the effect being if you move your head a small amount the high end will alternately disappear and re-appear! The LOW frequencies will couple to the floor and the ceiling. If you stack the cabinets like this, make sure you tie off the top boxes to the lighting stands for support.

A better way would be to fly the upper speakers, thus separating the HIGH horns and angling them towards the rear of the room. Provided they are small and light (12" and horn), they could be flown from the lighting truss; otherwise they will need to be flown from specific rigging points in the venue's ceiling.

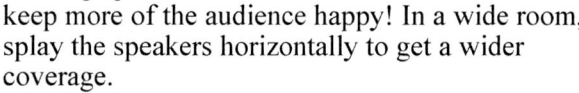
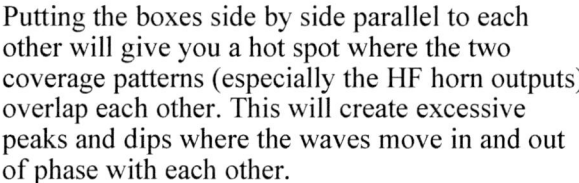

## How do we stack speakers up?

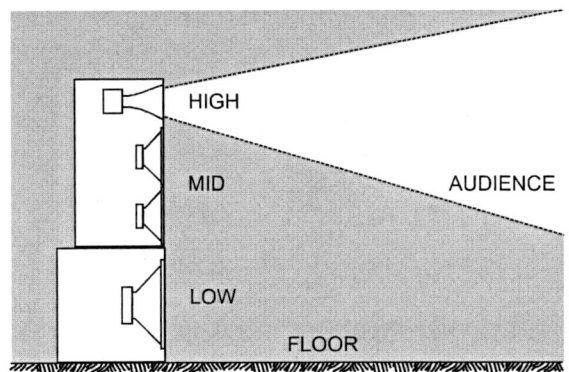

Here are some basic rules.

1. Keep the Low Frequencies low down

2. Keep the Mid Frequencies in the middle

3. Keep the High Frequencies up high.

Sounds simple really. But why?

### Keep the Lows low down.

Low frequency wavelengths are long, and below 100 Hz they're pretty well non-directional. Once they leave the speaker, they look for a surface to radiate along. For our purposes, the nearest surface is the floor. If you have a wall as well, even better.

If you have 2 walls and a floor, then you might have to turn the bottom end down. But that's better than not having enough.

## What about concert systems flown in the air?

These systems have to make their own radiating surface, and they use the other boxes around them to do it. A flown cluster 4 boxes wide by 4 boxes deep can have a frontal area of 256 square feet - not a bad size wall. Even so, these systems frequently have extra bass cabinets down on the ground.

## Keep the Mids in the middle.

The human ear is most sensitive to sounds in the Midrange area, so aim these straight at the audience, and they'll easily hear all the vocals.

## Keep the Highs high

High frequencies are very short wavelengths, and are the most easily dissipated by distance (and cigarette smoke!). So give them the best chance and keep them high, aimed over the audience's head towards the middle back.

The vertical spread of the horn will ensure that the people down the front still hear enough, and give an even spread of highs down to the back (provided the horn is well designed).

## Dispersion Patterns: The theory

Horns for the Mids and Highs have coverage patterns that are described in degrees: for example, a 60°H x 40°V. This means that if you draw an imaginary line out of the centre of the horn, it will give good coverage 30° each side of that line horizontally, and 20° each side of that line vertically.

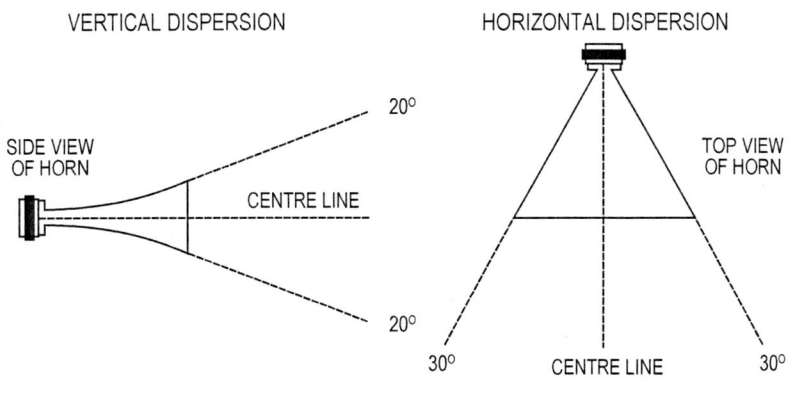

A 90 x 40 would be 45° each side of the line horizontally, and a 120 x 40 would be 60° each side of this line.

### Dispersion Patterns: The truth

Actually the sound spreads out further than this at some frequencies, and less at others. It's an average. Speaking in general terms, the pattern tends to get narrower at higher frequencies, and broader at lower ones. Lower than 100 Hz, as I mentioned before, it just leaps out of the box and runs around everywhere.

## Speaker Safety

People go along to gigs for enjoyment; they don't normally expect to end up in hospital after seeing their favourite band or artist. Yet even a quite small speaker box can do serious damage to someone if it falls on their head or their back. A larger one can do worse...!

Make sure that however you stack up your speakers, you do it with safety in mind.

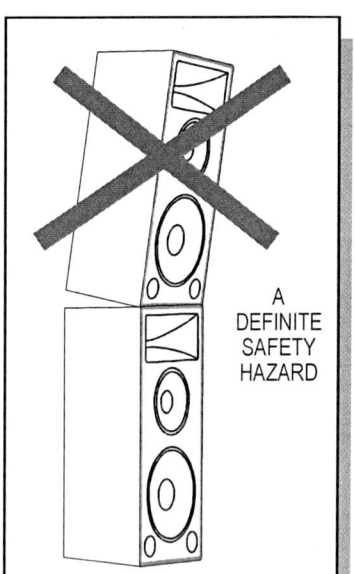

A DEFINITE SAFETY HAZARD

Don't stack them all up on top of a small bar table. Stack them on a piece of ply laid over several roadcases on their side or a specially designed stand.

*Never* tilt a speaker box downwards so that it is only standing on the front edge of the box. It instantly goes from being a fairly stable heavy box to a very unstable heavy box. When it vibrates with the music (as it definitely will) it has every chance of going walkabout on top of the poor audience member standing in front of it!

I once set up the subs in front of the stage at a small gig, to save space, and laid the front line of monitor wedges on top of them. We were only 3 songs into the set when the lead singer announced that her monitors had just disappeared off the edge of the subs into the crowd. The monitors had just vibrated off, and luckily only dropped 2 feet onto the floor. But what if it had been a front of house box falling off the top of the stack?

If you have multiple speakers stacked up, strap them together using a ratchet tie down strap, not copious amounts of gaffer tape! Check it thoroughly, and make the venue security people aware that letting the crowd climb up on them (and dive off them) or get too close to them is a no-no.

Try and be aware of what could happen, and be prepared.

If you have to fly speaker boxes in the air, make sure you get a licensed rigger to do it with the proper load rated equipment. Be warned - this is not something to do yourself with some chain from the hardware store. Most states and countries have very strict safety regulations on flying equipment over people's heads, so get a professional to do it who knows the ropes (no pun intended!).

## Speaker Phase/Polarity

Multiple speakers must be wired up 'In Phase' or with the correct Polarity. This means that the positive lead must go to the same terminal on every speaker - usually the Red one, and the negative lead must go to the other, usually Black or unmarked.

This ensures that when the speakers receive a signal, they all jump in the same direction at the same time. If they don't, the speakers are wired up 'Out of Phase' with each other (incorrect polarity); some will jump forwards, some backwards. This will cause Phase Cancellation' and big problems.

The following diagrams show what I mean:

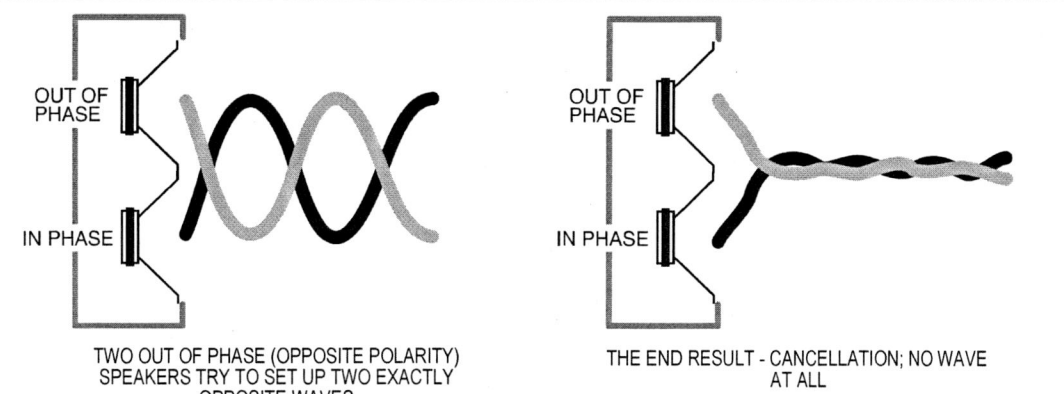

TWO OUT OF PHASE (OPPOSITE POLARITY) SPEAKERS TRY TO SET UP TWO EXACTLY OPPOSITE WAVES

THE END RESULT - CANCELLATION; NO WAVE AT ALL

If you have two bass speakers wired up out of phase with each other, you'll get virtually no output from them, no matter how much level you try to pump into them. Each speaker will cancel out the other's signal. The speaker that jumps forward first sets up one wave, and the one that jumps backwards first sets up the exact opposite wave.

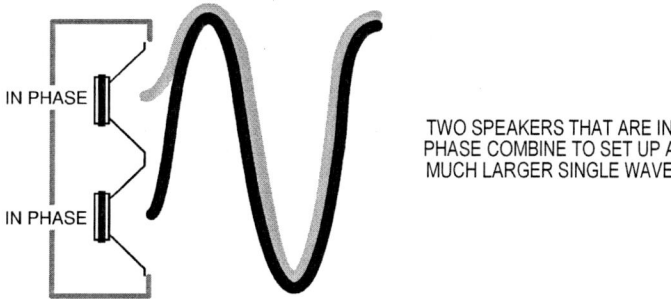

TWO SPEAKERS THAT ARE IN PHASE COMBINE TO SET UP A MUCH LARGER SINGLE WAVE

Two speakers (or more) that are wired up correctly all push together and set up a bigger, single wave, and bigger equals louder.

We'll talk more about coupling later, in this chapter, but this phenomenon is particularly important at lower frequencies since their wavelengths are so long.

### Checking Speaker Polarity

You can check speaker polarity easily if you have direct access to the actual speaker.

Here's how you do it: Plug a short speaker lead with bare wire tails into the box. Put one hand on the speaker cone, connect the negative tail of the lead to the negative terminal of a small battery, and TOUCH the positive tail to the positive terminal.

You should feel the speaker cone jump forwards (on JBLs, backwards). All the speakers in the same frequency band - all the LOWs, all the MIDs, should jump in the same direction. If they don't, rewire them until they do.

This test is fine *if* you have easy access to the speaker to put your hand onto it. This is not always possible without pulling the box apart, so to help

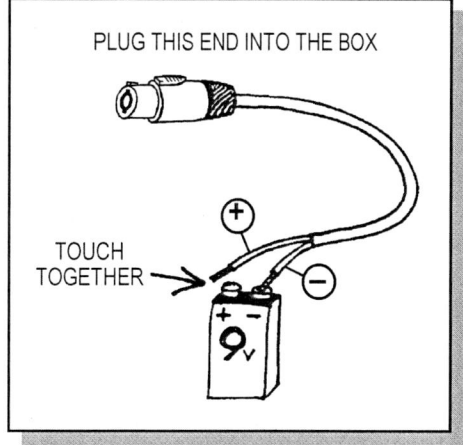

PLUG THIS END INTO THE BOX

TOUCH TOGETHER

engineers check out PA systems easily, a number of companies make "Phase Checkers", which are 2 part units consisting of a Sender and Receiver.

You plug the Sender into the mixing console, switch it on, bring up the level, and you'll hear a pulsing click through the system every second. Hold the Receiver in your hand, switch it on and and stick it in front of each speaker (each speaker driver, not each box; get in as close as you can).

The receiver will analyze the waveform and flash a Green LED for IN phase, and a Red LED for OUT of Phase.

RECEIVER:
POINT THIS AT
THE SPEAKER

SENDER:
PLUG THIS INTO
THE SYSTEM

You can also use one to check out the speaker box, by standing about a metre or so back from it and running the same test. And, if you sit it on the console and point it at the system, you can check out the system the same way.

However, if you get a drastically different reading, then try it from other points in the venue. You might have set the console up in a particularly odd part of the venue, where the reflected signals are louder than the signal from the system, and are causing phase cancellation. Try getting a bit closer to the system.

These gadgets are quite expensive, but are a valuable addition to your tools of the trade. If you've ever wondered why you seem to be pushing heaps of power into your system, but not getting much level out, then a Phase Checker could solve your problem before you start needing some expensive repairs.

## Watts vs SPL

Speaker loudness is not a matter of how many watts you put in, but how much SPL comes out. SPL stands for Sound Pressure Level, a measure of a speaker's efficiency. SPL is measured in dB - decibels - and the standard reference point is 1 watt at 1 metre distance.

For those of you in non-metric countries who've often wondered what a metre is, it's nearly 40 inches.

As an example, let's say our speaker has a Sound Pressure Level of 100 dB at 1 watt, 1 metre. This is known as its 'sensitivity'.

Doubling the amplifier power gives us a 3 dB increase in SPL; so at 2 watts, 1 metre this speaker will deliver 103 dB, at 4 watts 106 dB, 8 watts 109 dB and so on up to the maximum power handling capacity of the speaker.   Here's a chart to show this:

| 1 watt | @1 metre | 100dB |
|---|---|---|
| 2 watts | @1 metre | 103 |
| 4 " | " | 106 |
| 8 " | " | 109 |
| 16 " | " | 112 |
| 32 " | " | 115 |
| 64 " | " | 118 |
| 125 " | " | 121 |
| 250 " | " | 124 |
| 500 " | " | 127 |
| 1000 watts | @ 1 metre | 130dB |

INCREASING THE POWER FROM 1 WATT
TO 1000 WATTS PRODUCES A
**THEORETICAL** 30 DB INCREASE IN SPL

Of course if our speaker is LESS efficient than this example, say only 97 dB@ I watt 1 metre, then it is going to need **twice** as much power to reach the same SPL as our previous example. And, by the same token, if it is MORE efficient, say 103 dB, I watt 1 metre, then it will only need half as much power to reach the same SPL.

From this you can see why the efficiency of a speaker system is very important for large touring systems. If you can deliver the required SPL from half as many boxes and amplifiers, then your trucking costs will be lower, your fuel costs will be lower, your crew costs will be lower, your load in and out times will be faster, and so on. Compact efficient amplifiers driving compact efficient speaker boxes are the current and future solution to the ever increasing costs of touring live sound production.

Similar rules apply to doubling up on speaker boxes and amplifiers.

Let's use a hypothetical *NoNamo* brand One Box system to illustrate the point, with an average efficiency over the LOW, MID and HIGH of 100 dB, 1 watt 1 metre.

If one of these boxes puts out 100 dB, then 2 of them (and 2 amp racks) will put out 103dB; 4 will deliver 106 dB, 8 will deliver 109 dB, and so on, until you run out of boxes (or truck space).

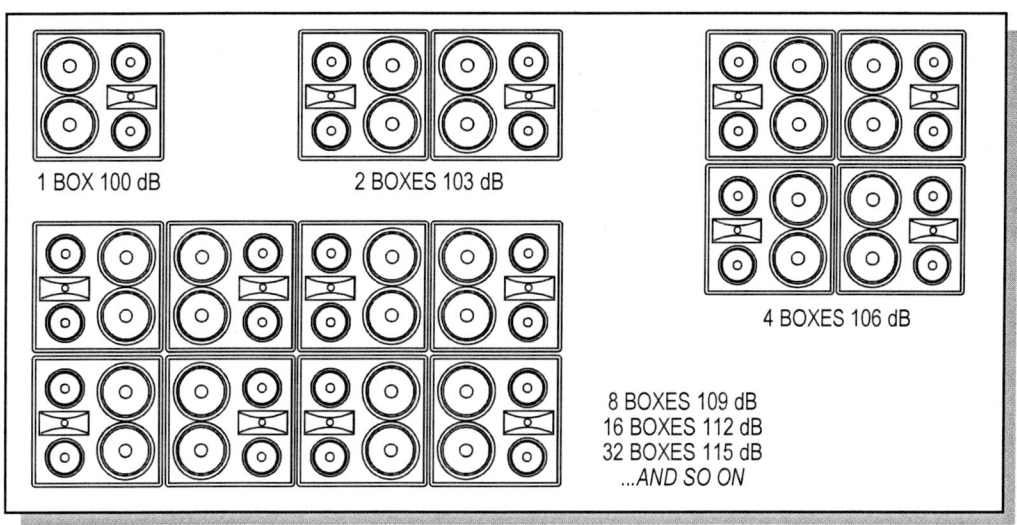

1 BOX 100 dB    2 BOXES 103 dB

4 BOXES 106 dB

8 BOXES 109 dB
16 BOXES 112 dB
32 BOXES 115 dB
...AND SO ON

*An ineffi-
cient PA
speaker is
an expensive
way to heat
a room*

### The Good News

Our hypothetical 32 box concert system will theoretically produce 115 dB, 1 watt 1 metre. At 1000 watts per box at one metre it should produce 145 dB!

### The Bad News

This is the theory. In practice there are many factors that will affect the absolute SPL from a system:

1: It is impossible to get 1 metre away from every box at the one time; that many boxes is too dispersed a point source for accurate concentration at one point.

2: Low Frequency speakers will 'couple up' when placed in close proximity to each other, but overlapping coverage of Mid and High horns can create peaks and dips when placed near each other. In other words the whole system won't get equally loud at all frequencies

3: Different frequencies will reflect differently from different surfaces throughout the venue; some will be absorbed more easily, others will bounce around more.

4: The speakers themselves do not deliver such a linear increase in output. Worse still, as they warm up their resistance increases (the wire in the voice coils gets hot) and they need more power to keep putting out the same SPL.

### SPL vs Distance

But wait, there's more! Things get rapidly worse once you start moving back from that 1 metre position. The SPL drops off in accordance with the Inverse Square Law, which in our case means that for every doubling of distance from the sound source, the area to be covered QUADRUPLES.

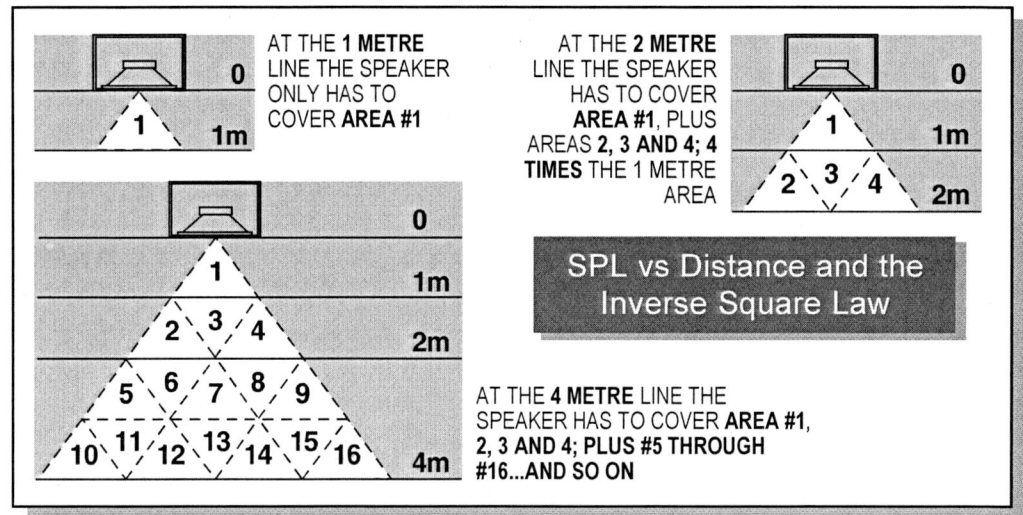

AT THE **1 METRE** LINE THE SPEAKER ONLY HAS TO COVER **AREA #1**

AT THE **2 METRE** LINE THE SPEAKER HAS TO COVER **AREA #1**, PLUS AREAS **2, 3 AND 4; 4 TIMES** THE 1 METRE AREA

SPL vs Distance and the Inverse Square Law

AT THE **4 METRE** LINE THE SPEAKER HAS TO COVER **AREA #1, 2, 3 AND 4; PLUS #5 THROUGH #16...AND SO ON**

What this does to our SPL figures is that for every doubling of distance from the speakers, the SPL drops by 6 dB.

Looking at our 32 box system, at 500 watts per box we have a theoretical 151 dB at 1 metre. At 2 metres distance this would be 145 dB, at 4 metres 139 dB, and so on.

At a concert most of the audience is going to be between 16 to 64 metres from the speakers, and so will get a much slower SPL drop off that if they were closer. In the first 16 metres the level drops 24 dB; in the next 78 metres it only drops another 12 dB.

For a gig the size of the one pictured at the bottom of the page, 30 to 40 metres (100' or more) would be an ideal mixing position; loud, yet far enough away from the stage sound (over which you have no control) to be able to pull a good mix

## Speaker Systems

### Discrete (or Component) Systems

This is the classic early big system, where each frequency band (Low, LowMid, High Mid, High) is handled by a separate speaker in a separate cabinet. A folded horn with Dual 15" bass drivers for Low, a horn loaded Low Mid cabinet with a single lighter cone 15" (4560 type design), a large radial horn flare and large diaphragm compression driver for Hi Mids, and a couple of Supertweeters for Highs. The classic 4 way system.

Other configurations changed the Low Mid cabinet for one with 2 x 12" drivers, which were able to handle higher frequencies, and so a different compression driver could be used which

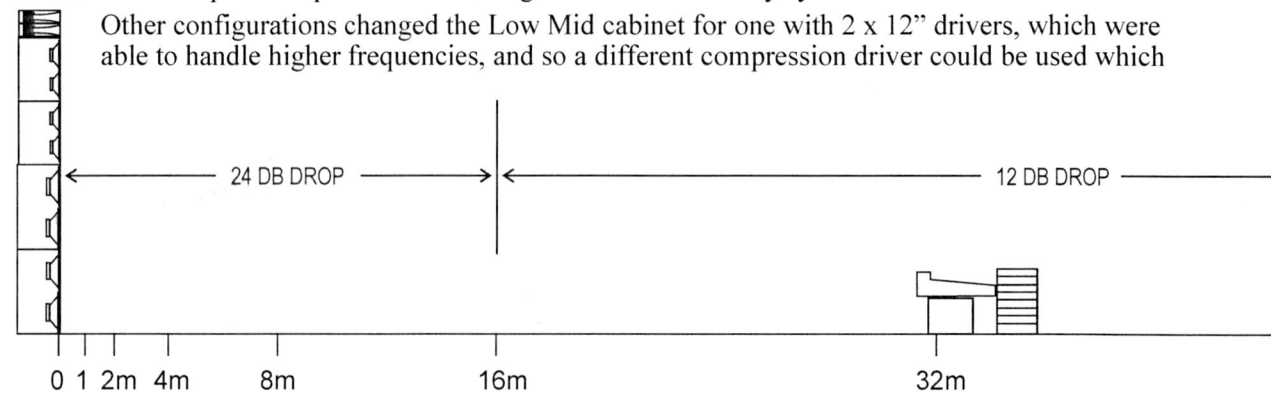

24 DB DROP ← → 12 DB DROP

0  1  2m  4m      8m              16m                    32m

Live Sound Mixing 4th Edition  ©2005 D.R.Fry

went right out to the edge of hearing, without needing supertweeters - giving us a 3 way design. Multiples of these systems were the backbone of club and concert sound for many years.

Set up correctly they provided sound that was loud and pretty good (for their time), and individual components could be aimed at all parts of the venue, giving good coverage. But, they were big, very heavy and could be stacked up wrongly by inexperienced crew, giving considerably less than perfect coverage or sound. Because it was hard to fly them they had to be ground stacked, creating bad sightlines for the audience.

CLASSIC EARLY 3/4 WAY - W BIN, 4560 MID CABINETS, RADIAL HORNS

### One Box and Two Box Systems

During the mid to late 80's there was a growing trend to fit all the speakers - Low, Low Mid, High Mid, High either in the one cabinet, or all except Low in the one cabinet, with separate Low cabinets. See our hypothetical system on P.1051. These are known as One Box or Two Box systems, and are designed with the following parameters in mind, although not necessarily in this order!

1. Sound better
2. Set up faster
3. Pack neatly into trucks in as little space as possible
4. Easy and Safe to fly in the air.

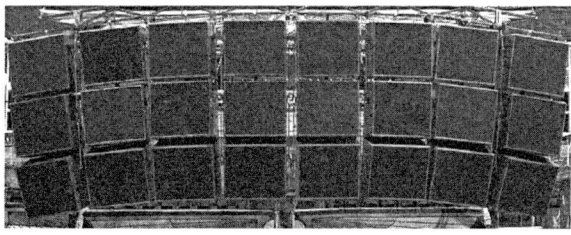

ONE-BOX CURVED ARRAY FORMED WITH RECTANGULAR SPEAKER BOXES

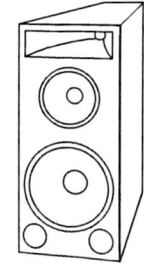

TRAPEZOIDAL SHAPED SPEAKER CABINET - TAPERS TOWARDS THE BACK

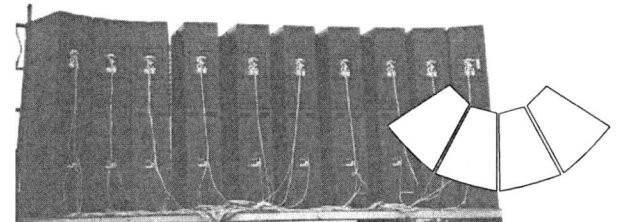

CURVED ARRAY FORMED WITH TRAPEZOIDAL SPEAKER BOXES

Most speaker cabinets in this type of system have multipin connectors (Cannon/Amphenol EP or Neutrik Speakons) on the back so that they can't be wired up incorrectly (the plug only goes in one way), and instead of a crossover they have dedicated Control Units, or Speaker Management Systems, which provide all the electronics necessary to deliver good sound night after night. *(See Chapter 8 - Crossovers)*

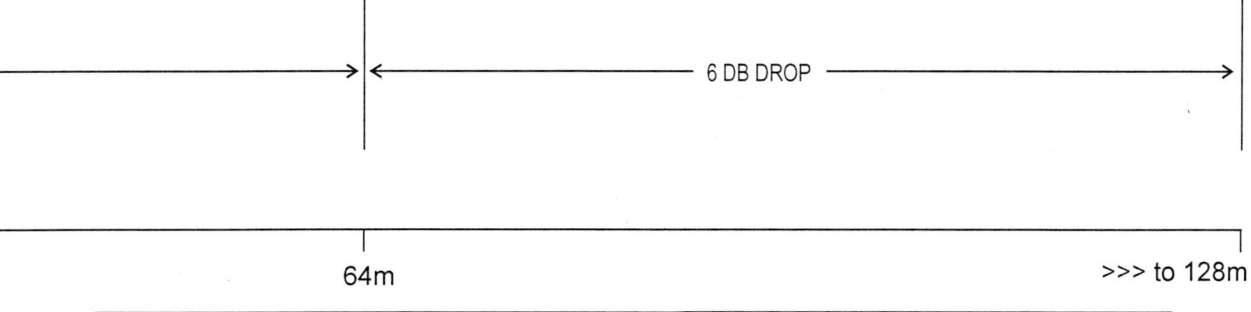

6 DB DROP

64m                                    >>> to 128m

Many of the cabinets are trapezoid shaped, tapering towards the back so that they can be formed into a curved array easily.

Speed in setting up and pulling down is a big plus, and also, because the options for stacking are limited, the possibility of user misuse is reduced. If you can only stack it up one way, you can't go far wrong. On the other hand, coverage can be uneven if the whole cabinet has to be aimed rather than individual components.

For smaller systems though, the 12" or 15"and horn with optional Sub are the standard worldwide. In smaller clubs and venues a well-designed couple of these a side with a Sub can provide more than enough sound to let you demonstrate your mxing ability to the audience.

### Line Arrays

Line arrays are the current favourite in larger live sound systems, although smaller versions will be found anywhere from ballrooms to school halls. The line array concept is not new - but its application to live sound for music rather than train stations is! A line array relies on 'coupling', a phenomenon we have touched on earlier in this chapter.

Any speaker will couple to its nearest neighbour if their centres are closer to each other than the size of the highest wavelength they will handle.

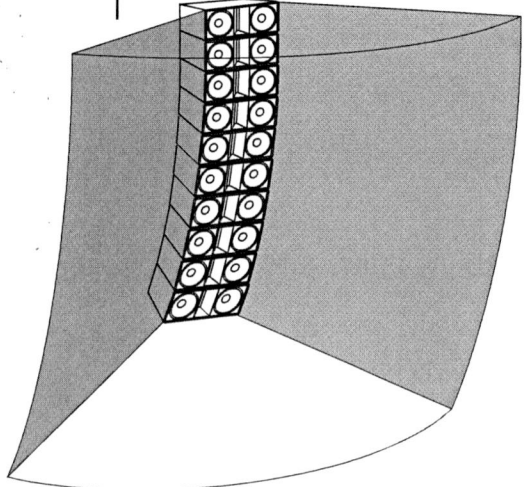

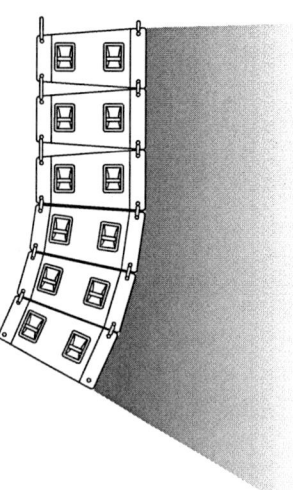

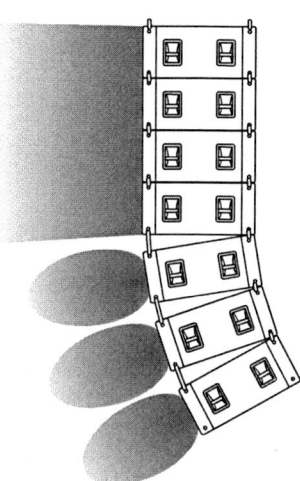

THEORETICAL COVERAGE OF LINE ARRAY SYSTEM - A WIDE FLAT CURVED SLICE OF CAKE!

TAPERED CABINET CAN PIVOT FROM THE FRONT TO STOP ANY GAPS APPEARING AND BREAKING THE LINE

RECTANGULAR CABINET MUST PIVOT FROM THE REAR, ALLOWING GAPS TO APPEAR AND BREAK THE LINE

Coupling in a vertical line brings 2 major benefits:
1. An increase of 3dB in output for the speakers
2. A reduction in the vertical coverage - the sound from each speaker tends to lean towards each other. Given a long enough array, usually a minimum of 10 to 12 boxes and often many more, the sound comes out in a wide horizontal arc.

Low Frequency drivers will couple up easily, since a 100 Hz wave is about 10 feet (3 metres) long. Mid drivers can do it too, if they are close enough - a 1KHz wave is about 12 inches (300mm) long. High Frequency drivers have a harder time; since their wavelengths are so small, it's impossible to get the drivers that close, so each box has to have more HF drivers than you would expect to see in a cabinet designed to be used in ones or twos.

With a little bit of judicious angling, the array can be curved to cover virtually the whole venue in a wide sweep. You'll notice that each cabinet is angled slightly, pivoting from the front so that the line of coupling isn't broken, as it would be if they pivoted from the back.

## Repealing the Inverse Square Law?

Much of the appeal of line arrays lies with their apparent breaking of the Inverse Square Law *(see page 105)*. Instead of the level dropping 6dB for every doubling of distance from the source, with a line array it only drops 3dB, because the sound wave only expands horizontally, not vertically as well.

But that's only part true. Yes, it does drop 3dB, but only in the near field, which can vary from only 1.3 metres (5 feet) at 100 Hz, to over 100 metres (300+ feet) at 10 KHz. After that the beam of sound is no longer so tightly focussed, and subject to air absorption and dissipation, reverting back to the regular 6dB drop in the far field. However that initial near field response can be enough to increase the throw of the system considerably, but not equally at all frequencies. In large venues there will be extra Low frequency cabinets either hung alongside the main array, or ground stacked.

## Setting Up

Setting up any large system these days is usually done with the help of brand-specific software programs, and line arrays are no exception. These programs have all the parameters of the cabinets, and can work out the optimim hanging height, curve and number of boxes required to fill the venue with sound. The theory is that every seat can be a good seat. The reality is often different. No matter what type of system you are using, 'power alley' is directly facing the system, on axis with the front of the speakers. Response does taper off the more to one side or the other you get, but if you have enough cabinets you should be able to cover pretty well all the audience with sound. Don't assume that everywhere in the venue sounds as good as it does where you are mixing from. During the soundcheck it is essential to 'walk the room' and listen for any dead sounding areas. Very often the system level and EQ can be modified on a box by box basis, boosting in some areas and cutting in others, to provide good sound throughout the room.

*Don't assume that everywhere in the venue sounds as good as your mixing position*

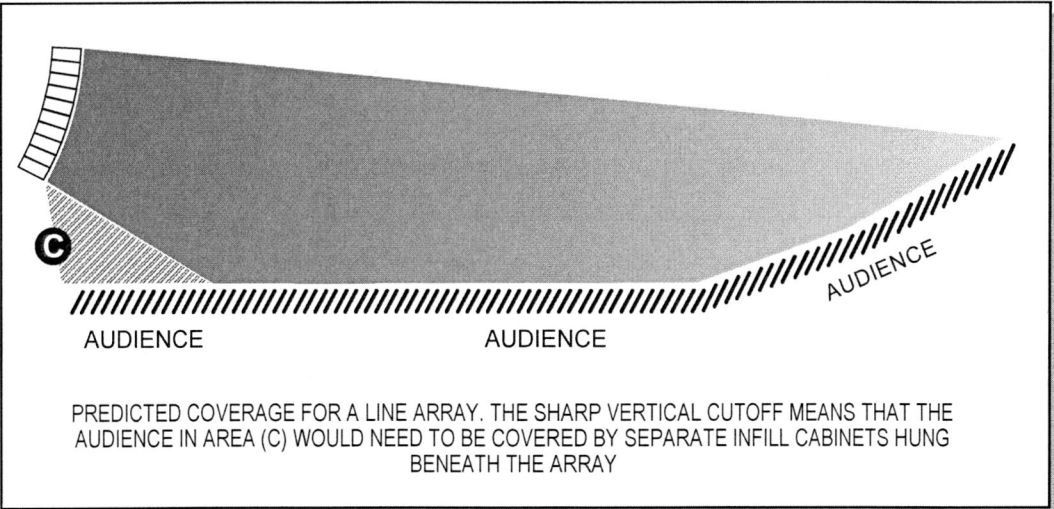

PREDICTED COVERAGE FOR A LINE ARRAY. THE SHARP VERTICAL CUTOFF MEANS THAT THE AUDIENCE IN AREA (C) WOULD NEED TO BE COVERED BY SEPARATE INFILL CABINETS HUNG BENEATH THE ARRAY

## Powered Systems

With all of the speaker systems we've talked about so far, the amplifiers have sat backstage and run long lines of speaker cable out to each cabinet. Some systems do it differently - the amplifiers are located inside each speaker cabinet. Meyer Sound pioneered this concept, and it has been adopted by other companies too. Without long lines of thick copper between amplifier and speaker, this type of 'close-coupled' design delivers greater actual power at the speaker and improves the damping factor.

Each speaker gets exactly the amount of power it can handle, and all speaker management - EQ, phase correction, crossover functions, speaker protection limiting - is built-in. The reduced number of connections is designed to eliminate mis-patching and lessen the possibility of ground loops.

Powered systems have proved very popular for theatre and stage shows, since they can be virtually silent without the droning fan noise from amp racks.

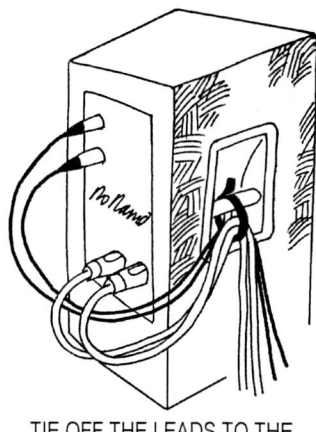

A common feature to all professional powered systems is locking power connectors. Just as the Speakon connector is changing unpowered systems, the PowerCon lockable AC power connector is finding a home in powered speaker cabinets. After all, a power lead vibrating out is a nuisance if the cabinet is on the ground, but in the air it's a nightmare!

TIE OFF THE LEADS TO THE HANDLE AS A WEIGHT AND STRAIN RELIEF

NEUTRIK POWERCON AC CONNECTORS - BRIGHT BLUE FOR IN, WHITE FOR OUT

XLR input connectors are already latching, so are less of a problem in this respect.

Note: Always tie off and support the cabling to any speaker system, especially if it's a powered system being flown. Signal leads are much more fragile than heavy duty speaker lead, and you don't want all the system cabling hanging off one solder joint!

Powered speaker systems make a lot of sense, and represent the current state of the art in live sound. They come in all flavours - small, large, line array and curved array - all you have to do is run out some AC power and a signal to the cabinets.

In any good speaker system, the time consuming chores are already done for you, leaving you free to do what you originally wanted to do...MIX!

## Speaker Checklist

- ☑ Make sure the correct speakers are wired to the correct amps
- ☑ Make sure the speakers are wired 'in phase' - when one jumps forwards, they all do
- ☑ Try not to drop them
- ☑ Set them up with audience (and performer) safety in mind; if they need flying, get a professional licensed rigger to do it
- ☑ Aim the speakers to give maximum audience coverage; position yourself so you can hear what the majority of the audience hears
- ☑ Don't overdrive the speakers by pushing in more power than they can handle
- ☑ Listen for any distortion or strange sounds from the speakers; check out the reason straight away

## 11      *Monitors*

## Monitors

*Also known as Foldback*

This is the single most important part of the system as far as the band is concerned. Why?

Because it is the only part of the system that they can hear.

Imagine yourself onstage, as say a guitarist. Even if you don't have a Hendrix/Who size speaker stack behind you, most small combo size amplifiers can deliver enough SPL to make a dead man's ears bleed. You can probably also hear way too much drums and cymbals, some keyboards, maybe feel a bit of bass, but any vocal sound will only exist in your imagination unless lots of it comes through the monitors. If you can hear everything you need, without stressing out, you and the other band members can concentrate on the playing and it'll be a great gig.

So if you want to keep the band happy (and keep your gig) then you need to deliver what they want in the monitors. Forget front of house – the band's girlfriends/boyfriends will tell them what it sounds like out front, but the quality and level of the monitor sound will determine what the band thinks of both the system *and* your job of handling it.

More than anything else, the monitors have to be as LOUD as necessary for the band to hear themselves above the music level on stage. This is not an easy thing, as to do this you have to bend all the rules. It's no wonder that control of feedback can be a major problem when setting up the monitors.

*The monitors are the only part of the system that the band can hear*

---

I'll repeat something from *Chapter 5 - Microphones:*

'The monitor system is blaring out across the stage and also up from the wedges.

'We want to get this monitor sound into the singer's ears, but we don't want it going into the microphone.

'Ears are at the most only 5" (100mm) from the mouth, and the mouth is about ¼" (5mm) from the microphone!'

So you are trying to get a large amount of level out of a speaker that is usually no more that 6 feet away from a sensitive vocal microphone.

There is a technical formula for working out gain before feedback, and it's a very useful tool for consultants and designers. Personally, though, when the monitors are feeding back, the band is yelling at me, and the audience has their hands over their ears screaming "Make it stop!", then give me a decent equalizer over a calculator any day!

## Tools of the Trade

Let's run over some of the monitor tools we have available.

### *Equalizers and other signal processors* (see Chapter 3)

The 30 band graphic equalizer is the primary tool for massaging the monitor sound to produce something that doesn't feed back all night. It's going to be your best friend; constantly practise with it until you know instantly what each frequency sounds like, and how much cut or boost is required to achieve the desired sound. When used in conjunction with the console EQ, you should have enough EQ to handle whatever the laws of physics can throw at you.

Another development is the automatic feedback eliminator, which hunts down feedback as it happens and pulls down the appropriate frequency just enough to stop it. There are quite a few available, some excellent and fast reacting, some slower and thus not so good.

### *Wedges*

Also known as Slants, Stage Monitors

These are the angled monitors across the stage, directly in front of each singer. They will usually have a 12" or 15" speaker and a compression driver/horn in them, the size of which will depend on the size and purpose of the wedge.

Depending on the absolute SPL the wedges are expected to produce, they will either be 2 way (Bi-amped) or have a passive crossover.

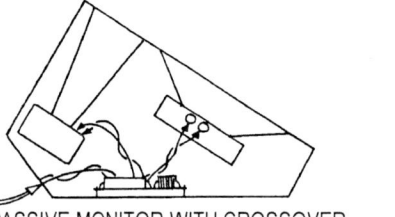

PASSIVE MONITOR WITH CROSSOVER
INSIDE, POWERED BY A SINGLE
AMPLIFIER CHANNEL

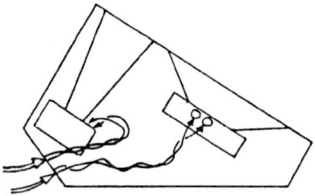

ACTIVE MONITOR, POWERED BY
2 AMPLIFIER CHANNELS AND AN
ACTIVE CROSSOVER

Amplifier wise, one with a passive crossover will only need one side of the amplifier, whereas a Bi-amped monitor will use both sides of the amplifier and need an active crossover. *Refer back to Crossovers, Chapter 9 for the difference between Active and Passive.*

The configuration will depend on the SPL you need. Any band whose on-stage level from the instruments is not too loud would probably be happy with the SPL from passive monitors. A full-on hard rock or heavy metal band would need to go for Bi-amped monitors, and a lot of them, if they are going to compete with multiple stacks of guitar amplifiers.

*When the audience is screaming "Make it stop!"*

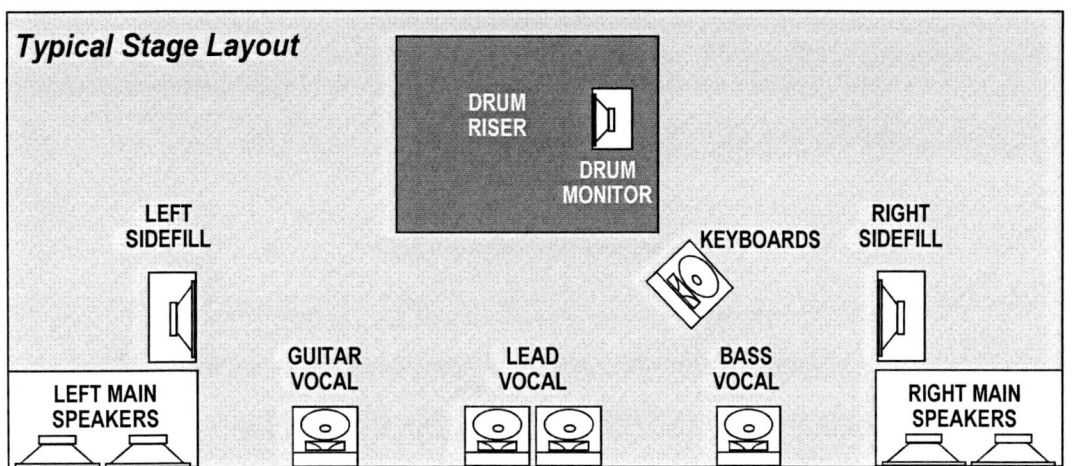

### Side Fill

This is the way to get some real level into the monitors. Side fills are speaker stacks set up behind the main stacks, angled across the stage facing the band. In large systems they are frequently one or two of whatever box is being used out front, ensuring system flexibility and compatibility. Properly set up, and EQ'd the same way you would the main system, good side fills can turn a whisper into a roar, and cut through the on-stage instrument level.

### Drum Monitor

This is a small PA system in itself. Usually set up at the side of the drummer, up next to one ear, or pointing up from the floor if the previous position interferes with sightlines too much.

The main prerequisite of a drum monitor is that it is loud, with a good low end response. The drummer will need it to hear himself (mainly Kick and Snare), the bass player, and probably some vocals to cue him for various parts of the song.

### In-Ear Monitors

A great idea if the artist likes them; some do, some don't. From the monitor engineer's point of view they alleviate all of the feedback problems; from the artist's point of view it can be a bit like singing along with a Walkman - they can feel isolated from the rest of what's happening on stage. This may not be a good thing if the band or artist likes to interact with each other to pull off a good performance. We'll look at what needs to be done to handle in-ear monitors later in this chapter.

### Where do you put the monitors?

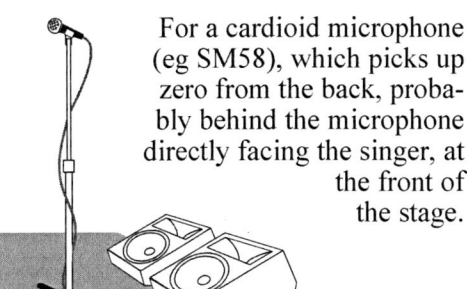

For a cardioid microphone (eg SM58), which picks up zero from the back, probably behind the microphone directly facing the singer, at the front of the stage.

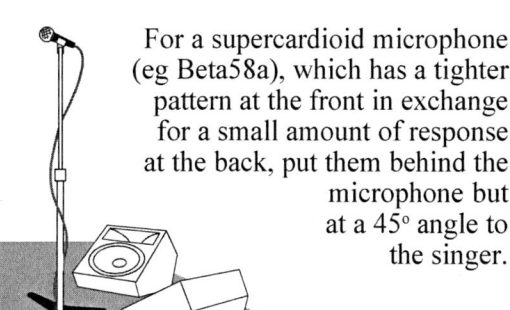

For a supercardioid microphone (eg Beta58a), which has a tighter pattern at the front in exchange for a small amount of response at the back, put them behind the microphone but at a 45° angle to the singer.

For others in the band, position the monitor behind the microphone, making sure that its line of fire is kept well away from the lead vocal microphone.

*The drum monitor is a small PA system in itself*

### Controlling the Monitors

We'll do a complete monitor setup checklist at the end of this chapter. Right now we'll look at some of the ways in which you can get greater control over the monitor sound.

Looking after the monitor mix from the main House mix console is not too hard if the requirements are fairly simple; 1 send going to 3 wedges across the front of the stage, for example.

Once you get more complicated than that, you can start to run into problems.  Even with 1 send and 3 wedges things are not always easy. Think about these two things.

1. Any change of the channel gain control will result in the same gain change being applied to the monitors. Here's an example.  Let's say you've set up the singer's monitors so they are nice and loud on stage, and running just under the feedback point.

   The band starts playing away on stage and you find that the singer is singing a lot softer than you had anticipated, and even with the channel fader all the way up there is not enough vocal level in the main house mix.

Here's the problem; if you increase the channel gain to bring up the vocals, you will also raise the monitor gain by the same amount, which will usually tip the monitor over the edge into squeals of feedback.

Well, about all you can do is to gradually wind back the monitor send slightly at the same time that you bring up the channel gain. The two may or may not cancel each other out, but you really have no choice.

2. In the section on mixing consoles we looked at the Pre-Fade sends, which are the ones to run the monitors from. Ideally they should not only be Pre-Fade but Pre EQ as well. Frequently they aren't, and we are back to problem #1 above; any change in the channel EQ in the main house mix will also change the monitor EQ, and could easily start up a feedback squeal.

In both these examples you are facing the same basic problem - the Main System sound, for all the paying customers, is being controlled by the sound of the monitor system, because you daren't make the necessary changes.

This is quite a dilemma. If they band isn't happy they won't get you to do the sound again; if the audience isn't happy they won't get the band again!

## Monitor Console

The way around all of this is to use a separate console to run the monitors.

> *Any change in the channel gain will also change the monitor level*

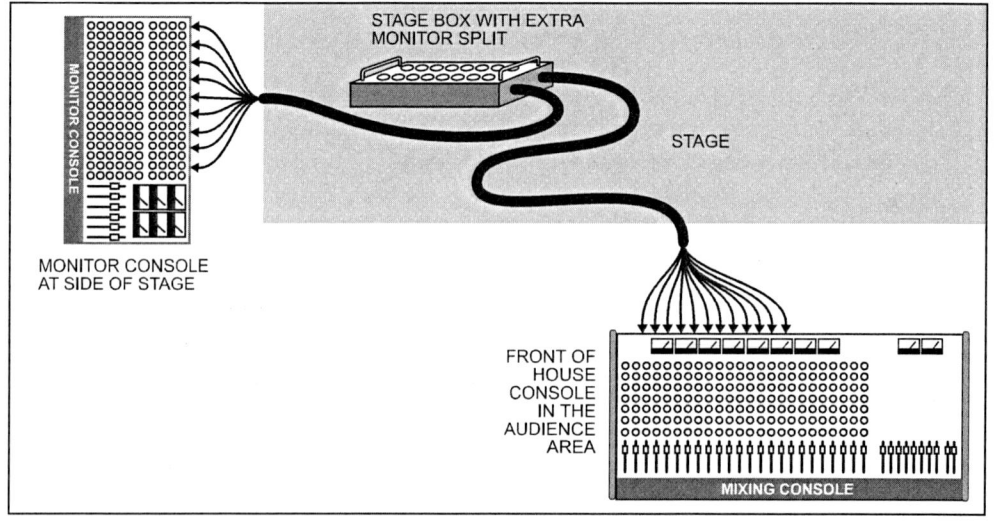

## How does this work?

An extra multicore snake runs from the stage box to the side of the stage.  This has the same number of tails as the main snake, and the two are wired together inside the stage box. In high end systems these are actively split, using electronic circuitry or transformers. Personally I used to just hardwire the Monitor split in parallel with the Front of House feed and never had any trouble.

In theory your monitor mixer should have the same number of channels as your main mixer, but for all but the most complicated situations you can survive with quite a few less. For example, out of all the drums you really only need Kick and Snare; then you need Bass guitar, Guitar, Keyboards (if the keyboardist runs his own mix you can get away with only one channel for them), and all the vocals.

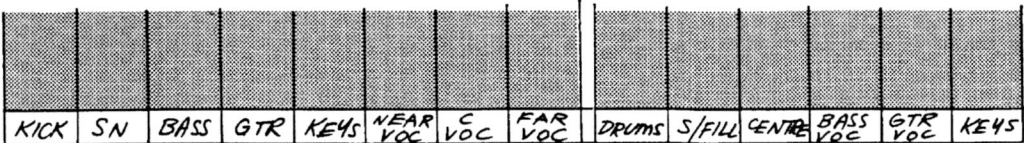

| KICK | SN | BASS | GTR | KEYS | NEAR VOC | C VOC | FAR VOC | DRUMS | S/FILL | CENTRE | BASS VOC | GTR VOC | KEYS |

For all except big touring and concert work you can probably get away with a 12 channel console for monitors, although extra channels obviously make your life easier.

A dedicated monitor mixer does not have a main fader for each channel, but a set of knobs like the Auxiliary sends on a normal mixing console. These sends run to a set of Master sliders which control the Output level of each send.

From the mixer each send should run into its own equalizer, then to its own amplifier(s), and then to its particular speaker - wedges, sidefills or drum monitor.

The monitor mixer should have at least 4 separate sends, and more often will have from 6 to 16, depending on the size of the system.

A lot of today's larger mixers can handle both House or Monitor mixing.They can have up to 16 Aux sends on each channel, and the Group Faders and Aux Masters can be swapped so you can have faders to control each mix. This gives rental companies maximum flexibility with their rental stock

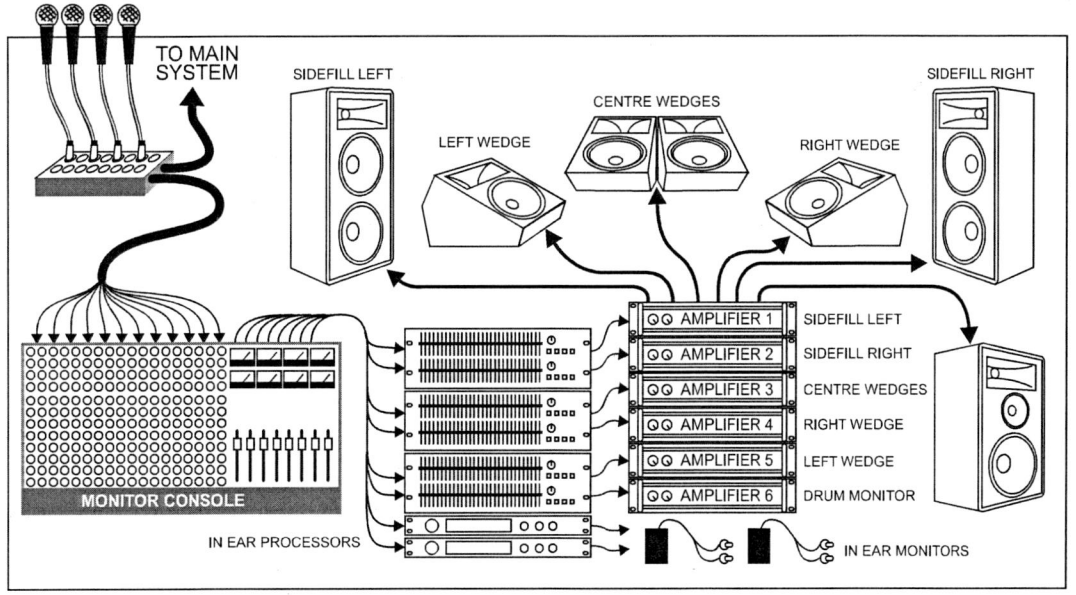

MONITOR MIXER AND MONITOR SENDS LAYOUT

A TYPICAL MONITOR MIXER CHANNEL WITH 8 SENDS

### Mainly me, plus ???

The basic concept behind monitor mixing is that each musician can have a different mix, with just the things that *they* need, in their monitor.

- The lead singer may only want his or her own vocals in their mix;
- The other singers may want to hear mainly themselves, but just a little bit of the lead vocals.
- The keyboard player will probably want to hear all the keyboards and his vocals, and a little of all the other vocals;
- The drummer would usually want the Kick and Snare drums, some Bass guitar, and a little of all the vocals.

With a separate monitor mix all of this and more is possible. The only drawback is that once you have set it up, someone knowledgeable needs to stay by the monitor console throughout the performance to make small adjustments as the musicians need them.

 It's very difficult for you to run backwards and forwards during the performance. A lightning dash through a crowded gig to adjust monitor levels can be very risky. The audience have no idea who you are - all they see is someone trying to push their way to the front. Be warned; take it easy if you want to get back in one piece!

For this reason you should try to anticipate any problems during the soundcheck before the show starts.

Touring Concert systems have a specific Monitor Engineer on the crew whose only job is to get the monitor mix together. This may be a luxury for you and your band, but a monitor console isn't. Using one will improve your main mix by taking away the monitor worry, leaving you a free hand out front to get the sound the audience wants to hear.

## Monitor mixing

### When you are the monitor engineer

Mixing monitors is very different from mixing out front. Mixing for the audience only needs one mix, while monitor mixing can have you in charge of 8 to 16 or more separate mixes, all at the same time.

So, let's have a look at a monitor mix for our typical band: 3 vocals, Drums, Guitar, Bass and Keyboards.

1. Lead Vocal - 2 wedge monitors, set up for maximum volume and usually with just the lead vocal in it
2. Backing Vocal Left - 1 monitor, with mainly this vocal in it, plus a small amount of lead and the other backing vocal
3. Backing Vocal Right - 1 monitor, set up same as above
4. Keyboards - 1 monitor, with mainly keyboards in it, plus some lead vocal, and maybe a bit of Snare drum to keep in time, if necessary
5. Sidefill - 1 each side, with a vocal mix, some Kick and Snare drums, small amount of instruments if necessary
6. Drums - drum monitor, with drums (especially Kick and Snare, but all if you have the spare channels and can keep the toms under control with some gates), lead vocal so he can hear where he is in the song, and Bass so that drums and bass can work together to get a solid rhythm happening.

You'll be able to listen to each monitor yourself with the PFL buttons, on each channel and output group. You may have your own monitor, or if the budget is tight then a pair of headphones.

Ideally the monitor equalizers are patched into each output group via the insert points, which means that when you listen to each of the groups with the PFL/SOLO buttons you hear the

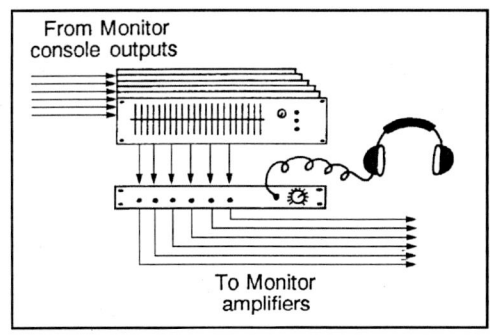
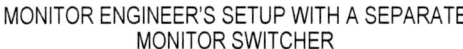

MONITOR ENGINEER'S SETUP WITH A SEPARATE
MONITOR SWITCHER

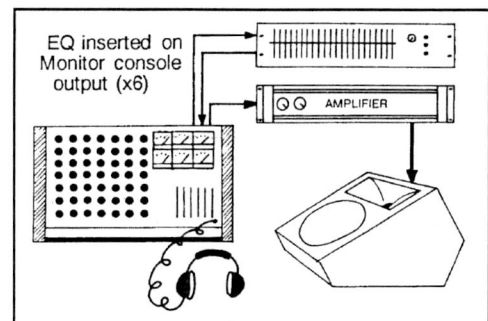

A SMARTER SETUP – THE EQUALIZERS
INSERTED ON EACH OUTPUT OF THE MONITOR
CONSOLE

same equalized sound that comes out of the monitors. Otherwise you only hear the unequalized sound, unless there is a monitor switcher plugged in after the EQs, with any output switchable to your monitor.

All of these features are designed to let you hear exactly what's occurring on stage. This way you can keep on top of the situation at all times, give each musician what they want, and kill any feedback as soon as it starts.

The mixes listed above are just a suggested starting point. When mixing monitors it's a great idea to talk to each of the musicians and see what they need.  For example, when they say "more of XYZ in the monitor", do they really mean "The level of XYZ is fine, but I want less of everything else" Once your levels are approaching maximum, it's advisable to start subtracting unwanted things rather than adding in more of the wanted ones.

It's far easier to find out what they DO want beforehand than to try and work out what they DON'T want once they've started playing. There are limitations to sign language, especially when you're trying to play a guitar or keyboards at the same time!

At the soundcheck, get up there on stage and check out each monitor thoroughly before the musicians come on. Make the equalization is as good as you can, check that every instrument you need is plugged into the monitor console, and that it is marked out so you can easily read it in low light conditions.

You'll need to try and have some level in reserve. Levels that were perfect at the soundcheck can mysteriously become too low when the gig starts. The adrenaline starts pumping, everyone plays harder and - Bang - suddenly there's the lead singer waving madly that he can't hear his vocals so turn them up!

This is *exactly* what can happen, so try and keep some extra level up your sleeve.

## Monitors from the Front of House console

*"You can't always get what you want, and you very rarely get what you need!"* So here are some basics for the times when you have very limited monitor setups.

### One monitor send

This will have to have just the vocals in it. Try and add anything else and the singer(s) will instantly say they can't hear themselves. On a small stage the level from the rest of the musicians will be more than enough.

### Two monitor sends

Send 1 will be for the lead vocals; send 2 can be for the backing vocals and may have a little extra instrument in on *two* conditions:

   1. That everyone listening to send 2 is happy with the extras. If the keyboard player wants some keyboards in the monitors, then the guitarist and bass player (if they sing) will have to live with it too. Check with them first.

*Ask the band what they want to hear in the monitors before you do anything*

2. That the monitor speaker can handle the extra signal. For example, it's not much use putting some bass guitar or kick drum through a wedge that is designed for vocals only. You'll end up with distorted levels of everything, and possibly a dead wedge at the end of the night!

### Three monitor sends

Once again, send 1 will be for the lead vocals, send 2 for the backing vocals, and send 3 you could either use as a drum monitor if you have a suitable box with lots of low end capability, or if it's a wedge, use it for a backing vocalist who need some instruments as well.

### Four monitor sends

With four monitor sends from front of house you're going to be kept on your toes alright, but it could be done! Set them up as for 3 sends (above), but this time make sure you have a suitable drum monitor and use it for the drummer.

It goes without saying (I hope) that each of these sends, whether it's 1, 2, 3 or 4, has to have its own equalizer and amplifier.

### Acoustic instruments

Acoustic instruments can be a problem if they need to be in the monitors. Since most of them make a sound by vibrating in some way, they can be easily set off into feedback by the vibrations from the sound onstage.

*Check and adjust the crossover before you touch the EQ*

As an example of what traps lie in store with acoustic instruments, a friend worked with a South American band who had an instrument called a Billanbao. This consisted of a coconut with a hole in it, attached to a stick with a piece of nylon fishing line stretched along it! An awkward thing to get much of a sound out of; after all, as he said, it's just a bloody coconut. Worse still, the band wanted it really loud in the mix and in the monitors! Trying an SM 57 on it didn't work, as the musician kept getting excited and banging the billanbao against it, which given the enormous amount of gain on the mic kept causing huge bangs through the whole system. Eventually using an SM58 with an external pop filter jammed over it to cushion the blows worked much better.

So be prepared for anything.

## Monitor EQing Checklist

This is a complete checklist of all steps for EQing monitors. It'll repeat things we've mentioned before, but it's meant to be a step by step guide. We'll use the lead vocal monitors as our example, as these are usually the most critical, but the same steps apply to all of the onstage monitors.

1. Position the monitors carefully, making sure that nothing points directly into the vocal microphones except the singer's mouth
2. Set the Gain structure of the channel up carefully so that you have about 6dB of fader (or knob) in reserve. See Gain structure setup, Chapter 2, page 14.
3. Check all amps, EQs and monitors are on, turned up, and working.
4. Slowly bring up the channel monitor send level. If something starts to ring, stop there and reduce the level slightly until it stops.
5. Go "Check 1 - 2" into the microphone and listen to how it sounds. It's got to sound good at a low level if it has any chance of sounding good flat out. You're looking for a very clean, crisp sound, not muffled.
6. If the monitors are active 2 way (bi-amped), adjust the crossover until it sounds as flat as possible *before* you touch the Graphic EQ
7. Bring up the level some more and listen for the next ring
8. By a process of elimination, intuition or knowledge, identify that frequency on the

equalizer. Start in the approximate area and push each slider up a fraction until you find the one that is hot

9. Reduce this fader's level until the ring stops, then reduce it a couple more dB

10. Go "Check 1 - 2" into the microphone again, check the sound, see what the level is like, and go back to step 8 again.

11. Keep going until you either have all the level you think you'll need, or until the fader on that first feedback ring is as far down as it will go.

12. Check the microphone in various positions, cup your hand around the back of it (singers will *always* do this!) and pull out any extra feedback rings with the EQ.

That's about as far as you can go for level. If it's not enough, check out *Chapter 14 - Problems*, for more help.

## Mixing In-Ear Monitors

As the price of in-ears drop to affordable levels, they are becoming more and more popular, especially with lead singers or solo artists. Less expensive ones are usually dynamic, with a tiny version of a regular speaker inside. The more expensive models have a dual driver system - a miniature 2 way system with technology borrowed from hearing aids and toughened up for onstage use. All models plug into a beltpack, usually with a wireless receiver just like wireless microphones.

A singer/guitarist can have three wireless beltpacks - one for the in-ears, one for a headset microphone, and one for the guitar! That's a lot of hardware to carry around.

Although they can be supplied with generic foam rubber sleeves that squish into the ear, for the best isolation custom ear moulds are better, and the most expensive models include this in their price. The better the isolation, the better the high and low frequencies are reproduced in the ears, and thus the better the sound and performance.

Mixing for in-ears could fill up half the book on its own, but there are a few basics to remember if you have to set some up.

*Pan the instruments as they would appear to the artist*

### *A complete mix*

With stage monitors there is usually so much onstage volume from the different instruments that a good vocal level can often be all that is required. Not so with in-ears. Although not totally isolated, because the bones in the head carry sound, especially low end, their isolation from the outside world means that a mix of what is happening onstage needs to be blended in with the vocals. For the best results the mix needs to be stereo so that the singer can have a reproduction of the stage positioning in their head, with themselves panned centre. As the monitor mixer, it's important that you position the various instruments and vocals in the in-ear mix *as they would appear to the artist.*

Imagine yourself onstage facing the audience; you know the guitarist is behind you on your right, but if the guitar seems to be coming from the left it's confusing. Multiply that by keyboards, extra guitar, drums and there is the potential for severe disorientation. You get one reality in your head from your ears, and a different one from your eyes. Singers using in-ears have stressed this point to me over and over again, so I'm passing it on to you!

As well as onstage sounds, you may need to have a couple of audience microphones mixed in  to allow the singer to hear the audience, especially in big shows or where people might yell out requests. Pan these to the artist's left and right, so they can look in the correct direction to acknowledge an audience member.

At the other end of the scale, a more simple mix is often sufficient for other musicians, especially if their position on stage doesn't change much during the set and they are in constant visual contact with each other.

For drummers, in-ears may not provide enough of a physical thump and so are often used with a 'Buttkicker' or 'Shaker' unit that actually vibrates the drummers seat.

### Handle with care

With in-ear moniotrs you have complete access to the ear canal, and with this comes a big chunk of responsibility. No buffer of air or distance from the speakers is available to soften any sudden changes in level; you're squirting audio right at the ear drum. So what this means is you must not make any sudden gain changes, switch pads out, disconnect or reconnect when the levels are up. Although all in-ears have built-in limiters, sharp transients can be very loud up next to the eardrum. The onboard limiters also won't make much difference to a signal that is being overdriven at the mixer and the wireless transmitter before it even gets to the singer's beltpack. So pay close attention to your mixer levels.

### In-Ear Tools

We'll need an effects unit to provide some reverb/delay effects in the mix and stop it sounding too dry, a stereo compressor/limiter to keep the levels under control, and a mixer to blend and pan the various signals.Since you don't have any feedback to worry about, adjust the mixer EQ for a sound that is clean, clear, but not excessively sibilant. Work closely with the artist to get the sound they feel comfortable with

A digital mixer is useful for a stereo in-ear mix; for smaller setups something like a Yamaha 01V or 03D would be fine. Any effects and limiting can be done with the onboard units and routed to Aux 1 and 2 which can be the in-ear sends to the wireless transmitter

Some good microphones for using with in-ear monitors (and a good singer) would be the Sennheiser 821, Neumann TMS 105 Live, Røde S1 Live, and the Shure SM 87

If the beltpack for the particular in-ear setup you are using has Volume and Pan controls, adjust them during the setup and soundcheck, then tape them in position so they can't be accidentally knocked and changed.

And last, don't have them up *too* loud. Apart from potential ear damage, the fact is the louder things are in the in-ears, the softer the artist will sing. Not good for an exciting front of house sound. Take a tip from studio engineers, and keep the level down to just enough so that they can hear themselves comfortably – if they want to hear it louder they can sing louder.

=**"**=

*Give an image of confidence when you are the monitor engineer*

=**"**=

### So what do you do?

Most of all you need to have an air of confidence when setting up the monitors. Bands can get quite paranoid about them, and rightly so, since they depend on good monitors to put on a good performance. Listen to what they want, do your best to give it them, never lose your patience (this can be hard!), and soon they'll be asking for you all the time.

And remember the gig isn't over till the band has walked off the stage for the last time. A friend of mine was doing monitors for a band; they finished the last song and walked off stage. He heaved a sigh of relief, pulled the masters down, took off his headphones, tossed them onto the monitor console and relaxed. After 30 seconds of continuous applause, the band walked back onstage to do an encore. So, he pushed the masters back up, only to be confronted with a persistent squealing from *every* monitor! The stage was in chaos as he tore his hair out trying to stop it, but to no avail. The band reluctantly did their encore without any monitors and were not happy.

When the house lights finally came up, he checked out the console thoroughly, only to find that his headphones had flicked the 1 KHz test tone switch as he had casually tossed it onto the console!

Some things you only do once!

THE MONITOR
ENGINEER'S EMPIRE

## 12      Setting Up

Before you can start connecting everything up and start soundchecking and mixing, you've got to get it all out of the truck. So, here's a run through of a complete gig set up, from start to finish

### Unpacking the truck

At the ideal gig, every case has wheels, every truck has a ramp, and every venue is a flat load from the truck to the stage. And, at the big concert end of the business this is usually true. However, at the end where you'll probably be starting, you'll find that most venues were designed with little or no thought given to live music and its production. Several flights of stairs and a narrow door at the top of them are all too common.

So, to try to prevent wrecked backs and hernias, here are some basic rules for unloading the truck and carrying things.

   1. Get yourself some thick leather gloves

   2. Always let the box do the work. Use its inertia to help you; don't fight it.

HOOK FINGERS
IN FRONT LIP

> = **"** =
> *Always let
> the box do
> the work;
> don't fight it*
> = **"** =

   3. Tip speaker boxes out of the truck into your hands. Just about every box can be carried face down by its front lip. Hook your fingers into the lip and the box won't fall out of your fingers going up and down stairs.

---

TIP OUT OF TRUCK INTO YOUR HANDS

4. A large box needs someone at each corner. A medium size box needs 1 person at the front, 2 at the back when going up or down stairs.

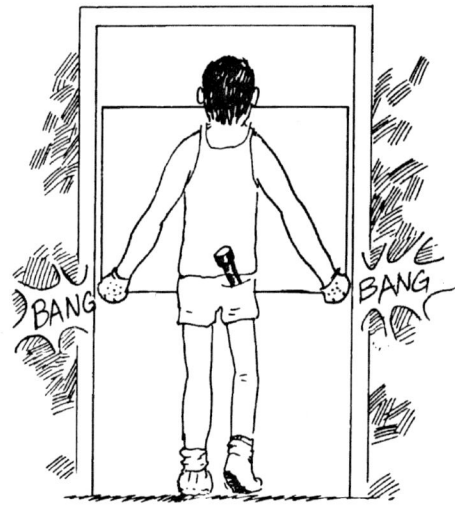

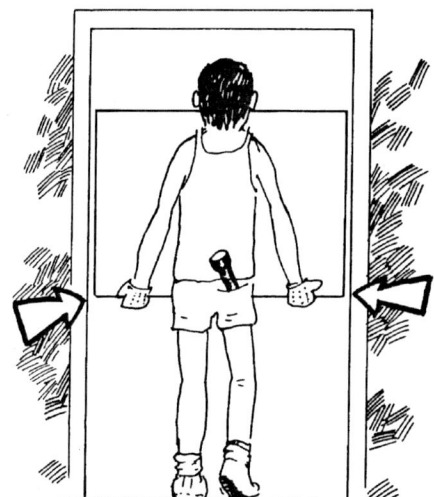

5. When you're carrying a speaker box through a doorway, **don't** have your hands on the outside edge. Keep your hands **inside** at all times. The inertia of the box will crush your hand painfully if it bangs into the doorway, causing you to probably let go. The guy on the other end won't be able to hold it all by himself, so he'll let go too, and the box will fall, often causing severe damage.

6. Pick up amplifier racks, effects racks, etc., by their bottom corners, not the handles. They won't come off if you lift up the case with them, but you probably won't be able to get it up to the right height. Generally speaking, the handles are there to lift the lid off, and to manoeuvre the case off its wheels when packing the truck.

Live Sound Mixing 4th Edition  ©2005 D.R.Fry

7. When you pick things up, bend your knees, NOT YOUR BACK! This is the single most important thing to learn about lifting. Keep your back straight and squat down - don't use your back as a crane. Bad backs are very common in this industry and can easily be avoided with a little care.

8. Don't carry too much by yourself. Just by looking at a box you can usually estimate whether you can pick it up by yourself or not. Get someone to help you if you think it is too big or too heavy. If you bite off more than you can chew, and you feel the box or case starting to fall, don't let go - try and fall onto it, and cushion the shock. If you just let go it may crush your toes.

9. Try to avoid double handling the gear. Before it comes out of the truck work out where it will go, so that you're not rearranging everything each time a new piece of equipment gets unpacked.

Take a tip from big concert productions and write on each case whereabouts on stage it should go. "Monitor mixer - Stage Left" "Monitor Effects - next to Monitor mixer - Stage Left", and so on. That way when there are extra people helping you, you're not forever stopping and explaining to them where each piece goes.

10. If you've got an upstairs load, allow yourself plenty of time. Stop and have a break when you feel tired, and don't push yourself too hard. Remember, what goes up has to come back down again!

## Putting the system together

Be systematic when you're putting the system together, and you can't go wrong. Start at one end, plug it together, and move on to the next part.

*Be systematic when putting it together and you can't go wrong*

Try not to get distracted. This is very hard, especially when you are halfway through connecting up a complicated monitor system, and the guitarist interrupts you to say that his "Tube Flangeriffic Screamer" pedal has just died, and can you have a look at it?

Immediately your chain of thought is broken. What can you do? You can think of exactly where you would like to stick his dead pedal, but then you'll lose the gig. Be tactful.

The best thing to do is to let people know beforehand that you'll be happy to look at anything that needs checking, or discussing a holistic approach to sound mixing, or whatever, but only after you've done your job and set everything up. Tell people not to bother you until they can hear music coming out of the system.

### Dead Leads and Spare Leads

Put suspect leads aside for later checking. I always wind them up and join the two connectors together; others tape the ends together, anything to stop people using them.

Which leads neatly on to the next point.

Always have **plenty** of spare leads. If you run 16 microphones, then have 20 microphone leads, and so on. Big stages will eat up a lot of leads, and leads have a habit of dying when you least expect it. Try and have spares handy, and fix faulties as soon as possible. We'll have a look at putting connectors on to leads in *'Old Dunk's Quick and Dirty Soldering Lesson' in Chapter 15.*

A good idea is to keep a mains AC powered soldering iron, solder, wire cutters and a small screwdriver in a drawer in the effects rack. That way you can sit at the mixer and work on faulty leads, plugs etc. while you're waiting for showtime.

### Multiple Bands

When there is going to be more than one band using the system during the gig, be prepared. Label every microphone and DI lead with its function - Vocal Left, Guitar Right, Keyboards 1, etc. Don't leave anything to chance or memory during the changeover and everything will go much smoother and faster. There is nothing more time consuming than having to trace each lead down to the stagebox and then to the mixer, to see which channel it is in. I've recommended labelling the leads, not the microphones, because that way you can unplug unused microphones/DI's and keep them in the microphone case. If you leave them plugged in they can have a habit of disappearing during the changeover! Especially nice slim compact pocket-size expensive active DI boxes!

Have a list of each microphone with its channel number taped down next to the stagebox, for quick reference should things need re-patching in a hurry. If one band is using your Guitar Left lead as their Keyboards Left, mark that on the list as well. It may take you 5 minutes longer when setting up, but it will save you tearing your hair out back at the mixer, when you can't find Keyboards Left anywhere.

If your monitor mixer has less channels than your Main House mixer, make a second marker strip of tape when you mark out your Main House mixer. Copy the same instrument listings onto it, and also write down the Channel/Multicore Snake line next to each instrument.

*Label every microphone and lead and the change-over will go smoother*

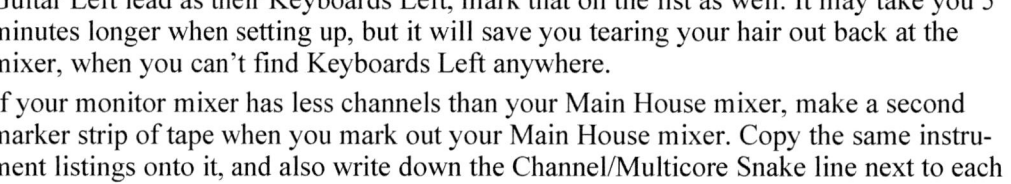

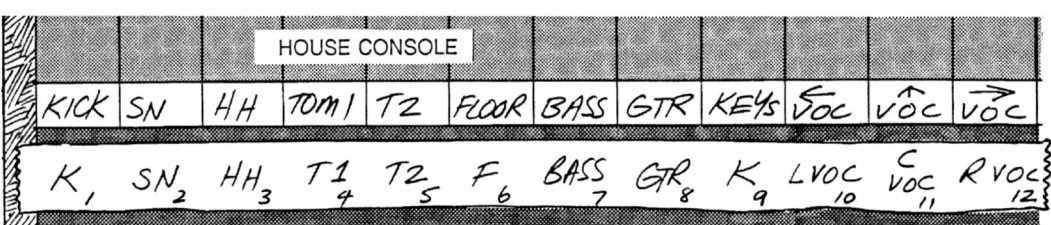

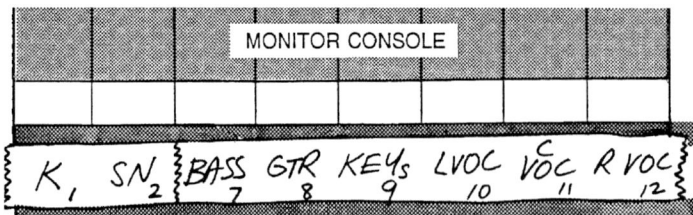

Peel off this extra line of tape and take it down to the monitor mixer. Now you can see at a glance which line has which instrument or vocal. You only need to plug in those particular ones that are needed in the monitors.

### Organizing your channel layout

Let's assume that you have a typical band to mike up, consisting of Drums, Bass, Guitar, Keyboards, and 3 vocals. If you are planning on putting all of them through the PA system, then you need an absolute minimum of 8 channels on the mixer.

### 8 Channel Layout

1/ Kick drum  2/ Snare drum  3/ Overhead  4/ Bass 5/ Keyboards 6/ Vocal Left
7/ Vocal Centre  8/ Vocal Right

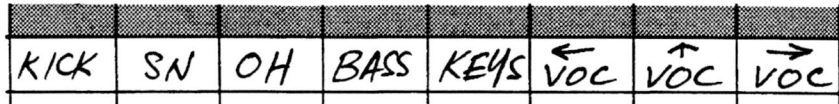

Tune the drum overhead so that it picks up the Toms, but reduce some of the High so that it's not all cymbals. Use the Auxiliary returns on the mixer for the Effects returns, and manually change one over for a CD input if you need one in the break.

With 12 channels you have a bit more accuracy in drum miking.

### 12 Channel Layout

1/ Kick drum  2/ Snare drum  3/ Toms 1 and 2  4/ Floor Tom 5/ Bass  6/ Guitar
7/ Keyboards 8/ Vocal Left  9/ Vocal Centre 10/ Vocal Right  11/ Delay Return
12/ Reverb Return

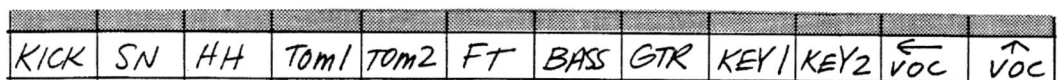

This is a better layout as far as ease of mixing goes. The effects are much easier to control when they're on channel faders. If you need a CD input, use the Line input on Channel 12 but don't forget to switch it back to Reverb when the band starts again.

### 16 Channel Layout

1/ Kick drum  2/ Snare drum  3/ Hi Hats 4/ Tom 1  5/ Tom 2  6/ Floor Tom  7/ Bass
8/ Guitar 9/ Keyboards 1  10/ Keyboards 2  11/ Vocal Right  12/ Vocal Centre
13/ Vocal Right  14, 15, 16/ Effects and/or CD/tape returns

With this layout the drums are pretty well covered, and now you can split the keyboards (assuming there are more than one) for greater mixing control. You also have 3 spare channels for the Effects returns, or 2 and one dedicated CD input.

### 20 Channel Layout

1/ Kick drum  2/ Snare TOP  3/ Snare BOTTOM  4/ Hi Hats  5/ Tom 1  6/ Tom 2
7/ Floor Tom  8/ Overhead Left  9/ Overhead Right  10/ Bass  11/ Guitar
12/ Keyboards Left  13/ Keyboards Right 14/ Vocal Left  15/ Vocal Centre
16/ Vocal Right 17, 18, 19, 20 Effects and/or CD/tape returns

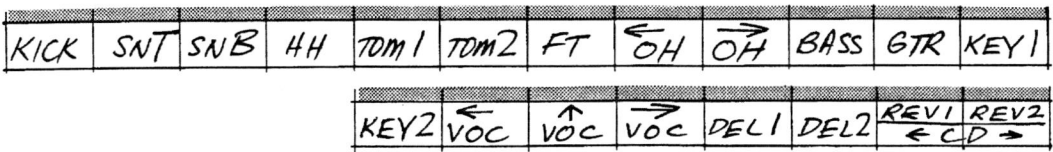

This is everything our band is going to need for the moment, unless as the mixer gets bigger then they get more instruments! So, here's the final layout.

## 24 Channel Layout

1/ Kick drum  2/ Snare TOP  3/ Snare BOTTOM  4/ Hi Hats  5/ Tom 1  6/ Tom 2
7/ Floor Tom  8/ Overhead Left  9/ Overhead Right  10/ Bass D.I.  11/ Bass Microphone
12/ Guitar 1  13/ Guitar 2 (maybe acoustic)  14/ Keyboards 1 15/ Keyboards 2
16/ Keyboards 3  17/ Vocals Left  18/ Vocals Centre  19/ Vocals Right
20, 21, 22, 23/ Effects returns  24/ CD in

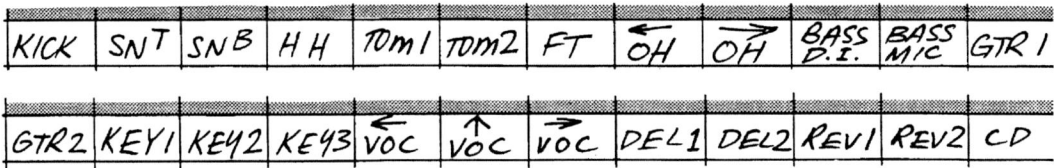

| KICK | SN T | SN B | H H | TOm 1 | TOm2 | FT | OH | OH | BASS D.I. | BASS MIC | GTR 1 |
|---|---|---|---|---|---|---|---|---|---|---|---|
| GTR2 | KEY1 | KEY2 | KEY3 | VOC | VOC | VOC | DEL1 | DEL2 | REV1 | REV2 | CD |

Of course, you may not have all these instruments, and this type of layout may be a bit of a luxury. But you may have more of anything - vocals, keyboards, extra percussion, so if you go back to the 8 channel minimum layout then you can see where you can start saving channels if you run short of them.

You don't have to stick to this order, either, but I find it easier to work from Left stage to Right stage in layers: first drums, then instruments left to right, then vocals left to right. Work out what comes easiest to your fingers.

## Subgroup Layouts (Groups, Submasters, Busses)

### Four Subgroup Mixers

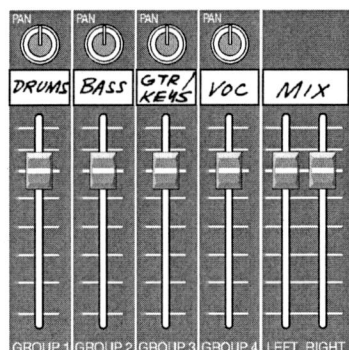

This is a basic 4 group layout. It's the most straightforward to set up, but it is a bit limiting if you have a stereo system and want to pan the drums or vocals.

Here's a simple stereo layout on 4 groups. Groups 1 and 2 are panned hard Left and Right, and so are 3 and 4.

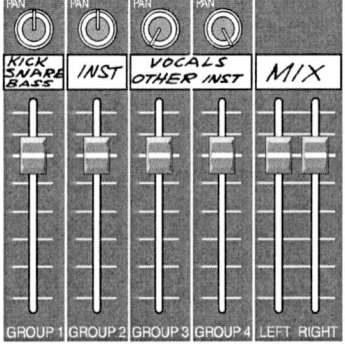

This layout groups all the Mono rhythm signals - Kick, Snare and Bass to Groups 1; the Keyboards and guitar on Group 2; and sets up Groups 3 and 4 as a stereo pair for the Vocals, plus the Toms, Hi Hats and Overheads of the drums. This layout keeps rhythm signals solidly in the centre of the mix, and lets you pan the Vocals and the Toms.

Live Sound Mixing 4th Edition  ©2005 D.R.Fry

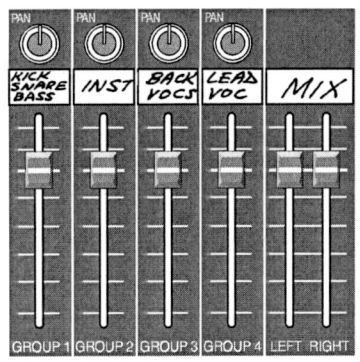

This next layout is similar to the previous one, but we are grouping all the backing vocals together so we can insert a gate over them.

In this final layout, we're using the Left/Right masters as a stereo group as well. Kick, Snare and Bass are again on Group 1, and this time all the effects and the CD/tape are on Group 2. The Toms, Guitars and Keyboards are on the stereo Groups 3 and 4, and the Vocals are going straight to the Left/Right master outputs.

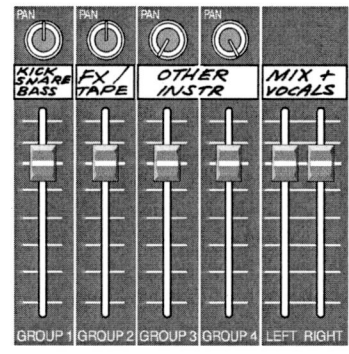

This last layout is extremely flexible, letting you pan all the Instruments, Toms and Vocals while controlling the overall effects level on one fader, which lets you pull them all down in between songs without having to reset them all again in the next song.

## 8 Subgroup Mixers (8 Bus)

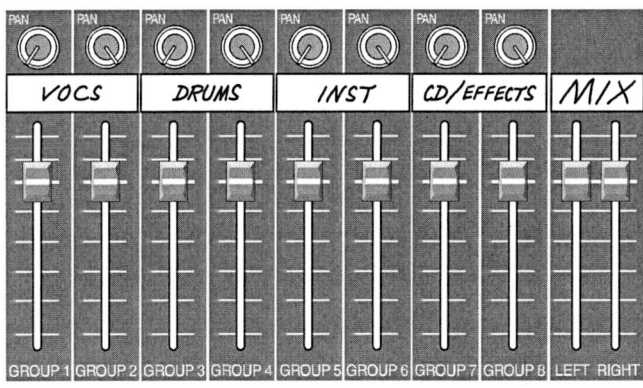

With 8 Subgroup (8 Bus) mixers, you can have all of the above different options in stereo.

Groups 1/2 can have all the vocals, Groups 3/4 the drums, Groups 5/6 the instruments, Groups 7/8 the effects returns and the CD/tape.

Or you could split the vocals so you can gate the backing ones, and separate the Bass to its own group.

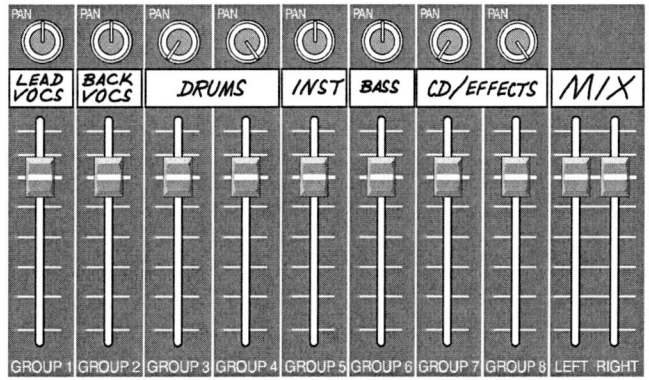

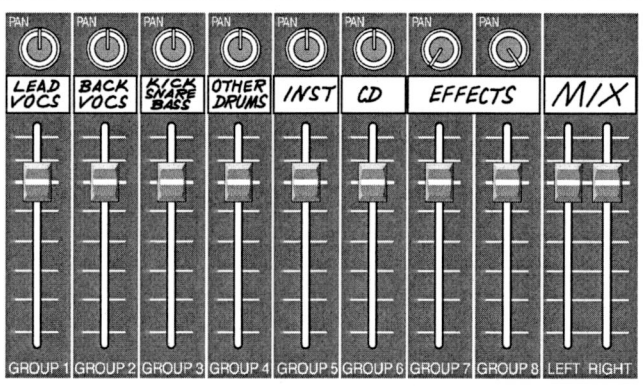

Another option is to group the Kick Snare and Bass together, as these are all typically mono signals. You can give the CD/tape its own group if you like

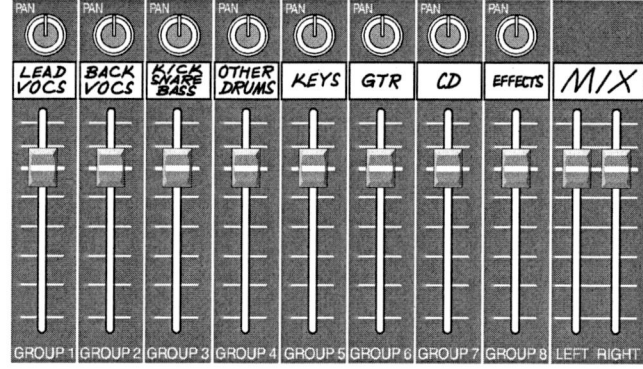

Finally, if you are running a mono system, you could give everything its own group!

However, this last one does rather over-complicate things. If you remember back to when we started out discussing groups, the reason behind them was to make your mixing job easier, not harder!

*These layouts are only suggestions*

These layouts are meant as food for thought, and are *only* suggestions. Use bits of each of them to make up your own favourite group layout, but be flexible - you should always use whichever one suits the particular band you're working with best.

Just make sure that however you decide to lay them out, you don't spend so much time on them that your concentration slips away from the job that you're being paid to do...MIX!

## Setting up

There are no rules for the order in which you set things up, but *before* we get to audio things, there is one very important piece of business to do first of all, and that is:

*'Identify and make contact with the person who'll be paying you!'* Organise a time to get together, preferably in a break during the gig, to get the money. At load out time, there are a heap of things to take care of on stage, and when you're all done, sometimes the promoter is nowhere to be seen!

OK, now back to audio matters. Here is a checklist that can be used as a starting point.

1. Put the Main Speakers in position. Take them straight out of the truck and put them where they are going to go. Avoid double handling if possible.

2. Put the Main and Monitor amplifier racks in place.

3. Unpack Main mixer and effects rack. If you are unsure of the mixing position, check with the venue manager. It's much easier to change positions now rather than later. Ideally the mixing position should be somewhere around the centre of the audience area, but you will often have to compromise on this.

    Try very hard not to be under a balcony, and keep away from walls, especially the back, as the sound that you hear will be bass heavy. This means your mix may be bass light in the rest of the venue, as your ears compensate for the increased bottom end at your mixing position.

4. Organise your AC power, and then run out the multicore snake, a power cable and your send loom down to the mixing position, and from the stage box across to the monitor mixer position if you're using one.

If at all possible, get the main snake and cables up in the air, or around the walls if it's long enough, to stop people tripping on it or damaging it. If you absolutely have to run it across an aisle where people will be walking, consider making a small ramp of plywood to go over the cables. Lay some carpet over this, and tape it down securely.

5. Lay out microphone leads on stage, position monitors and monitor mixer.

6. Run out Main speaker cables and plug up Main speaker stacks.

7. Run out Monitor cables and plug up Monitor system

8. Plug Multicore snake tails into Main mixer, and connect up all effects.

9. Check all amplifiers, crossovers, mixers are turned DOWN.

10. Turn on power to everything except amplifiers. Wait 10 seconds and then turn on amplifiers, one after the other.

11. Play a CD through the main mixer and bring up channel and master levels. Not too high - about half way. Then bring up crossovers to normal operating levels.

12. Turn amplifiers up slowly, and only until you start to hear something. Stick your head into the main speakers and check that the sound is OK. If there is no sound, turn them back down, go back and check your wiring, CD player, mixer channel and masters. Try again. When everything sounds happy, wind the amplifiers up fully.

13. Plug in main vocal microphones and check monitors. Don't EQ yet, just check that it's all working. Then plug in all the microphones and DIs.

14. EQ the Main system.

15. EQ the Monitor system.

16. Label the main mixer if it's not already labelled. Run another piece of tape underneath and copy down microphones and channel numbers. Take this extra piece of tape over to the monitor mixer to give you the correct lines for each microphone.

17. Check all microphone lines down to the main mixer.

18. When everything checks out OK, tape down all leads on stage to stop anyone tripping over them.

19. If the band has to walk down steps to get off the stage, put a line of white tape at the edge of each step. After a couple of hours under stage lights, it's very hard to see where any steps are. The last thing you want is for a band member to break a leg or an arm! Bang - there goes your gig!

20. You're ready for the soundcheck.

*Don't mix from under a balcony or near walls - you won't hear the same sound as everybody else*

## Soundchecks and how to handle them

"I love soundchecks but I hate rehearsals". The sound check is just that - a chance to check out the sound prior to the gig with the band up there on stage. It's for you to set up the mixer EQ and levels, the effects, iron out the monitor sound, and solve any problems. It is *not* an opportunity for the band to rehearse.

As the sound engineer you must keep control of the soundcheck until everything sounds the way you want it to. The sound is your responsibility, and you're the one who'll be blamed if something sounds terrible.

Once you have checked everything (EVERYTHING - there is no second chance once the show starts) and you are satisfied that every microphone signal runs down to the mixer, all the effects sound right, all the levels are right, the speakers aren't going to feed back, then the band can play whatever it likes.

Remember to keep things moving right along; don't give the musicians a chance to get bored waiting for you to set up something. Save problems till last. If there is a problem with a lead, go to the next channel. Get everything that is OK out of the way first, then go back and fix up any problems.

You can start with each instrument as they are ready, or start from one end of the mixer and work your way along it, checking as you go. My advice is to start with the drums first, since they frequently take the most time. When they're all OK (or as close to OK as you think you'll get) then bring the rest of the band out.

Tactfully get the drummer offstage while you check the rest of the band, or he'll quite likely keep banging away all through the soundcheck.

### Drums

*Keep control of the soundcheck, and don't let the musicians get bored*

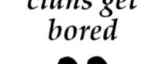

1. Listen to each drum individually and adjust the mixer EQ until you get the sound you're after. Don't set the channel gain too high. Check it on the PFL/SOLO meter. Kick and snare can run just up to 0 dB, but keep all the others bouncing up to -6 dB. You can always increase it later once the band plays something.

   Drums are one of the hardest things to get right; an acoustic anachronism in the world of electronics.

2. If there is a drum riser, use it - it helps separate the drums acoustically from the rest of the stage equipment.

3. If you have gates, use them. There's no doubt that they tighten up the sound a lot, as each microphone only picks up its own drum. There's no spill, which if you are running in stereo makes your mix more open and spacious.

4. If you have no gates then keep the LOW MIDs under control, especially on Kick and the Toms, as a LOW MID boom can start feeding back at any time.

5. If you are running top and bottom snare microphones, then check the phase switch on the bottom microphone channel; remember the 3 to 1 rule.

6. Work fast. Learn how to make the mixer EQ work for you. Know the sound you're after and get as close as you can as quickly as possible. There is nothing worse to a club owner or an audience then the steady "Thud...thud... thud" of someone endlessly checking a drum kit. Sure, you need to get it right, but you also need to get it right quickly.

7. Set up the drum effects, usually Reverbs and gates, once you have got the drums sounding right. Check out the various reverbs that you'll be using, then set up the one for the first song. When the drummer plays some 'time' (steady Kick and Snare, rolling around all the Toms), make sure that the Reverb unit is not overloading. If it is, back off the channel sends until the overload LED on the Reverb goes off.

8. Finally, check that all the drum channels are assigned to their correct subgroups. If you are running stereo, use two groups for the drums, one panned hard Left and one panned hard Right. Then you can position each drum in the stereo field using each channel's Pan control. As a start, run Kick and Snare centred, Hi Hats maybe slightly to one side, say Left, and the Toms equally spaced - if there are 3, then Tom 1 panned ¾ Left, Tom 2 Centre, Floor Tom panned ¾ Right. This will make the drums appear to move across the stage

when the drummer plays rolls or fills. Experiment to find what works best for your band and the venue. Don't Pan anything fully hard Left or Right because half the audience won't be able to hear it.

## Bass

1. Set the channel gain so it bounces up to around -6 to -3 dB, with the fader on 0 dB. Make sure the channel Overload/Clip LED doesn't come on when the bass player plays a few 'slap' notes.

2. If you have one available, a compressor inserted on the bass channel will take care of too much percussive level. Set it at a ratio of about 3 or 4:1 and the bass should sound good and tight.

3. Listen to the sound of the bass as it comes through the bass player's own amplifier rig. Unless he has made a special mention of something to you, this is the sound the bass player wants. If you recreate that same sound through the PA, then you can't go wrong. Just make sure the LOW MIDS are kept from booming, and maybe add some HIGH to the sound to give it a bit of an edge.

4. If you have enough channels, you might try a DI box AND a microphone on the bass, varying the sound between them for different songs and effects.

5. If the stage is very 'live', causing the bass to spill into every microphone on stage, then raising the bass speaker up off the stage can help isolate it. Sit it on a couple of milk crates with some black material draped around them for good looks!

6. Basses can be susceptible to humming (maybe because they don't know the words? Sorry). If the noise can't be fixed, you could either insert a gate on the bass channel, or 'gain ride' it yourself. By this I mean that you pull the bass channel fader down in between songs, or even switch the channel off between songs. This way the sound of the music will mask the hum, making it less noticeable. Don't forget to bring it back up or switch it on at the start of the next song, though.

7. Once again, check that the bass channel is assigned to the correct group.

*The stage power must be on the same Earth/ Ground as the PA.*

## Keyboards

Keyboards are usually DI'd unless it is acoustic piano. Be wary of synthesizers - they often have only a 2 pin power lead and a floating earth, or a 'wall-wart' power supply. Since everything is plastic and double insulated this is quite safe, but sometimes they will buzz unbelievably and other times they will be absolutely silent.

If the synthesizer has a balanced output (usually an XLR type) then use it; if it doesn't, then plug the output into a DI box and then into the stagebox.

If you get a buzzing one, then you should:

1. Check the leads. Not all musicians are great shakes with a soldering iron, and their concept of what makes a good lead can be very interesting, to say the least! Remember the golden rule of leads from Chapter 4: *"Every lead that comes before the amplifiers must be made from shielded cable."*

2. Lift the Audio Ground on the DI box.

3. Check the power point. You may well find that the synthesizer is not plugged in to your network of mains AC power, but into a convenient power point that the player has found over on his (or her) side of the stage. Since the synthesizer is directly connected to the PA system through the DI, you've now got 2 paths to Earth/Ground. In sound systems throughout the world the difference between these 2 paths translates into hum.

When checking the levels, get the keyboard player to play at maximum solo level as well as backing chords, so you don't get any sudden surprises. You could let the gain just reach 0 dB on the maximum solo level, otherwise keep it around -6 dB.

**Keyboard Mixer**

In a multi keyboard setup, the player will often have his instrument plugged into a separate sub-mixer on stage, so he can set up the levels the way he likes them. The output from this mixer will usually be split, one to the keyboard stage amplifier, and one to the PA system. This only takes up one channel (2 if in stereo) but you are stuck with the keyboard player's idea of the mix.

If there is a critical keyboard passage that is regularly not right, send another separate line down to the mixer from that particular keyboard so that you can control it individually.

Check any extra effects are set up right, and check subgroup assign.

### Drum Machines and Electronic Drums

Use the same rules as for Keyboards, and wherever possible use a DI on them. Some older ones will buzz no matter what you do, so a gate would come in extremely handy.

### Guitars

Not too many problems here. Keep the gain quite low, as you can get some powerful levels running down that microphone line. Check both rhythm and solo levels, plus make sure you have a bit of level in hand to control the parts you think should be brought up in the mix.

Nearly all guitarists have their own collection of foot pedal effects patched into the guitar line, and are often all they need. If you think you might want to add some delay or reverb yourself, then get the levels set up beforehand.

Check subgroup assign.

### Vocals

This is a very important area to check out properly. Vocals need to be clean, crisp, loud and clear. Get the singer(s) to sing into the microphone. "Check 1-2" is not enough. You need to know how the voice will sound when the adrenaline is pumping on stage, so a few lines sung at a high level is essential.

My particular favourite is the first line of Led Zeppelin's "Black Dog", which goes *"Hey momma said the way you move, gonna make you sweat, gonna make you groove..."* I don't think it's humanly possible to sing this softly!

1. Set the channel gain so that the meter just hits 0 dB on loud parts, with the channel fader at about 3/4 the way up. You need a bit of spare level with vocals, since they can range from a whisper to a shout. Make sure the microphone doesn't feed back when

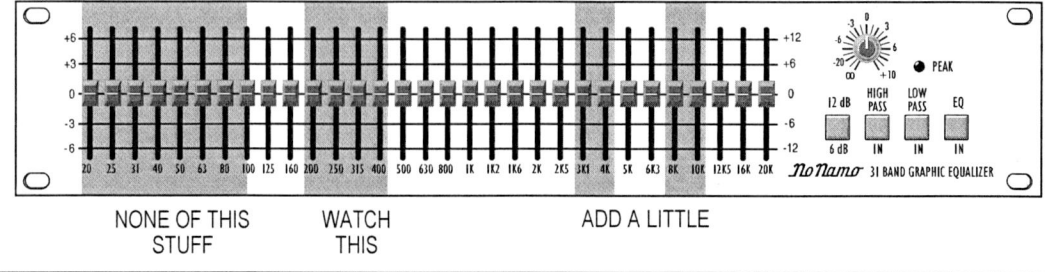

NONE OF THIS STUFF            WATCH THIS            ADD A LITTLE

Live Sound Mixing 4th Edition  ©2005 D.R.Fry

you push the fader all the way up (or at least 3 dB higher than you think you're going to need it!). Spend as much time as you can spare getting the vocal channel EQ sounding right.

2. Watch for boominess at 200 to 300 Hz, and cut it back in the LOW MIDs. You'll rarely need to add any LOW, more often to cut it back considerably. If there is a High Pass Filter or LOW CUT switch on the channel then switch it IN. This will roll off the low end and take away annoying stage noise and give a cleaner vocal sound. If there's a booming, popping sound on every word starting with 'P' or 'B', then you've got way too much bottom end on the vocals

3. A little HI MID 3.5 KHz boost will put some 'bite' into the vocals, to help them cut through the band's sound, and a little HIGH 8-10 KHz with put some sparkle into them. Remember that the audience will want to hear the vocals. They should be layered just slightly on top of the music, at the same level as a guitar or keyboard solo. Never let them get buried in the mix; although the singer can rarely hear what's going on out the front, his or her friends can, and won't hesitate to spill the beans.

4. If you're using a compressor on the lead vocals (a good idea) set up the Ratio at about 4:1, and the Threshold around 0dB. If the compressor has a Peak Limiter in it as well, then set that at about +3 to +4dB, so a good yell won't cut out the rest of the band.

*Please* note that these settings are just my suggested start points - your requirements may be quite different.

5. Gate the backing vocals if possible, so you won't have 3 or more microphones wide open on stage picking up all the ambient sound when they're not being used. If there are no gates spare, then 'gain ride' the backing vocals yourself to get a clean mix.

6. If you are running the vocal monitors from the main mixer, then now would be a good time to see how they sound. Wind up the Monitor send level slowly, until it just starts to 'ring'. Find that frequency on the monitor Graphic and pull it down about 3 dB, then check out the sound level in the monitor. If it is loud enough, and sounds good, leave it. If not, keep going with the same technique until it is. When that first frequency slider is all the way down, then that's pretty well as loud as you're going to get it.

7. Cup your hand over the microphone and see if it feeds back; if it does, pull down that frequency about 3 dB or reduce the overall level slightly.

8. If this is a ***really*** important gig, it is a good idea to have a spare vocal microphone, lead, snake line and channel ready to go in case of emergency (and ***especially*** if you're using a wireless microphone for the singer).

Set it up exactly the same as the lead vocal channel, but perhaps assigned directly to the Left/Right masters, so that in the event of a major problem with anything in the lead vocal line, the singer can go straight to another microphone and carry on as normal. Loss of lead vocals is a major catastrophe and must be avoided at all costs. With luck, just about anything else can be fixed up without the audience noticing too much, but not that.

As an example, I once had a cymbal stand fall over off the drum riser, and when the cymbal hit the stage it neatly chopped the lead vocal microphone lead in half! We put the stand back up again straight away, but it took quite a few minutes to find out why there were no vocals coming through.

9. Finally, check that the channels are assigned to the correct groups.

### Effects Returns

Check out all the effects you will be using, and make sure they are all working properly. A lot of delays, reverbs, gates and compressors have jack INs and OUTs, and these connectors are prone to wriggling half out. Give them all a push and a half twist just to make sure of a

*For more on Monitor levels, see Chapter 14 - Problems*

positive connection. All the leads that are usually left patched into the back of the effects rack should be checked and wiggled to make sure everything is OK.

Check the gain settings on the effects return channels. These should be on the low side, since the returns are coming in at Line level (around +4 dB), and you should have just enough

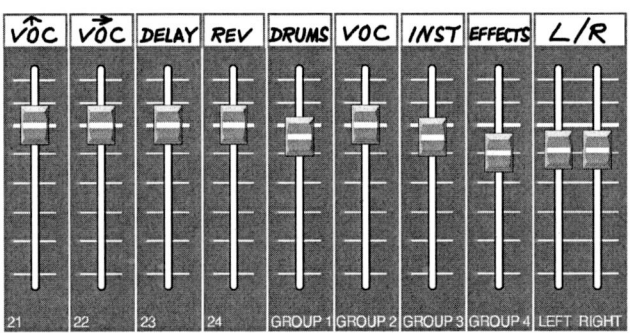

effect level with the fader 3/4 the way up. It is quite common to assign the effects straight to the Left/Right masters, but often more convenient to assign them to a spare group. This way you can pull them all down with one fader at the end of songs, without losing the individual effects balance. It's up to you which you find the most convenient.

Finally, get the band to play something all together. If you have done your checks pretty well, all the levels should only need final balancing. With the system running at the level you want, you should end up with all the channel faders at or near the 3/4 position, or about 0 dB; all the subgroup faders about the same; but the master Left/Right faders maybe a little below 0 dB, so that you have something in reserve for when the place is full of audience.

### Fine Tuning

Use the channel EQ to remove any acoustic interaction between instruments so they all sound good together. Vocals, guitar, most keyboards are all essentially midrange devices. Make the channel EQ enhance the differences between them so one stands out from the other. You should be able to mentally step back from the mix, close your eyes and hear each instrument individually.

Cue up any intro tapes or CD tracks that are required, make sure the mixer light is not shining into the audience's eyes, switch off the channels, but leave the faders where they are, pull down the Left/Right masters, and wait for showtime.

### Support acts

If you're supporting an act that's using a digital mixer you'll either

- Use a separate analog mixer,
- If you're lucky, get your own page/layer of settings on the digital mixer that you can recall when it's time for your set. This is the better option, so if you get this chance, grab it as it can be a great learning opportunity. The next paragraphs won't apply to you.

If you have a support act that will be using the mixer, or if you're the support act and someone else will be using it, mark your channel settings on a piece of paper for easy re-setup during the changeover. I've included a page of channel sheets on page 169. Draw up something like this, make a few copies, and keep them to mark your settings on. If you have done your Main system EQ properly, and you are working with the same band, then your mixer settings should remain fairly constant from gig to gig.

If you have a switch pushed IN, like the PAD for example, mark it with a tick.

Mark your GAIN setting with a line, and maybe with the appropriate calibration setting for greater accuracy

Mark your EQ settings with lines. It doesn't matter if you don't have all these EQ controls on each channel - just fill in the ones you have. If you have 3 way fixed EQ, just fill in the High and Low sections, and any one of the mids. If the mixer has 3 way EQ with sweepable Mids, disregard the High Mid section. If it's 4 way fixed, leave one circle per Mid section blank...and so on

*Check the console over COMPLETELY in the changeover*

The same goes for Auxiliaries - just fill in what you've got.

Mark out the Groups and Pans as you have them set up on the mixer. Tick whether you're sending it to L-R, 1-2, 3-4, 5-6, or 7-8 and mark the Pan control accordingly. If you don't have groups, don't fill them in!

This plan assumes that your channel fader will be at 0 dB or thereabouts. If not, you could include a fader note. eg -10 dB, 50% or whatever you find easiest to remember

Check the mixer over COMPLETELY in the support act changeover. Make sure everything has been switched ON, and the assigns are all correct. If you don't check everything you can have some nasty moments.

One support band engineer switched off the subgroups at the end of their set and didn't mention it to me. I didn't notice and set up the mixer for the main band; they came onstage, I pushed up the faders and NOTHING HAPPENED!

It's hard to describe the sinking feeling in your stomach and the cold sweat that breaks out on your skin, but it's not pleasant. I thought the end of the world had come. I was using an unfamiliar mixer and was at my wit's end, frantically looking over the mixer to see what could possibly be wrong, when I noticed that the group switches were OFF. I switched them back ON one after the other, the group faders all the way up, and the sudden wall of sound nearly flipped people over the back of their seats!

I don't think I stopped twitching for a week!

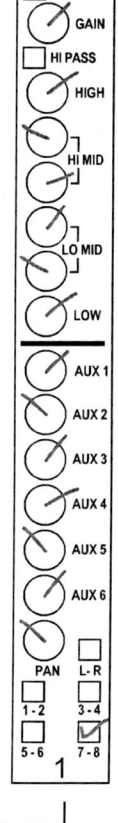

## Small Systems

Not everyone is running around with a truckful of equipment playing at larger venues. There are a huge amount of bands working night after night with very basic systems such a a 12" and horn box each side, maybe a sub, and an 8 or 12 channel mixer.

Other times you'll just be setting up a vocal only system for a corporate lunch, or maybe a press conference. Either way, you'll only need a subset of our Setting Up section on page 128.

Naturally, point #1 - *'Identify and make contact with the person who'll be paying you'* will stay the same!

2. Bring in everything and put each piece in its approximate position as you go, so you won't have to move it afterwards (no double handling)

3. Find a convenient power point to use, and run a lead from it to a multi-way plug board When all necessary power boards are connected, tape the plug to the wall socket so it can't easily be pulled out. I also suggest that you switch it on, and tape the switch in the 'on' position as well.

4. Put the speakers on their stands.

5. Connect the mixer to the amplifier, and the amplifier to the speakers

6. Put the microphone(s) on stands in their correct positions.

7. Make sure all the microphones are *behind* the speakers

VOC ✗    VOC ✗    VOC ✗

KEEP MICROPHONES BEHIND THIS LINE

8. Connect the mics to the mixer, and mark out who is in which channel

9. Turn the amps and mixer down, then switch on the mixer, then the amplifier.

10. Push up a channel fader, and slowly bring up the level controls on the amplifier

11. Try a "Check 1-2" and something similar should come out of the speakers

12. Once you know it is all working, then you can fine tune the levels and the channel EQ as required.

If you can't make any noise because the room is full of people, then use a combination of headphones and watching the meters to check levels. A small amount of soft background music from a CD will check that the speakers are working without annoying anyone.

At weddings, parties, anniversaries and similar gigs you always find the oldest, crankiest, most important people are seated at the tables closest to the band! Disregard them at your peril, because one of them is usually the person who'll be paying you.

However, careful placement of the speakers can minimise this problem.

At these functions I set up each speaker so it points diagonally across the dance floor, focussing somewhere in the middle. It's the people on the dance floor who need to hear best. More importantly, these tables of VIPs won't be in the direct firing line of the speakers; instead, they'll have the buffer zone of the dance floor to lessen the impact.

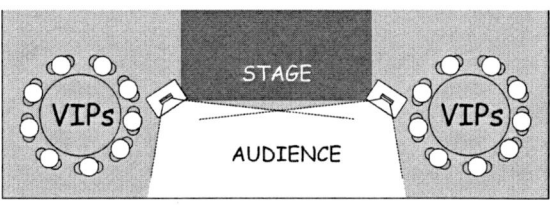

An added bonus for this layout is that the edge of the horn coverage travels just across the front of the stage. Not too close to the microphones to cause feedback problems at reception centre sound levels, but close enough for the singers to get some idea of how they're singing.

### Packing Up

Packing up at the end of the gig is basically the reverse of setting up, with a couple of exceptions.

1. Pull all the levels down on the mixer, and on your way up to the stage do the same to the amplifiers. This stops any bangs or thumps coming out of the main speakers as the band starts to pack up and disconnect the AC power to their stage equipment.

2. Grab all the microphones and DI boxes before you do anything else. Put them into the microphone case and put that box inside a bigger case. These are the first things to go missing at the end of a gig. They slip into pockets and bags really easily!

If the management of the venue wants to have some music playing as the audience drifts out of the place, just pull down all the channel faders on the mixer and make # 2 the first thing that you do. It's also a good idea to let the amps idle for about 5 minutes before you turn them off, and not move them for another 10 minutes after they have been turned off

Once all the leads are rolled up (see Chapter 4) and put into the leads case, work out a logical flow of equipment back into the truck. If you have some loaders to help you, then you are probably better off inside the truck calling the load. That way everything goes into the truck in the position that you want it.

There is **nothing** worse at 3 am than having to unpack and then re-pack the truck because a certain case didn't go in at the right time.

### AC Power Ground Rules

All power that you use MUST be on the same circuit, and share the SAME EARTH/ GROUND. Don't plug instrument amplifiers, keyboards etc. into different wall sockets that may be around the stage; run everything from your own network of power outlets.

Also, don't be tempted to plug the mixer into a convenient power point at the rear of the venue. It probably won't be on the same circuit as your amplifiers up by the stage, and the difference in the Earth/Ground will be picked up as Hum.

Another potential power problem is the Lighting. Try to keep your leads away from the lighting ones, and make sure your power is different to the power the lights are using.

If your leads have to cross lighting cables *(see pic)*, then make sure they cross at 90° angles to minimize noise. A loud sweeping buzz every time the lights change or dim can be very annoying.

THIS IS OVERKILL IN ALL BUT TH.E NOISIEST SITUATIONS!

## Organizing your AC Power Supply

Before we start, remember that *any* A.C. (Alternating Current) wiring modifications should *only* be undertaken by a licensed electrician. OK?

The importance of a solid AC mains supply to all electronic equipment, and sound systems in particular, cannot be overstated. Have you ever sat at a mixer and seen the mixer or effects rack lamp dimming in time with the kick drum? This indicates that the AC mains is sagging (the voltage is dropping) and if you can *see* it, then it must be sagging a lot, since light globes are fairly forgiving indicators. A good solid AC mains is also important to eliminating AC noise (dimmer buzz, switch noise, etc.) from your sound system.

For example, if your mains supply sags by 20-30% your expensive, heavy 500 Watt/channel power amplifiers have just become expensive, heavy 250 Watt/channel power amplifiers, and the headroom of the System has just disappeared. It's equivalent to unplugging half your loudspeakers during loud transients, which doesn't really make a lot of sense.

Unlike the signal processors, mixers, digital effects, etc. in the system which have a regulated power supply, power amplifiers (for reasons of size, weight and cost) cannot afford this luxury. This means that the Power Supply feeding the output stage of your amplifiers has a fixed ratio to your AC mains. If this mains voltage is low, then the power available to your loudspeakers is less.

### How do we get around this?

For a start make sure all your AC cabling, extension leads etc. are at least 15 amp cable. Don't use thin figure-of-eight desk lamp cord. Make sure your AC distribution box is wired with 20 or 25 amp cable.

Remember one piece of thin cable can affect the output of the complete system! It acts like a governor on an engine.

*A thin power cable acts like a governor on an engine*

### Single Phase supplies for smaller systems

Once you've checked that your wiring is up to standard, let's start looking at the origins of your AC supply. No, not as far back as the Power Station, but the socket on the wall you plug into. Have a look around and check:

- Is the cigarette vending machine plugged into the same socket?
- Is the flashing sign out front plugged into it?
- Are the refrigerators on the same circuit?
- Are the hand-dryers in the Toilets on the other side of the wall? Check it out otherwise you'll get a thump through the system every time someone goes to the bathroom!
- Make sure the lighting guy hasn't got 8 Par 64 cans running from the same circuit, otherwise the band hits the stage, lights go up, circuit breakers blow, and the band's in darkness with NO lights and NO sound!

### Three Phase supplies for Medium to Large systems

In this case the venue has a large chunky socket on the wall, usually put there because the venue owner doesn't want your power leads taped all over his designer pastel walls. If it looks fairly industrial, well that's because it is. It's a 3 phase outlet, and you plug the chunky plug from your distribution board into this. And by the way, we're talking seriously life threatening voltages here, so handle it with some respect!

The other end of your distribution board usually is a box, with an array of AC socket outlets marked 1, 2 or 3. These numbers refer to the phase that they are connected to. The type of 3 phase connector that you need has to have 5 pins - 3 active, one Neutral and one Earth/Ground (the most important of the lot). Some sockets only have 4 pins - 3 active and no Neutral. These 4 pin types CANNOT be used for sound systems. They are for large electric motors, kitchen cookers etc.

Assuming you have the correct 3 phase socket, if there is only one of them you're going to have to fight over it with the lighting guy. So compromise. Give him two phases and keep one for yourself and the stage gear; this should minimize dimmer buzz and noise and stop your AC supply sagging whenever the lights go on.

Some venues have the added luxury of a 3 phase outlet just for the PA System and stage gear, primarily for concert systems. Normal usage for this situation in a larger system would be:

Phase 1 Main system Left

Phase 2 Main system Right

Phase 3 Monitor System, Front of House mixers, effects and the stage gear.

In a smaller system, it would probably be:

Phase 1 Main System

Phase 2 Monitors system

Phase 3 Front of House mixers, effects and the stage gear.

Whatever you do about buzzes and hums, don't be tempted to start disconnecting electrical Earths/Grounds.

NEVER disconnect the Earth/Ground on the whole PA system; if you do, you run the risk of killing someone. Worse still, it could be YOU!

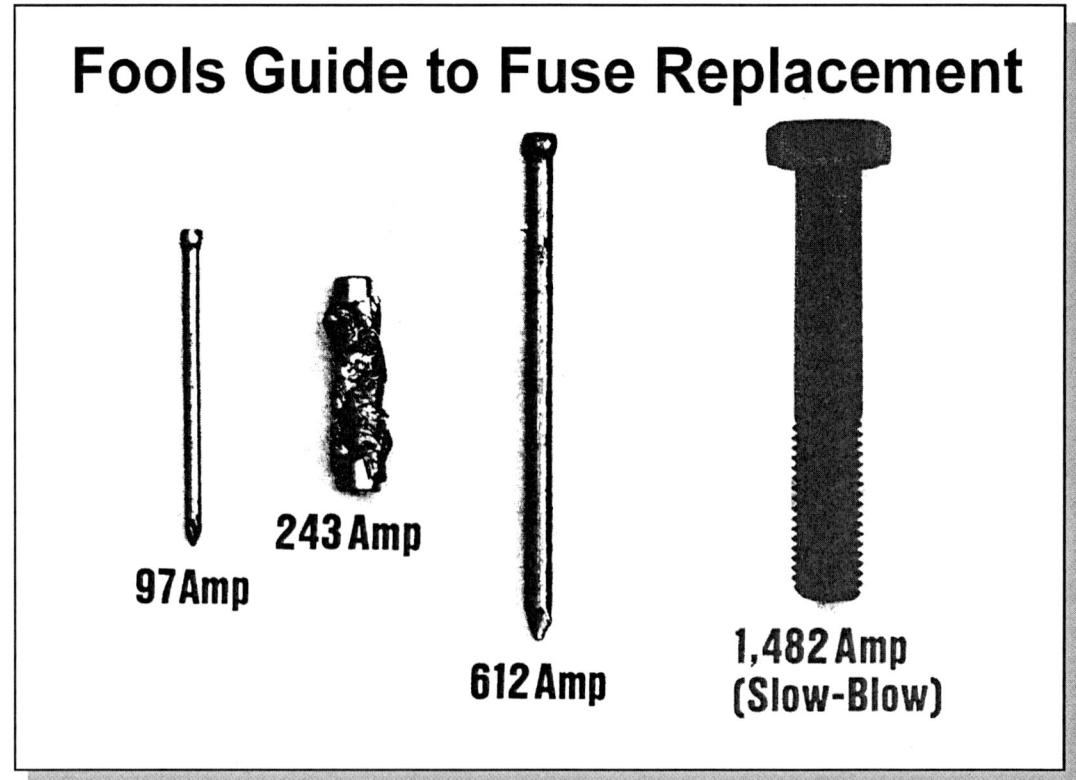

# Fools Guide to Fuse Replacement

97Amp

243 Amp

612 Amp

1,482 Amp
(Slow-Blow)

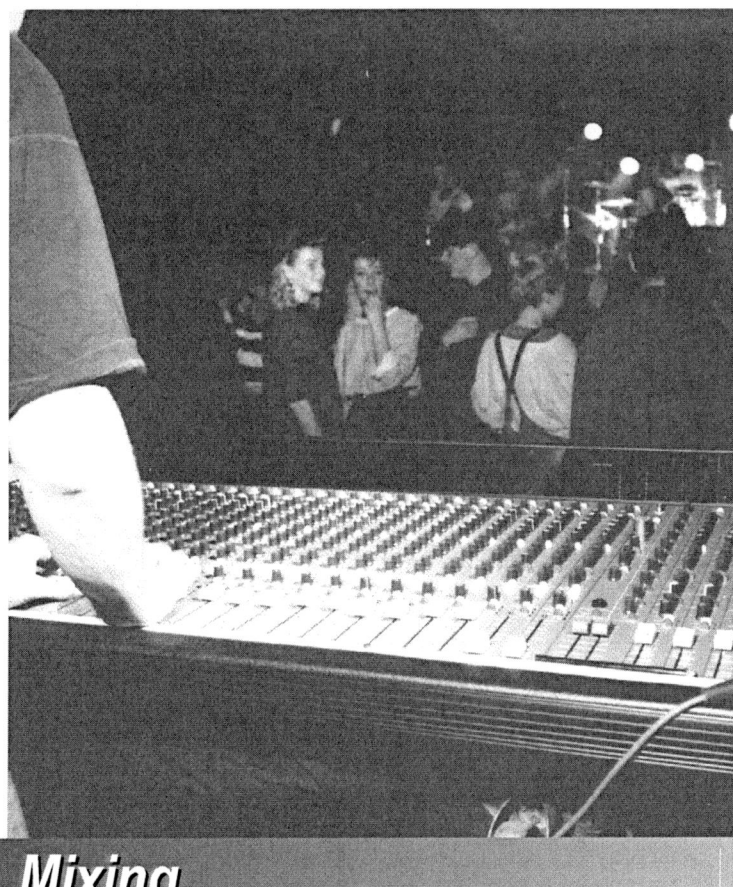

## 13      Mixing

## Putting the mix together

OK, so it's all put together, set up, soundchecked, the band has just walked out on stage and started playing. Now what do you do?

Well, to successfully mix live music you must know what 'sounds good'. In other words, you've got to have some kind of ear for music. All the technical knowledge in the world won't help if you can't distinguish what sounds pleasing to the ear and what doesn't.

You also need to have an idea of the overall sound you want to achieve with the mix, so you can aim towards it. In other words, if you don't know where you want to go, you won't have much chance of getting there!

It's not too hard to move the faders up and down to get the right levels for the various instruments and vocals - that's the easy part. What is harder is getting each one of them to sound good at the right level, and this is where practice and EQ knowledge comes in. For example, if you have too much LOW on everything, the whole band will sound like it's playing inside the Kick drum, no matter how carefully you set the levels!

### Listen

So, if you've got the main faders up and there's something recognizable as music coming out of the speaker stacks, then you just take a couple of seconds to *listen*. You're listening for things that don't sound right.

### Vocals First, Music Second

The vocals have to be heard or else there's not much point in having them. Never let the instruments drown them out. On the other hand, the vocals should never drown out the instruments. How do you achieve this balance? Personally, first I like to make sure the vocals can be heard, and then I make sure that the music is pumping away at just fractionally below the vocal level. Then, once I have got everything sounding just about right, I try to get

> *=❝=*
> *If you want
> to mix then
> you have to
> know what
> sounds good
> and bad*
> *=❞=*

the two of them interacting and swapping at the same level.

The reason I do it this way is that while people are listening to the words of the song, I can be working away at the individual sounds and levels of the drums, the bass, the keyboards and the guitars, making sure that they are right before I make them as important in the mix as the vocals. With a bit of luck and hard work it should be together by the end of the first song.

So, don't start off with everything flat out. Leave yourself a bit of room in the mix and ease into it.

### What Next?

Establish a solid rhythm sound. Watch out for too much LOW MID 'boom' in the Kick drum which can start everything feeding back on stage; if it's not clear enough add a little edge to it with some HIGHs.

Make sure the Snare drum doesn't 'klonk' too much. If it gets too annoying, pull back some of the MIDs. Make sure the Toms level is nice and high so that they really cut through when the drummer hits them. Gates make this easy, otherwise you have to be quite savage with the LOW and LOW MID EQ to stop them feeding back.

Keep the drums and bass working together as a foundation on which to build the overall sound. You could assign them all to the same group if it makes life easier. The bass may need a little LOW added for some grunt, and a little HIGH to let the individual notes cut through.

### Listen some more

*LISTEN -*
*for things*
*that don't*
*sound right*

After each change you make, mentally step back and listen. Is the sound better? Is that guitar too loud? Just because you have a microphone in front of the amp doesn't mean that it has to be up in the mix. Often in small venues the guitar is so loud off the stage that it hardly needs to be in the mix unless it is time for a solo. And even then just a small increase will be plenty

Keep an eye on the Keyboards. Don't let them gurgle away buried in the mix; adding a little HIGH MID and HIGH will give them some sparkle, and cutting the LOW will stop them sounding muffled. If they are taking a solo, bring the level up the same as you would for a guitar solo, which should be the same as lead vocal level.

*Only* when you have all the instruments and vocals running at roughly the correct levels should you pop on the headphones and do some fine tuning with the PFL/Solo buttons, and even then just for a few seconds at a time. It's very easy to lose track of what's happening with the headphones on because you're isolated from everything except the channel you're listening to. The on-stage performance is your main concern, and nothing should distract you from it.

### What's a good mix?

A cynic might say that a good mix is one where the band's girlfriends and boyfriends don't complain! And from a keeping your job point of view that's probably true!

Still in a musical sense, a good mix is one where you made the correct decisions duyring the performance, with all the levels balanced, nothing drowning out anything else, solos coming to the front at the right time, and a mix that the audience liked.

A mix where:

-The singer's fans hear all the words

-The drum fans hear all the drums.

-The guitar fans hear all the guitar solos

-The keyboard fans, etc., I'm sure you get my drift.

Sounds hard? It can be at times, because live sound mixing is not like studio mixing. You can't dump the track and do it again. You've got to make decisions there and then, and pretty quick, too. Things happen fast on stage, and your reaction time must match them.

### Don't Panic

It's not easy. There can be upwards of 6 or 7 musicians on stage, all playing something, and each of them demanding your utmost attention. If the drummer slips in a quick little extra fill, or the guitarist decides it's his turn to sing, you've got to catch it so the audience can hear it.

If the keyboard player starts a solo, you've got to recognise it as being one, work out which keyboard or synthesizer he is using, if there are several, find the appropriate channel fader, and push it up to the right level. If you don't do all this quickly, it can be finished before you've had a chance to start.

### Mistakes? What Mistakes?

If you make a mistake, don't worry, everyone does. If you push up the wrong fader, add in way too much reverb or delay on the vocals, leave something out of the mix for a couple of songs, sure, it's a mistake but it's not the end of the world. Knowing what you did wrong, and working out why you did or didn't do something is what is important. Learn from your mistakes and you can only get better.

Luckily you've got a couple of things on your side. One is that for the audience, everything is fleeting. The whole live sound experience is a transitory thing; something happens, the audience sees and hears it, BANG it's gone and something else takes its place. If you are taping the gig then you're the only one who'll be able to sit back and listen to your mistakes over and over again!

The other point is that live sound is big and loud. And, guess what? Music sounds better when it's loud! (We're back to those Equal Loudness curves again!) Not *too* loud, but at that critical level where the sound just grabs you and catches you up in it. This dynamic presence will cover up a lot of things in your mix that may not be quite perfect.

When you take the tape of the gig back to your hotel room and sit there listening to it with critical ears you will hear a lot that the audience probably didn't notice, so don't be too harsh on yourself.

Remember, you're listening to the band from a completely different point of view from the audience. Things that scream out at you from the tape, they won't notice; they are there to have a good time and hear their favourite songs, and you are there to reinforce and enhance the band's performance.

Of course, if you work with the same band all the time, then you'll know the songs and what happens in them. But if you are a freelance sound engineer, working with a different band and system each night, then the ability to work fast and accurately will help you establish yourself as the band's preferred mixer.

### Practice, Practice, Practice

Live mixing takes a lot of practice before it becomes second nature. You have to be able to hear a drum and think, "Uh oh, too much LOW MID in there, better pull out some 300 Hz", or "Maybe I'll compress that guitar a bit more so the chords don't overpower the single notes", or "Is that feedback in the monitors or main system? I'll just pull down 1 KHz slightly and see if it stops." Once you can do this automatically, you can work fast and get it right fast.

### Concentrate

Until you are totally at ease with mixing, it will take more concentration that you ever thought possible. As you get better at it and do more of it, you'll instinctively know when you have to take care of twenty things at once, and when you can relax a little. Even when you are relaxing on the surface, though, you'll still be listening and watching for things that need attention.

And no matter how many gigs you do, things will always surprise you. Like the time a friend of mine had the show all under control and thought he could take it easy, since everything was going so well. It had been a hard room to EQ, but he had persevered and now

*A good mix is one where the band's girlfriends and boy-friends don't complain!*

everything was sounding great. He leaned back on his mixing stool, and relaxed for a few moments.

WEEEEEK - a blast of feedback brought him back to reality. He looked up on stage, to see that the band had all suddenly put sombreros on! The reflections off the wide brims of the hats had started the monitors feeding back, which had set off a sympathetic howl in the front of house system! It was back to work with a vengeance!

Things like this will always happen when you least expect it. A singer may suddenly pull out a harmonica, cup his hands around the microphone with it and blast away, his solo blending in with a burst of feedback. It's happened to me; I'm sure it will happen to you.

These are the sort of things that you'll have to be continually watching for, as well as setting up different effects, changing the levels, bringing instruments up and down for solos, keeping people's drinks away from the equipment, and lots more.

### Overnight Success?

None of this is going to happen overnight. It takes a while before you can make the system do what *you* want it to do, and not what *it* wants to do. Let's face it, the PA will be quite happy sitting there all night going 'boing boing', but *don't let it*. If you have a certain sound in mind, you have to work hard at the EQ, effects and levels to get that sound.

Don't give up until the sound coming out of the speakers is the sound you want to hear.

### Recording the gig

*The system will be quite happy going 'boing boing' all night if you let it!*

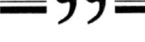

It's a good idea to record every gig that you mix *for your ears only*, just so you can sit back and listen to it critically later. You'll often hear things that slipped by you in the heat of the moment. However, if you have done a recording with leads split from the Left/Right outputs of the mixer, what you will definitely hear is lots of vocals. The vocals will be the softest instrument on stage, so proportionately they will be the ones that will need the most gain in the mix, and so they'll come out the loudest on the recording.

If the band wants a recording of the gig, then that's a totally different matter. I know quite a few sound engineers who will *never* make a tape of the gig for the band. If you decide that you will, then make sure you stress to them that it is a *raw* recording, straight off the L/R feeds, and so won't sound the same as a remixed live CD! A lot of bands find this difficult to understand, and believe that what they hear on the desk tape is exactly what the audience heard.

With comments like "It's all vocals" "It's all drums" "Where's the guitar?", forgetting that the guitar was so loud that all night long people were asking you to turn it down and you didn't even have it in the mix(!), you can understand some engineers' reluctance to tape the gig for the band.

I've suggested using a cassette deck because it's cheap, convenient and set-and-forget. There's nothing to stop you using a CD burner, or even an iPod/Minidisk/MP3 player as a recording medium. If you have access to one of those compact digital multitrackers then you could record each subgroup *plus* stereo ambience tracks and mix it down to stereo later.

Just remember that the *live* mix is your primary concern. Don't get distracted.

### A Better Way

What I like to do is record one channel off a mono feed from the console, and the other channel off a microphone sitting on the effects rack. This way you can have the clarity of the mixer combined with the actual live room sound on the one tape. Adjust the two levels when you play it back, maybe switch it to mono if you like, and you have a surprisingly 'real' live tape that really conveys the feel of the gig.

It's not perfect, but it's quick, requires no checking once you've set the recording levels, and if it's no good you can record over it at the next gig. If it sounds good you can transfer it to a computer, delay the console track by the length of the multicore snake (to bring the tracks back into sync), and *then* give a copy to the band.

Of course, things don't always go according to plan. I set the cassette deck up this way one night, and recorded the whole thing. The following day on the way to the next gig I popped the cassette into the truck's tape deck to have a listen.

The channel from the console was fine; but the live microphone channel had two guys complaining all night about the band, the lights, the PA, and the mix! So watch where you put that microphone!

## Other Mixing Situations

There will be times when you'll be called upon to mix very different things - solo artists, rap artists, corporate presentations, church services, stage shows. The last three especially have requirements that are quite different from bands, and need to be the subject of their own books. But I can guarantee that at some stage you'll get asked to handle all of them.

Why? Because you're the sound expert; it's what you do! Don't knock these opportunities back, because they can keep you going in lean times, and the more experience you have, the more work you'll get asked to do (and the better you do it, the more you can charge!). And then we can all retire in luxury to the Live Sound Mixing yacht moored in Monaco harbour.*

## Solo Artists

There are a whole lot of solo artists out there, either working by themselves or with backing bands, and these need a slightly different approach to mixing them.

### Handle with care

Solo artists are very different to bands. Don't forget this basic fact. They don't have other band members they can unload their troubles onto; they have to cope with things by themselves. They need constant reassurances that everything is sounding good, and this is where you need a really positive outlook.

Don't burden them with any problems you might have with the system; it will immediately assume enormous proportions for them and be a constant source of worry. So when they ask (and they always will) how it's sounding, *never* say 'All right I guess but there's something wrong with the reverb/EQ/console/whatever.' Tell them it's great, because they don't really want to know the truth, they want to be reassured that their sound is in good hands - yours. They depend on your confidence in order to deliver a confident performance themselves.

You are probably the latest in a long line of sound engineers they have worked with - some excellent, some good, some probably abysmal - and they may have very fixed ideas about how they want to sound.

If they know what they want, then give it to them. If you have some specific ideas for changing things, don't float them on the first gig, because they you might make them uneasy about changing what has probably been a successful format for them. Instead, save them until the artist has learned to trust your judgement, and then you can do whatever you like.

If they *do* ask for your input, be careful. You'll need to say something apart from *'it was great'* all the time, otherwise after a while they won't believe you. So don't criticise their actual performance, instead say something like *"perhaps you could extend/shorten that introduction to song aaa"* or *"where did you get that joke between songs bbb and ccc?"* or *"should we change the order of songs - there's a bit of a flat spot in the show between yyy and zzz."* You just need to say something that shows you've been paying attention!

With a band I like to keep the music and vocals swapping around about the same level, but with solo artists you need to re-assess this concept.

The golden rule is:

### "No matter what, the solo artist must be loudest in the mix."

Don't take this to extremes; just ensure that no matter what, they can be heard. If the artist is a singer, then their vocal level needs to be the dominant one. If you're using just a small system, compress the band harder, so that the vocals *always* lie on top of the music.

*Don't burden them with any system problems you might have*

If the artist is a singer *and* musician, say a guitarist, then keep their guitar just burbling away in with the band if it's just rhythm chords, but zip up the level as soon as they take a solo, then bring it back down and let the vocal back on top.

If it's a keyboard/piano and vocal situation, the same applies, but you could make the mix slightly more piano oriented all the time, hovering right under the vocal. Unless it's solo piano and no band, watch out for the LOW MIDS and LOW frequencies, as these can get lost and sound muddy in with the band. Add a little HIGH MID to get the piano to cut through.

### Monitors for Solo Artists

What they want is lots of themselves, usually as loud as you can get it.

### Give the Audience what it wants

Basically, it's a question of who the audience has come to see. Is it the famous solo artist or the backing band? Let's face it, at an Eric Clapton concert no-one has really come along to hear just the drummer, *no matter how good he is*; they've come along to hear EC's guitar playing, and you would expect his guitar to play a dominant part in the mix. Likewise Elton John and piano.

Just use a little commonsense, and everything will fall into place. Remember, solo singers often like to wander out into the audience in cabaret style gigs, so they will be able to hear how things *really* sound out front! Keep them happy and you've probably got a gig for life.

## Corporate Presentations

### Non existent mic technique

*Handle solo artists with care; if they know what they want, then give it to them*

This is the sort of gig that can be a dream or a nightmare. One of the first things you'll discover is that some presenters have absolutely no mic technique whatsoever. They will wave it around while they're talking, yell into it while almost swallowing it, or whisper into it at arms length. So don't give them a hand held microphone unless they specifically ask for one.

Use a microphone on a stand, or on a lectern if they need to have a bunch of notes in front of them.

One way or another, you've got to get the microphone as consistently close to the mouth as possible. The further the distance, the more of the room sound gets in - that typical midrange honk you can hear when people move too far from the microphone. The voice has got to be clear and natural sounding (everyone knows what a voice *should* sound like) but will need to be a bit 'larger than life' so it commands attention from the audience. This can be hard when someone is droning on about profit and loss figures or corporate mission statements, but work at it, and your efforts to make it sound better will be rewarded when you get the job next time.

WRONG - TALKING *OVER* THE MIC

RIGHT - TALKING *INTO* THE MIC

Put a compressor on the main presenter's microphone, and one across the subgroup if there will be extra mics. Personally I would also put gates on any other vocal mics, set at a low threshold so you won't miss any important words, but shut down when not needed and give you more gain on the main mic.

However I wouldn't put a gate on the main mic but would sit there with my hand on the fader all night, manually gain riding it as required.

Anything else will be pretty straightforward, usually consisting of playing a CD or pushing up the sound for a video presentation. Cue up the CD track using the PFL on the mixer, and don't start off with the fader too high in case the CD level is super hot.

Live Sound Mixing 4th Edition  ©2005 D.R.Fry

### Laptops

Corporate meetings these days mean laptops and PowerPoint presentations. You need to arm yourself with a good stereo DI box and a well-made stereo Mini Jack to dual XLR leads, or one of the new Audio Visual DI boxes with a Mini Jack input.

First of all, make sure the laptop is running from AC power, since you don't want it to kick into extreme power saving mode just before the presentation, and you especially don't want the battery in the laptop to go flat *during* the presentation. It's quite likely that the presenters have been rehearsing their presentations during the day, and when they get up on stage the laptop battery may be on its last legs. So AC power it should be.

Lift the Audio Ground on the DI box(es), and plug them into the stage box, so they run down to the Main mixer where you are. Depending on the sound quality you may need to gate them if the noise level is too high.

Like any mixing job, the key to it all is concentration and good EQ skills. Oh, and maybe a little 'shmoozing' the organizer! Operating on the old saying that "it's better the devil you know than the devil you don't know," companies will usually get the last person who did the job to do it again, provided that everything went smoothly the previous time.

## Awards Nights

While you're unlikely to find yourself mixing the Oscars, for example, without having any previous experience, there will be lots of other smaller events that run on similar lines. Football clubs, schools, industry groups, service clubs; everyone likes to get an award so there is no shortage of them!

However, in many cases you'll be dealing with people that are not professionals, so you'll have to be their mentor. Explain how close to stand to the microphone, how to speak clearly into it, and if the mic has a switch tape it up in the ON position!

For a function like this in a large auditorium, an automatic Feedback Eliminator such as a Sabine or one built into the EQ/speaker controller will be a lifesaver, especially if there are going to be wireless mics. Put a stripe of different coloured tape around each microphone, big and bright enough to be seen from the mixing position, and label the mixer channels with the same colours. That way, no matter *who* is using *which* mic, you will always know which one to bring up the levels on.

Ideally on big productions there will be a 'microphone wrangler' - someone whose only job is to organise which mic is being used and let you know through the talkback system before they come on stage.

If there is going to be live entertainment, try to keep the presentation audio channels separate from the band, so there is no need to reset levels and EQ. If the music is pre-recorded, once again try to have everything cued up ready.

## Rap/Hip hop/Beatbox/Dance Club Artists

Love it or hate it, you can't escape it. All the advice regarding solo artists applies here, but even more so! Nearly all the time they will perform to a backing track supplied on CD, MiniDisk, or increasingly an iPod or MP3 player. If there is a DJ/scratcher they will have their own turntable setup which will need to run into the main system with an AV DI or a couple of regular ones. A compressor over this would be a *very* good idea!

Mixing will mainly consist of blending the vocals with the backing track, and if there is more than one performer, then keeping the vocals constant, especially if they are swapping lead vocals around.

You'll need to work the desk EQ to get the best vocal sound, since cupping the mic in the hand and holding it upside down in front of the mouth is a major part of the image.

As for the system, too much bottom end is never enough!

## Church Sound

This is a specialised field that has its own books, but we can do an overview of the basics, in as non-denominational a way as possible.

Church sound can range from:

- A simple wireless microphone that reinforces the sermon, to
- A full-on stage production with a complete miked up band playing and a choir singing.

For the first option voice-only setup, you need to make sure the vocal sound is as clear as possible. Churches, especially older ones, are extremely reverberant spaces, and will need careful positioning of the speakers to keep them pointing at the congregation, and not bouncing off the walls too much. A good wireless microphone system and a good equalizer would be the first two things on my list.

The second option is a complete concert production. Larger churches can have congregations ranging from hundreds to thousands, and the production is scaled up accordingly.

Either way, it's similar to a wedding or similar function in that the older, most important people are often down the front! And they don't like it too loud, so keep them in mind when you're mixing.

Church sound people like to talk about 'the word'. 'The word' is the message coming from whoever is on stage at a particular time. *Nothing* gets in the way of 'the word', not lead guitar, choir, drums, nothing. Your mission is to keep the instruments and secondary vocals below the level of the person delivering 'the word'.

Many churches are on a limited budget, so they don't have the latest, most up-to-date equipment, but here are some options that you can aim for:

- Keep the mix lead vocal centred
- Make the musicians play softer
- Point amplifiers away from the congregation
- Put the drums on a carpeted riser, with perspex baffles around if necessary
- Try and get as many musicians on in-ear monitors as possible

Think of it as mixing for a top selling solo artist, but instead of their manager looking over your shoulder, it's someone a bit bigger!

## Theatre Shows

Unlike a typical rock music performance where the sound system has an 'in your face' impact, the system for a stage show should be transparent, almost as if it isn't there. The aim is to subtly enhance the natural sound of the voices, whether singing or talking.

### Know the show

It's a great help if you're familiar with the show beforhand. Maybe you've listened to the CD, seen a previous performance, read the play, or seen the movie. If you've got a good idea how things are meant to unfold, you can get a head start on the mixing.

### Walk the room

When you arrive in the theatre, a good start is to walk around the auditorium. Clap your hands to hear the reflections, and listen to how voices and music sound. You'll soon get an idea of the room resonances - maybe it's particularly lively at 800 Hz, for example, so when you tune the Front of House Equalizer you can be aware of that and compensate for it by cutting that frequency a bit more than you usually might.

In larger productions you'll probably be mixing from a position in the auditorium, as you would for a concert. For school productions, amateur theatre and other productions, it's more than likely you'll be mixing from the Bio box, a small glassed-in room at the back of the theatre (like the projection room in a cinema).

Bio box mixing is very different. You'll have a pair of monitors to listen, mix and refer to, and the only way to hear the actual Live sound is to open the windows. If you're *very* lucky the monitors will be on a delay! My recommendation is to have the windows open and monitors soft, so you can make comparisons between the actual and monitor sound.

### People skills

You'll be dealing with both the Director (for dialogue and staging) and the Musical Director (for the music and singing). Use all your people skills to keep things going smoothly between the three of you. Hope that the two of them get on well together, otherwise you'll be the meat in the sandwich!

Once the show starts, the Stage Manager is in control and should keep you informed of any changes or potential problems.

You'll need a mic plot - a list of all microphones used and who's using them, and a script with all the cues written on it. With any luck you should also get a script reader, someone whose job it is to follow the script and keep you one step ahead of any cues, effects, production numbers as the performance progresses.

The general rule is that once a performer is on stage, their mic is on, and then off as soon as they are off stage. If you can't see them, you can't hear them. The exception is when someone starts singing offstage before they come on, and that's where your script reader and your knowledge of the show will be useful.

Don't worry though - after the 20th performance you'll know everything backwards, and be singing the complete show in your sleep!

### Microphones

Theatre and musicals mean wireless mics and lots of them. In the Bio box you'll have a good line-of-sight to the stage, so it is safe to have the  radio mic aerials and receivers up there with you.

The common mic setup is a skin tone coloured omni directional mic positioned at the side of the face on a headband, and a beltpack under clothing at the side or back. The front of the face is usually kept clear, to create the illusion of no mic (and no sound system as I mentioned earlier!) hence the need for an omni mic.

Omni directional mics are tricky things to use live, because they pick up sound from all directions. You'll need good EQ skills to filter out the sounds you don't want - monitors, noise, room sound - and keep the ones you want up in the mix and not feeding back. Luckily the levels required are less than rock shows, and you'll soon figure out the right amount of Low Mids to cut and the right Hi Mid boost.

Just remember it has to be natural sounding, but bigger.

When you get two lead performers close together, you'll notice both voices can start to sound metallic and hollow. It goes back to the 3 to 1 rule, where 2 microphones are picking up the same sound but at different distances. The answer is to fade down one for as long as they are close to each other. As soon as they move apart, bring the fader back up.

On major productions, the lead performers will often have two mics and beltpacks, one mic each side of the head. So if one goes dead you can instantly switch to the other, hopefully without missing a beat!

If it's a show requiring rock concert levels of vocals, then a cardioid headset mic will be necessary, with the mic head positioned right in front of the mouth. In these shows the music

*After the 20th performance you'll be singing the complete show in your sleep!*

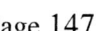

is the message, so seeing the mic isn't a problem.

To pick up non miked performers and the chorus line, you can use shotguns, but remember they often have a lot of pickup from rear - where the orchestra pit is! Use them carefully.

### Monitors

Monitors for stage shows are usually side fills, or hanging from the first lighting bar and pointing upstage (to the back of the stage). You only need to provide a limited monitor mix – essentially the performers need to hear the beat, to stay in time; and to hear the pitch of the music, to stay in tune. Putting a lot of vocals through them is usually not necessary (or desirable, with omni directional mics). The monitors should be audible but not rock star levels.

## Coping with advice

What can you do about that select group of audio connoisseurs who hang around the mixing console, full of beer and advice? An endless procession of audio expert wannabees, because it's often said that everyone is an expert on two things - their own job, whatever that might be *and* mixing audio - they'll tell you what's wrong with the sound at the drop of a hat. There is usually a cluster of them grouped around you at the mixer, saying things like "I can't hear the guitar (or drums, or bass, or whatever). Turn it up" or "Tell 'em to play something good!"

Well, relax. Everyone who's ever mixed sound has had the benefit of this kind of advice, so don't take it personally! But what should you do? My advice is firstly to listen to what they have to say, in case there is something going on that you haven't noticed.

On the other hand, if it's just something like "Make it go faster", or "That singer's hopeless, turn him down", then the best thing to do is to tactfully nod your head, say "I'll see what I can do", or something else non-committal; perhaps twist a few knobs on an unused channel then say "That should be a bit better".

The thing is, you don't want to get involved in a meaningful discussion and let the mix slip away from you, nor do you want a violent confrontation which may land you in hospital!

So take it easy, take a deep breath, smile and survive to mix another day.

### Mixing Quick Reference

- ☑ Listen, adjust, listen some more
- ☑ Get the vocals audible first; bring the music up under them, then get the two of them at a similar level. Remember the vocals have to be heard or there's not much point in having them
- ☑ Use the console's EQ to enhance each instrument and give each instrument an individual sound
- ☑ Ease your way into the mix; don't have everything flat out straight away or you'll leave yourself with nowhere to go
- ☑ Work quickly and know the sound you want. You've got to get it right, but you've got to get it right fast
- ☑ Handle solo artists with care; keep them well out front in the mix
- ☑ Concentrate, don't panic, and it'll all come together

## 14     *Problems*

### "The band says the monitors aren't loud enough"

Well, this is a problem and a half, but relax; there isn't a sound engineer who hasn't been faced with this problem, and quite often every night! Every time you try to increase the level in the monitors it feeds back in a deafening squeal.

In an ideal world, the following would be simple solutions for most monitor problems:

    1. Louder monitors with a flatter response

    2. Bigger amplifiers to drive them

    3. Better Equalizers to EQ them

    4. In-ear monitors

    5. Lots of space on stage

OK so it's a wish list, I know. For those of us without deep pockets, we'll just have to go with what we've got, and set it up as best we can.

The feedback problem is often worse on small stages, where everyone is playing on top of each other, and the singer's ears are only 2" from the cymbals. But before you even touch a fader on the equalizer, you should make sure you've done everything possible to create a better acoustic environment.

Thick drapes around the stage can help a great deal; so can moving the drummer and singer apart with a drum riser, and changing the way the instrument amplifiers are set out. Try to have as little as possible pointing directly at the lead singer's microphone, so that his vocal level in the monitors doesn't have to fight its way over the onstage sound being picked up by his microphone. And make sure there is nothing else but the vocals in the front wedges.

### *Why does it feed back?*

Basically one frequency is louder than all the rest coming out of the monitor, it gets picked up by the microphone, and comes out of the monitor even louder, it gets picked up by the microphone even quicker and comes out of the monitor even louder...and so on, in an infinite loop getting louder and louder. This loop is only broken when:

    1. The overall level is pulled down, or

    2. The offending frequency is reduced, or

    3. The speaker dies. *(refer to Chapter 10 - Speakers)*

Let's cast our minds back to *Chapter 3 - Equalizers and Equalizing*. We need to get as flat a response as possible from the speaker (equal levels at all frequencies) so that we can get the maximum out of our microphone/speaker combination. The equalizer is our interface between the sound of the room (or in the case of monitors, the sound of the part of the room facing the microphone) and the sound of the system.

Every room has a sound of its own. Every area inside that room affects the sound in some way. Different surfaces reflect some frequencies and give us a peak in the response, others absorb some frequencies and give us a dip. For us to have a fighting chance of overcoming this, especially the peaks, we need to have a speaker box that is pretty flat to start with.

Once you've explored all the basic EQ methods we've described earlier, try these ideas:

1. Tell the band to play softer. Not an option? It should be, but I know what bands are like! OK go on to the next.

2. Check that the monitor Equalizer is switched In, and set to the maximum cut/boost setting (12dB or 15dB). I know this sounds obvious, but it happens. *Note:* If you have no separate EQ for the monitors, then you'd better beg, borrow or buy one, because otherwise there is no way around the problem if you need some level.On a small mixer, the 5 or 7 band onboard EQ is not accurate enough for this type of work - you really need a 30 band.

3. Try reducing the Input Gain to the channel slightly, and bringing up the level slightly on the channel send to compensate. This will reduce the sensitivity of the channel and rearrange the gain structure. The channel may be close to overloading without you knowing it, and an overloaded circuit does not act in a linear way.

4. Pull down 80 to 100 Hz and all the frequencies below them. These frequencies are wasted in vocal monitors and can mask the higher frequencies that supply the vocal information. They will muddy up the sound and soak up the amplifier's power, leaving less for the critical vocal midrange.

5. If the peak feedback frequency is cut as far down as it will go on the graphic EQ, and it is still feeding back, you need an extra 2" of slider!

    Try this: bring down your level from the console slightly, then bring up all the other slid-

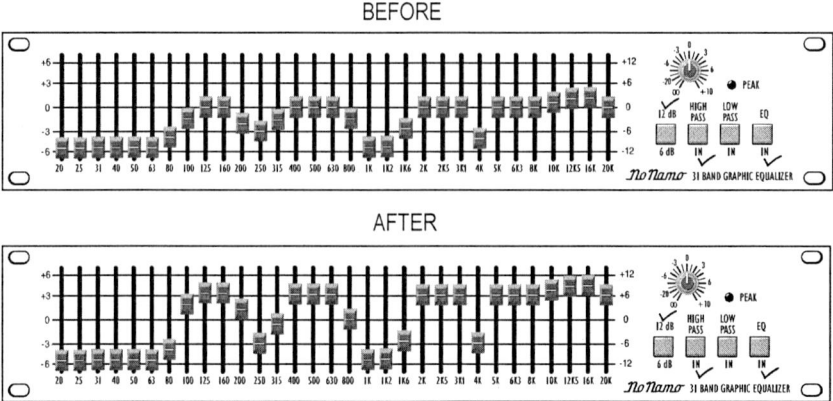

ers (other than the ones you want to cut), by up to 3dB if you can. By doing this you have dropped your peak frequency by up to 3 dB, and raised your overall level at the same time. Have a look at the example in the diagram on the previous page.

It won't be *quite* this simple, but this should give you some ideas when all else fails. Of course, 15dB cut is more than enough; the real reason you're looking for more cut is either a badly designed passive crossover or wrongly adjusted active one. Or else someone has replaced the original compression driver or speaker  with a different one, upsetting the overall frequency response of the monitor.

6. Sit the front wedge monitors up on a roadcase to get them closer to the singer's ears. This can help, but it looks ugly and spoils the sightlines for the audience. Here's an alternative:

7. Use the front wedge monitors as sidefills. You can hear better when the sound source is at ear height.

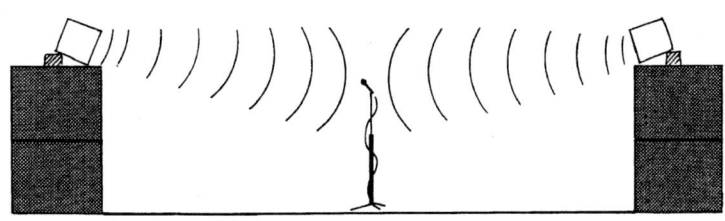

When all else fails, take the wedge monitors away from in front of the singer, and sit them up on their sides on a couple of road cases each side of the stage, in as close a direct line with the ears as possible. Re-EQ them for this new position, and this should allow you to kick up the level quite considerably, and give a dramatic increase in 'hearability' for the singer.

8. If you have a spare side to an Aural Exciter, then run it on the monitor send. What one side will do out front, the other will do for the monitors. You can run the Drive control harder on the monitors; you are not after smoothness but some 'bark' with plenty of bite'.

9. Try another microphone of the same type. The one you are using might have been damaged and not working properly, giving you excessive peaks and dips that weren't part of its design.

10. If your monitors are active 2 way (Bi-amped) back off the HIGH send from the crossover about 3 dB, then bring up the EQ sliders that are not excessively cut. If your monitors are passively crossed over, you could try poking a bit of foam or one of your old socks down the throat of the horn as a passive pad. This does increase the loading on the horn diaphragm, though, and may cause premature failure of the compression driver. Use this technique sparingly!
    Seriously, though, if you have a passive crossover it must be set up to deliver as flat as possible a frequency response from the speakers it's connected to. You may need to modify the crossover and have the Highs padded down with high power resistors to bring their level down closer to that of the Lows. This is a job for a competent technician, though, and not something you can do on the night.

11. Clean the microphone basket and pop filter. Unscrew the basket, pull out the acoustic foam pop filter inside, take them into the bathroom and wash them in hot soapy water. You will be surprised (and perhaps revolted) at the amount of gunge that washes out. Rinse the two parts well, and dry them under the hot air hand dryer.
    When they are dry put the microphone back together. If they were very dirty, the sound should now be much improved, with better HIGH MIDs and HIGHs. It will certainly smell better!

12. Get a better Graphic Equalizer. There are good reasons why one EQ is $200 and another is $2,000!

13. If your speaker management/digital crossover has a Feedback Eliminator module built in, then use it. If not, get your hands on a stand-alone one like a Sabine, Shure or similar. This technology can save your reputation and make your life easier, so why not embrace it?

## "I can't get enough level in the vocals out front; the band is over-powering them. The system is distorting and there's just no more left."

The most common cause of this problem is that you've got too little system for too big a room. Just as drag racers say there is no substitute for cubic inches, in a PA system there is no substitute for powerful amplifiers and speakers, and lots of 'em!

Another reason is bad gain structure; if you set up every channel to hit the 0 dB mark on the PFL/SOLO meter, that can be 32 volts appearing at the master section, which may strain the headroom capabilities of the mixer. Refer to the soundcheck section for more advice on this.

Still, we are left with a genuine problem that faces nearly everybody sometime. Here's some possible solutions:

1. Pull the level of the instruments down. I know this sounds obvious, and not always possible if you want to retain the 'punch', but you may need to revise your levels on some. Go back to one of the early pieces of advice on mixing in Chapter 13 - LISTEN.

2. Is the Kick drum drowning out everything? If so, bring it back a bit. Not everyone has come along to hear the drummer!

3. Is the guitar chugging away in the foreground instead of the background? Is it so loud off the stage that it doesn't need to be in the mix, anyway? Just because you've put a microphone in front of the guitar amplifier doesn't mean that you have to have the fader 3/4 the way up all the time.

4. Have you got too much LOW dialled up on things that don't need a lot of LOW? Low frequencies demand a lot of your system's available power, so keep it under control. In this situation, keep it out of vocals, guitars, keyboards, and only have just the amount the mix can survive on in the Kick drum and Bass.

5. Is there enough gain on the singer's desk channel? Or is there too much and it's distorting? Cut back the LOW and LOW MID and bring up some HIGH MID and HIGH (just a little - be careful). Listen. Does that improve things?
When you've tried all these, go on to this next suggestion.

6. Go back to *Chapter 7*, the section on using compressors, and revise your main system compressor settings.

   Harden up the compression ratio, from perhaps 4:1 to 10:1. This will effectively kill any peaks, and you don't need as much in reserve, so you can increase the output level of the compressor. Everything is now louder. Adjust the threshold of the compressor so that when the band is playing, with no vocals, the level runs just up to the threshold.

   Now, when the vocals come in, the input level to the compressor will go over the threshold and it will start to compress. In effect, the compressor squeezes down the instruments and the vocals jump in to fill the space, automatically coming out on top.

   Look at it this way. If you think of the PA system as being 100%, and you fill up that 100% with instruments, when you bring up the vocals you can't get more than 100%, so the vocals have to push the instruments out of the way. Sounds complicated? It's not, once you try it, and it does work. Basically you are controlling the level of one signal - the instruments, with another signal - the vocals.

   Just remember to gain ride the Left and Right master output levels at the end of each song to stop the extra gain in the compressor making the system feed back.

   Experiment with this technique and you will soon have the whole process sounding completely natural. It's a form of 'ducking' and is used to a great extent on TV and Radio commercial voice overs, although they usually set it up using the sidechain of the compressor *(see Chapter 7 - Signal Processors/Compressors/Sidechain insert)*. Listen to a few and hear how the music fades into the background the instant the announcer's voice starts, and how it returns as soon as he stops. It is also used in the recording and mastering process, but much more subtly, and this is the sort of effect you should aim at.

*Have you got too small a system for too big a room?*

7. Put a very short delay on the lead vocal, about 15 to 40 ms, and bring it up to the same level as the lead vocal channel. Give the delay channel a little boost around 3.5 KHz and see how that sounds. You should get an apparent increase in the vocal level.

   This effect approximates 'double tracking', stretching out the consonants in the words. The vocals are not really any louder, but they are in the mix twice, which makes them appear thicker and stronger. If you are running in stereo, pan the vocal channel hard Left, and the delay channel hard Right. The vocals should now appear to spread across the whole stage.

8. If you only have one delay and don't want to tie it up on this one job, get hold of a cheap Chorus or Flanger pedal. Set it on a slow shallow sweep and maybe kick up the HIGHs slightly. For a low cost version of the previous effect, it can do a surprisingly good job. Keep an eye on the hiss and try it out.

9. Insert one side of an Aural Exciter on the vocal channel. This will really pull the vocals out of the mix for you, but don't overdo it. See the section on Exciters in Chapter 7 for more details on how they work.

## "The drum monitor isn't loud enough"

Well, it never is. If it's not loud enough to knock the drummer off his seat each time he hits the kick drum, then he's not happy!

A good drum monitor is virtually a PA system in itself. It's hard to find the perfect drum monitor for all occasions, and for all drummers. If it sounds good it's often too big, and if it sounds bad then it's usually too small or has the wrong components in it.

Bi-amped is better, but not essential. To run a good drum monitor you must have a powerful amplifier (minimum 300 watts into 8 ohms) and good EQ. Try these suggestions for getting more out of your drum monitor.

1. Positioning is very critical. You've got to get it up off the ground and as close to the drummer's ears as possible.

2. Check that the snare drum microphone points away from the monitor. If it points into the horn you're going to have big problems with squeal. Refer to Chapter 15, and the "Rules for Singers #1...Keep the blunt end of the microphone pointed away from the speaker at all times".

4. The Kick drum must be well damped, with foam rubber, pillows and/or sandbag. If not, it will 'boom' like crazy and you won't have a hope of getting any level out of the monitor before it feeds back. Here you may run into trouble with the drummer.

   If he says that he doesn't want to dampen down the Kick drum, but likes it to sound live, tell him tactfully that you can add heaps of life into it out front, but if he wants to hear it in his monitor then you must take some of the boom out. You are going to need a lot of LOW MID cut out anyway, even with the foam and sandbag.

   A few moments spent discussing these points in advance can often solve any problems and stop you coming to blows! Once he hears how good it can sound, he'll be on your side for ever.

5. You **must** have a separate equalizer for the drum monitor. All of the LOW and LOW MID frequencies are dangerous, but especially watch 100 Hz to 200 Hz, and watch for squeals in the vocal range HIGH MIDs. Spend some time getting it as right as you can, no matter how drastic the EQ. Don't be afraid to make suggestions regarding the drum tun-

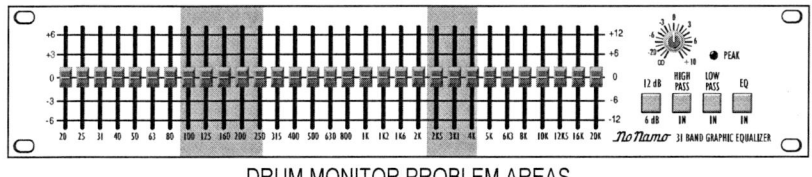

DRUM MONITOR PROBLEM AREAS

ing if you think it will help things. Remember, you're the sound engineer - the sound is your responsibility.

6. If you have any gates available, use them. Fine tuning the Threshold and Release can stop any excess 'boom' becoming feedback by turning the microphone off straight after the stick or beater has hit it.

### Another Drum Monitor Problem

What are the three words that a sound engineer hates to hear? No, it's not even "There's no money!" Even worse than that...it's "The drummer sings!" These words can strike fear into the heart of the most hardened sound engineer!

The problem is, a monitor that is set up for drums is very hard to also set up for vocals. The two things need approaching from totally different directions. Very often the frequencies you need to cut out of one, you need to keep in the other.

The easiest and best way around it is to give the drummer a separate wedge, EQ'd for vocal, as well as his drum monitor EQ'd for drums *(see pic at Left)*. This should give him the best of both worlds. It will also remove the risk of him swinging the vocal microphone around into the monitor when he's not singing.

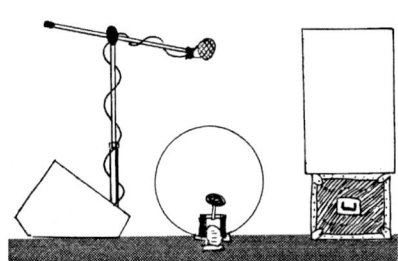

DRUMMER'S EYE VIEW OF DRUM MONITOR / WEDGE SETUP

Make sure also that you point the vocal microphone up towards the mouth, so that when you bring up his vocals out front you don't bring up the snare drum at the same time.

An alternative might be to give the drummer a pair of headphones, and the sort of mix you'd put into in-ear monitors. They don't have to be wireless (it's unlikely he'll be wandering around the stage during songs!) and can be a very economical solution to the problem.

*The drummer sings!*

### A final trick for all stage monitors

If endless checking is not getting the right sound for the person listening to the monitor, pull the level right down while they are still saying "Check One Two", wait a second, and then slowly bring it back up again.

The sudden change from high volume to nothing causes the ear to reset itself, and as the level slowly comes back up they are listening more closely. Chances are that as soon as the volume comes back up to where it was they'll say "Yeah, that's great, leave it at that".

I know this sounds too simple, but it works more times than it doesn't. Don't use it too often, though, and keep it to yourself. You don't want the band to know what you're up to!

## What to do when things don't work

Sooner or later something will go wrong. Luckily 99 times out of 100 it is something very simple. A lead has been connected wrongly because you're in a hurry, a fuse has blown, a solder connection has come adrift, or you've forgotten to switch something on. Whatever you do, don't panic, because then you won't be thinking straight and you could inadvertently cause more problems than you solve. Take a deep breath, don't listen to anyone yelling, and just get on with it. Run through the system layout in your head, and check it as you go. Delegate jobs to calm down people who are tearing their hair out, and you'll soon track down the cause.

Big system or small, the live sound industry is very hard on equipment. Being bounced in and out of a truck night after night, things are bound to happen. Which is why spare leads, mic clips, mic stands and more should always be available. The normal process of wear and tear is accelerated, which is one reason why speaker boxes and rack cases tend to be heavy - they are built to stand up to intensive road use.

When trouble shooting, remember these points:

Nothing will work unless you –

1. Run a signal to it

2. Run some power to it

3. Turn it on

Swap over suspect items with something that you know is working. If music is coming out of the Left stack but not the Right, swap over the Left and Right speaker leads. If the Right stack now works but the Left doesn't then it's not the speakers.

Check the leads, crossovers, equalizers, etc. Work your way down the signal chain and you'll eventually isolate the problem, and with any luck it will be a lead. If you're not big on soldering leads, check out *Chapter 15* for Old Dunk's 'quick and dirty' soldering section.

To quickly check out any signal processor or equalizer problem, just pull the input and output leads out of it and join them together. If there is no change then the problem is not that item; if everything suddenly works, then it is.

UNPLUG THE LEADS FROM THE REAR OF THE UNIT

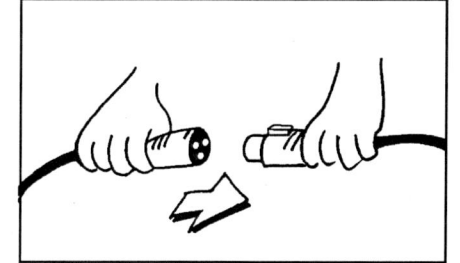

AND PLUG THEM TOGETHER

## Absolute Emergencies

In emergencies you have to do whatever is necessary to get the show going.

Let's modify the old show biz saying, and say "The show must go on, *especially if you want to get paid!*"

1. If the crossover dies, then you could conceivably use your equalizer as a sort of crossover. Using it as a 2 way system, you could run your LOWs full range, and run your HIGHs out of the equalizer, pushing all the faders above 2 KHz fully up, and all below fully down. With a stereo EQ, you could run the system mono, and run the console signal to EQ Channels A and B. Then you could run the LOWs out of Channel A, and the HIGHs out of Channel B.

    Avoid pushing the system too hard and the speakers should survive the night.

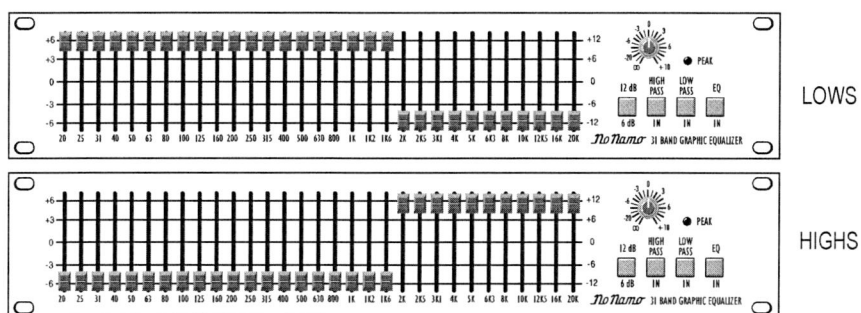

2. If the LOW amplifier dies, then use the MID amplifier and run the LOW speakers full range, bypassing the crossover. It won't be great but it's better than nothing. Do the same if your MID amplifier or speakers die.

*In emergencies you have to do whatever is necessary to get the show going*

3. If your HIGH horns die, then run half the MIDs as MID and the other half as HIGH. Once again, it may not be good, and will definitely call for some drastic EQ, but it's better than no HIGHs.
Don't run the LOW amplifier into your HIGH horns though. You can safely run any signal into a speaker designed for a lower frequency signal; it might not be the best sound you've ever heard, but it's unlikely to kill it. However, remember you *can't* run a signal into a speaker designed for a higher frequency than that signal. Refer back to *Chapter 9 - Crossovers*, and *Chapter 10 - Speakers.*

4. If the Main system dies, turn the Monitors around so the audience can hear them and use them as the Main system. If the Monitors die, angle part of the Main system across the stage.

5. You should always have some odd leads for these kinds of emergencies, so that you can wire things up differently quickly. Go through your system with a "worst possible case" scenario, and try to have the leads available to still keep things working. Keep these leads separate from the rest of the PA leads. Spend a bit of time on this and it will pay you back many times over if you have a system breakdown. Here are some suggestions that I've found useful:

- Speakons to bare wires
- Speakon lead joiners
- Male and Female XLRs to bare wires
- Mono and Stereo Jacks to bare wires
- Jack sockets to bare wires

*It's amazing what you can do wrong or forget to when you're in a hurry*

In an emergency you can quickly twist combinations of these together as necessary, wrap a turn of gaffer tape around the join, all without having to get out the soldering iron. However, remember they are a **temporary** measure only - fix the problem permanently as soon as possible.

You'll be surprised what you can get away with and still end up with a halfway decent sound. It's very likely that you and the other crew members will be the only ones who notice any change.

### Get to know the sounds of different problems

- A blown power fuse or a tripped circuit breaker on an amplifier will not turn on the power light or the fans, and the amplifier will be totally silent. No hum, nothing. Make sure you disconnect the power and the speakers before checking the fuse or resetting the relay.

- A blown rail fuse on an amplifier will make the sound very distorted at any volume, like playing through a distortion pedal under water.
Disconnect the power and speakers before checking this, too.

RESETTABLE CIRCUIT BREAKER, REPLACING POWER FUSES IN AMPLIFIERS. PUSH IT TO RESET

- If you ever hear a very low, very loud farting sound (sorry - there's no other way to describe it!) through the speakers when you turn on an amplifier, DISCONNECT IT IMMEDIATELY. The amplifier has 'gone DC' - the power transistors inside have stopped working and are dumping the internal DC (Direct Current) voltage from the power supply straight into your speakers and will burn them out almost instantly. This is why you should check out each amplifier as you turn it on by listening at very low levels with your head in the speaker.
An amplifier with this kind of DC problem can't be fixed on the spot, but will need expert treatment and repair. The technical phrase is – *'it's stuffed!'* Replace it with your spare amplifier.

- A speaker that is 'scratching' - rubbing its voice coil against the magnet - may sound OK at low volume but will give out sharp 'Crack' sounds on loud peaks. Get it fixed soon or it will eventually rub its way through the voice coil windings and then it will be completely silent.

- If there is no sound when you yell into a microphone, or it goes from soft to loud with a click and then back again, then this is probably a bad solder joint. Somewhere! These are extremely slow to track down, but you could start with the microphone lead. Swap it to another channel on both the mixer and the multicore snake, try another mic and then another lead, and within 3 changes you'll isolate the problem. It might help to pray that it's not an internal connection in the mixer, the amplifier or the speaker box. Think of how many connections there must be between your original signal and the speaker, and you'll have some idea of the number of possible things to go wrong!

- When something doesn't work after you've plugged the system up, stay calm. Remember our first 3 points of trouble shooting. Check that every lead in the signal chain from microphone to mixing desk to speakers is plugged in correctly. Check all the obvious things first and nearly every time you'll find that it is human error, not the system, that's at fault.

## Hummmmm

There will be times when the system will hum for no apparent reason. There is always a reason, though, but sometimes it can be hard to find. Firstly, go through the obvious ones from *Chapter 12- Setting Up/ AC Power Ground Rules,* rememberig that under no circumstances should you ever disconnect any AC Power Ground/Earth pins.

A gadget that can come in useful is an Iso Transformer box. This is a metal box about the size of a DI Box, containing a Line level (0dBV) audio transformer wound at a 1:1 ratio, so whatever level goes in one end comes out the other. It has XLR Inputs and Outputs, and its job is to 'lift' or 'float' the *Audio* ground, and also isolate the Hot + and Cold − Balanced lines. It breaks the Audio ground line, stopping the hum from travelling to the mixer

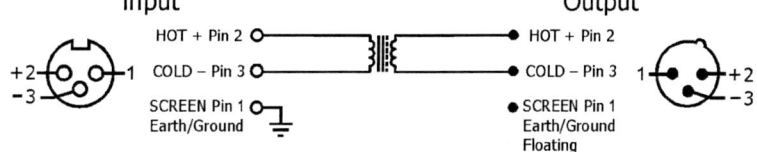

TYPICAL ISO TRANSFORMER CIRCUIT

### How do you use it?

You plug it in wherever one part of the system meets another; between Monitor system and Front of House; between Front of House and amplifier feed; it's a process of trial and error until you find the right spot where suddenly the hum stops.

## What to do when there is no time for a soundcheck

There is no substitute for a good soundcheck, and you should always allow enough time in the schedule for them. But if the truck breaks down and you're running 5 hours late, then you have to do something. If the band doesn't play, then you'll have an irate promoter on your hands, a disappointed crowd, no-one will get paid and you'll have driven all that way for nothing!

The usual situation is either that the audience is in the venue eating or waiting, or there is a DJ system bopping away. Whichever one it is, they don't want "Check ONE TWO" blaring out of the system at 130 dB!

So, for just such an occasion, here's a list of steps to go through when the unthinkable happens. It's only approximate, and the details will vary with the mixing console and system, but it's something to have up your sleeve.

### If the console is still set up from the night before

If you used the system at the gig the night before, then there's no real problem. Go with it as it is. If the Main System graphic EQ is still set from the night before, then just bring up the channel faders. Don't start off really loud; take it easy. Bring up the vocals first, then bring the music up under them until you have some idea of how the room is going to react to the system. Keep a hand close to the graphic EQ, ready for any surprises.

This is where training your ears is invaluable. If you can hear a feedback ring starting and can identify the frequency (even approximately), then you can remove the problem before it gets a chance to start.

Listen carefully to the problem. Is it caused by just the one instrument, in which case adjusting the channel EQ should solve it; or is it happening on everything as soon as it hits that frequency, in which case you should adjust the graphic EQ.

If you are the monitor engineer, then this type of ability will keep everybody on stage happy, and begging to work with you.

## When the console is not set up

Here you've definitely got problems, but you can still overcome them with a plan of action designed for just such an occasion.

Here's a checklist of what to do:

1. Pull down the channel faders, group faders and master faders.

2. Plug in your headphones.

3. Start with the vocals. Unplug the Lead vocal multicore tail from the console input, and plug in the lead vocal microphone.

4. Check that the PFL switch is not SOLO. If it is, bring the channel fader up to 0 dB or 3/4 the way up.

5. Press PFL/SOLO switch and talk into microphone. Adjust the channel gain until an explosive "TWO" just hits 0 dB on the PFL/SOLO meter. Check that it sounds OK in the headphones.

6. Unplug the microphone and lead and put them back on stage. Plug the lead back into the stagebox, and *don't forget to plug the tail back into the console channel!!!*

7. Set the other vocal gains the same. Roll off a little LOW and LOW MID, and add just a little HI MID. If in doubt leave it flat with just a little LOW taken out.

8. Set guitar gains to less than vocals; maybe start on half as much gain. Leave the EQ flat.

9. Bass. If you're using an active DI, then set the gain similar to vocals but switch a 20 dB pad in. If there's no pad switch, then set the gain very low. If you're using a passive DI, then set the gain similar to vocals; maybe a bit less if it's a loud, hard player. Leave the EQ flat. Set up the Keyboard channels the same.

10. Set all drum gains low apart from the Hi Hats and Overheads, which should be set similar to Vocals. Roll off lots of LOW MID in the Kick and Snare channels. Roll off everything except HI on the Hi Hats. Leave small toms flat; roll off lots of LOW MIDs on the larger toms.

11. Set Vocal faders at 0 dB mark (3/4 way up); guitars, bass and keyboards a bit less. Set Kick and Snare drums at 0 dB, the rest of the drums a bit less.

12. Check all group assigns are correct; set group faders at 0 dB.

13. Get someone (anyone) to go up on stage and talk into each microphone while you listen to each channel on the PFL/SOLO switches. Don't worry about levels, you've already set them. You just want to check that everything is coming down to the console properly.

    Check the DI lines by unplugging them and plugging a microphone into each lead. Listen hard - you should hear something. Don't forget to make sure the DIs are plugged back in afterwards.

14. To make sure the signal chain is OK down to the amplifiers and speakers, plug your own microphone into a spare channel, bring up the master Left/Right faders slowly, while you tap the microphone *gently* in time to the DJ, background music or whatever, until you can hear it. If everything is running right you should hear a 'thud' each time you tap.

15. If you don't hear anything, check that the EQ is turned up, the crossover is turned up, the amplifiers are turned on and up, and the speakers are plugged in. It's amazing what you can forget when you're in a hurry! When you've done all this, go back and try #14 again. Keep doing this until it works.

16. For the monitors, wind up the channel send on the lead vocal until you can just detect a ring about to start. Back off the level about 3 dB, pull down that frequency about 3 dB on the monitor graphic, and get ready to play it by ear during the gig. Set the monitor sends on the other vocal channels to the same level.

Well, that's about it in general terms, but you've probably got the idea and can modify these details to suit the system you're using. You'll have to set your effects up as you go, using your headphones and the PFL/SOLO switches on the effects returns.

When the band comes on, bring up the master Left/Right faders to just under three quarters the way up, and cross your fingers. If you've followed the steps above, then at least something should come out of the speaker stacks. That's good, because in my experience an audience is a lot happier when *something* rather than *nothing* comes out of the system, even if it is a little rough around the edges!

When the singer leaps onto the stage and yells "Hello Wandiligong" or wherever you are, and you can hear it, then you're halfway towards a successful gig.

In the first song you should:-

• Check and adjust the vocal sound and level, and maybe get some delay and reverb happening

• Check and adjust the general drum sound. You can do specific tuning a bit later, just get the levels right at the moment.

• Check and adjust the Keyboards and Bass levels

• Check and adjust the Guitars, and be ready for a solo.

• Check the level of your jug of lemon squash and get someone to top it up - you've earned it!

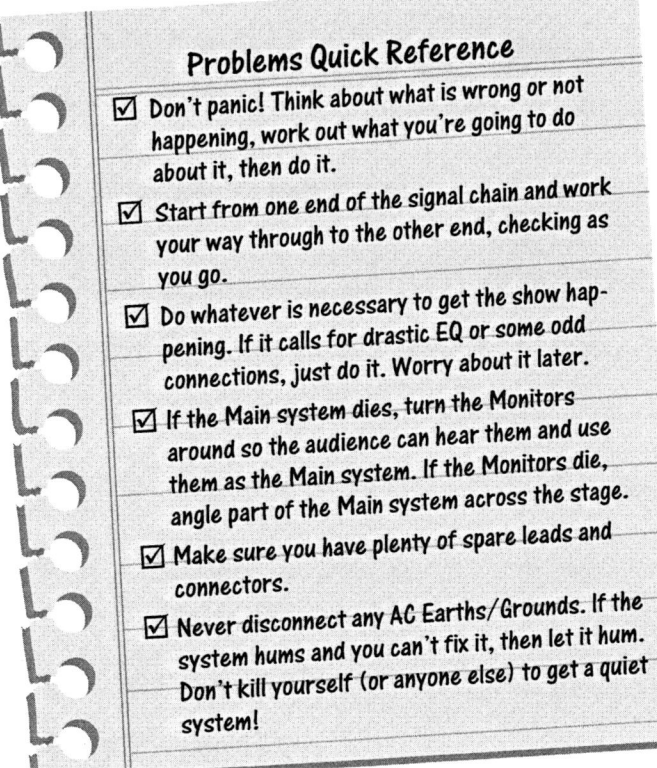

**Problems Quick Reference**

☑ Don't panic! Think about what is wrong or not happening, work out what you're going to do about it, then do it.

☑ Start from one end of the signal chain and work your way through to the other end, checking as you go.

☑ Do whatever is necessary to get the show happening. If it calls for drastic EQ or some odd connections, just do it. Worry about it later.

☑ If the Main system dies, turn the Monitors around so the audience can hear them and use them as the Main system. If the Monitors die, angle part of the Main system across the stage.

☑ Make sure you have plenty of spare leads and connectors.

☑ Never disconnect any AC Earths/Grounds. If the system hums and you can't fix it, then let it hum. Don't kill yourself (or anyone else) to get a quiet system!

*Things your case shouldn't contain?*

## 15      *Appendix*

## Top Ten things your own case should contain

### 1. A cellular/mobile phone.

These are no longer an option, but an ***essential*** tool, and until you've got one, you won't believe how useful they can be. Truck broken down? Call for help without having to find a phone box. Dispute over the rider once you get to the gig? Get the agent on the phone and put him on the spot to work it out with the promoter. See a once-in-a-lifetime event? Take a picture with the phone and send it a friend. Use it as your mobile office to book one gig as you travel to another. Some have built-in electronic organizers, can check and send email, and surf the net. For a lot of people these phones are an option; for the working sound engineer, they are a necessity.

### 2. A really good bright torch

Maybe a smallish MAGLITE® or something similar, with spare batteries. If you can stick it in your mouth that's an added bonus, because it leaves both your hands free. Never lend it to anybody.

### 3. A heavy duty pair of headphones

Something with good noise rejection. If you can't find any that shut out enough outside sound, try a pair of industrial Noise Suppressing Earmuffs, with high quality headphone inserts wired into them. I got hold of some earmuffs that were designed especially for airport workers, and I put a set of Sennheiser replacement inserts in them. Never lend them to anybody, either.

### 4. A favourite microphone

Ideally one that is the same as the lead vocal, plus a lead for plugging it into the console when tuning the system.

### 5. Some white or masking tape

Also a grease pencil and markers, to mark out the mixing desk, monitor desk, equalizers, amp racks, stage boxes, anything that will make setting up faster and more accurate.

### 6. Some CDs

To play when checking out the system and also during the breaks. You should be very familiar with the sound of these so you can make mental comparisons between the way they should sound, and the way that they do sound.

### 7. Accessories

Spare XLR, Neutrik Speakon and guitar jack plugs, preferably with some wire tails with bare ends already soldered onto them. You never know when you'll need to make up some instant adapters, and this way you can just twist the ends together quickly. Also: some shielded cable, a mains powered soldering iron, solder, wire cutters, pliers and *your own roll of gaffer tape.* Keep this tape away from the band, or one day you'll go to use it and it will be gone.

### 8. A small multimeter

For lead checking and for power checking. ***Don't stick the probes into a power point unless you are sure you know what you are doing!*** If you are unsure, then just get hold of a lead tester and a AC tester, the ones with 3 LEDs on them. I bought my Whirlwind lead tester back in 1988 and it has worked solidly ever since then. The instructions are on the front and you can't go wrong.

### 9. A book

Something to read in those long hours between setup time and showtime. Or a notepad, so you can write a book, like I did!

• I'm not being selfish when I say don't lend these things to anybody. People borrow them with the best intentions of giving them back later, but they hardly ever do. Then when *you* need any of these things, you have to go and borrow them from someone else!

### 10. Last but not least

Finally, don't forget to pack a sense of humour. This is Live Sound, not life or death brain surgery. It's meant to be FUN. If you aren't enjoying it, why should the audience?

## Ear Protection

Look after your ears; they are earning your living for you. Once *they* stop working, so do you. Can't hear - can't mix!

If you have to drive 6 hours in a noisy truck to get to the gig, wear some earplugs for the journey. If you don't, you'll arrive with a bad case of ear fatigue, or Temporary Hearing Shift. You'll lose all of your top end and dynamic range, and it will take a couple of hours of peace and quiet for your hearing to get back to normal. Of course, peace and quiet are the two things that are in very short supply in the rush to get things set up in time.

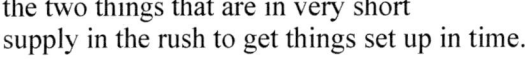
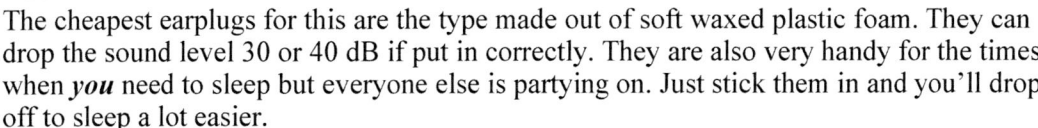

The cheapest earplugs for this are the type made out of soft waxed plastic foam. They can drop the sound level 30 or 40 dB if put in correctly. They are also very handy for the times when *you* need to sleep but everyone else is partying on. Just stick them in and you'll drop off to sleep a lot easier.

If you have the money, though, the Musicians Earplugs made by Etymotic Research (*www.etymotic.com*) are a better idea. They come in models that drop the sound level by 9, 15 or 25 dB. The same sound quality as you'd normally hear, only quieter. They are very handy if you have to go and check out the main stacks or monitors when they are running hard.

They do need to be custom made to fit your ears, though, and cost quite a bit more than the 75 cents for the foam ones!

Still, it's like the old saying about crash helmets: *"If you only have a ten dollar head, then get a ten dollar helmet!"*

## How to solder leads

You'll frequently have to fix up leads that get damaged, or make up special ones, so here's a quick run down on putting the connectors on and soldering them.

This is not Trade School Soldering 101, but Old Dunk's 'quick and dirty' get-the-job-done method. You'll need a soldering iron designed for electronic work (not plumbing), some rosin cored solder, a small pair of wire snippers (a razor blade in an emergency) and a pair of linesman's pliers.

### *Guitar Jack Connectors*

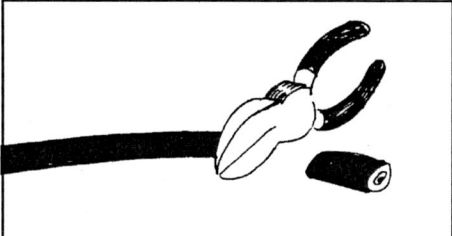

1. Cut the lead to the length you want with the snippers

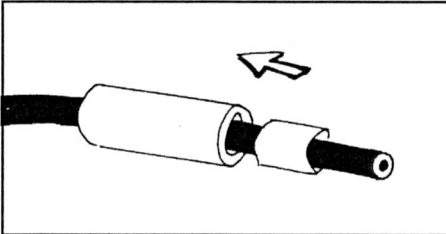

2. Slip the screw-on cap and the plastic inner shield backwards over the lead

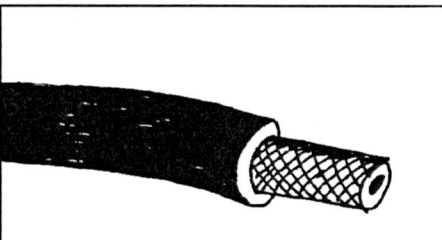

3. Cut about 15 mm (½") of the plastic sheathing off the lead with the snippers and expose the braid

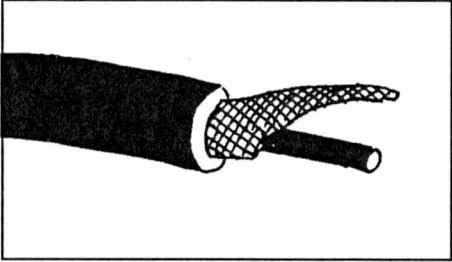

4. Spread the braid apart, pull out the inner plastic covered wire, and twist the braid back together

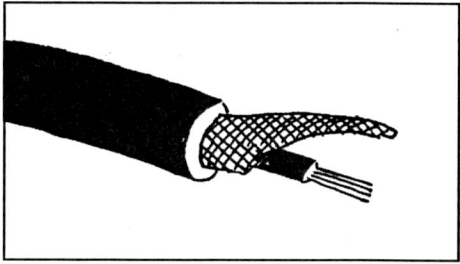

5. Strip 5 mm (¼") of the inner wire plastic sheath off with the snippers and expose the bare wire

6. Press the soldering iron against the solder and the inner wire at the same time. It will suddenly melt and fill the wire strands up so it looks like a little silver rod.
Do the same to the twisted together outer braid

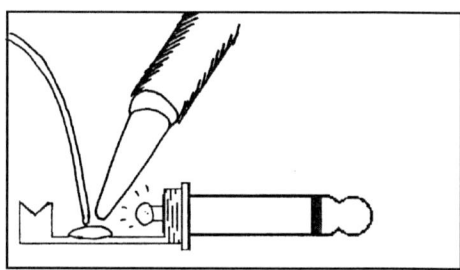

7. Press the soldering iron against the centre pin of the jack plug body and the solder at the same time.
When the solder melts onto the pin, pull it away and leave a small puddle of it on the pin.
Do the same to the centre of the outer arm of the plug

8. Bring the solder tipped centre wire up next to the solder tipped centre pin. Touch the soldering iron tip to the two of the at the same time.
As soon as the solder melts and flows, pull the iron away and let the joined up blob cool

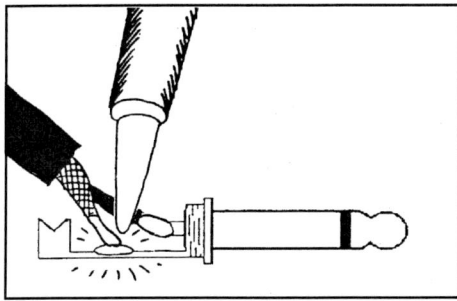

9. Use the same technique on the outer wire and the outer arm, shortening the wire if necessary to match it to the position of the solder blob

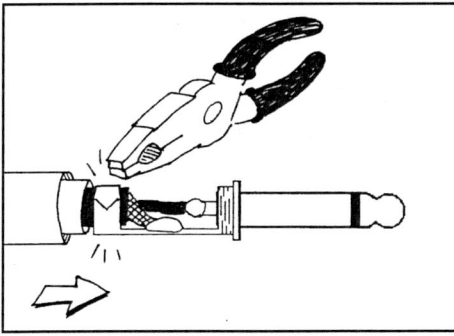

10. Let it all cool down, then crimp the end of the outer arm over the lead with the pliers, push the plastic inner shield over the connections, and screw the cap down tight.

## XLR Connectors

That wasn't too hard, was it? Now you've got some confidence, let's tackle a 3 pin XLR. We'll start off with the basic type and then look at different manufacturer's variations.

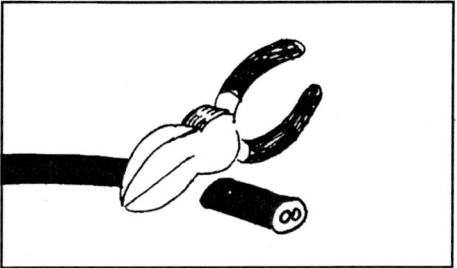

1. Cut the lead to the length you want with the snippers

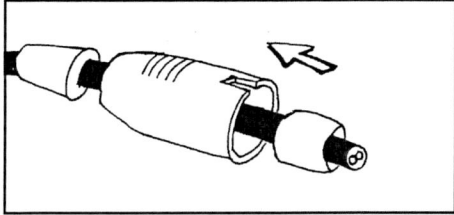

2. Slide the rubber boot, connector body and plastic inner shield (if supplied) backwards over the lead

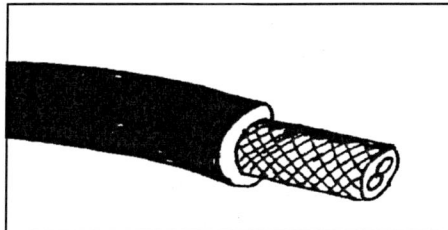

3. Strip 15 mm (½") of the outer plastic sheath off the lead with the snippers, and expose the outer braid

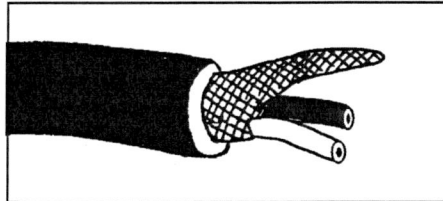

4. Spread the braid apart, and pull out the two plastic sheathed inner wires, and twist the braid back together

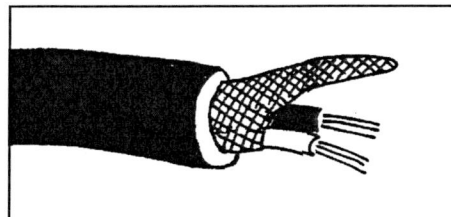

5. Strip 5 mm (¼") of plastic sheath off the two inner wires with the snippers and expose the bare wires

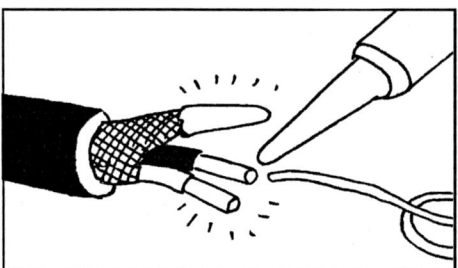

6. Press the soldering iron against one of the inner wires and the solder at the same time. It will suddenly melt and fill the wire strands up so it looks like a little silver rod. Do the same for the other inner wire and the outer braid

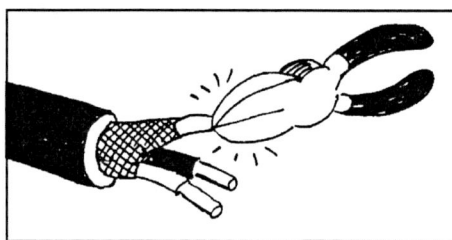

7. Snip the outer braid slightly shorter than the two wires

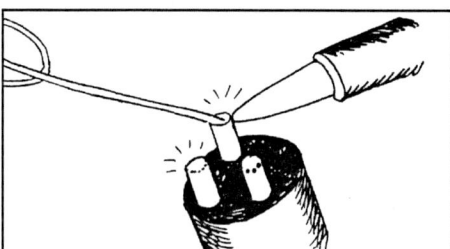

8. Put your soldering iron and solder against each of the three inner pins of the connector and fill them up with solder

9. Decide which colour inner wire will be + (Hot) to solder to Pin # 2. Put the soldering iron against the solder filled pin, and when it melts, push the wire into it. As soon as it all flows into one nice blob, take the iron away. Do the same for the other inner wire to Pin # 3, and also for the braid into Pin # 1

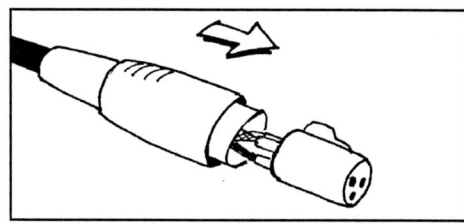

10. Slide the connector body and plastic inner shield (if supplied) down over the pins

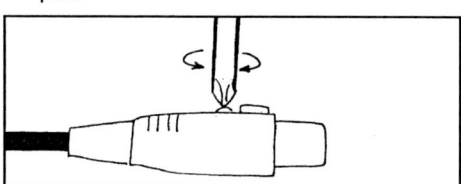

11. Tighten the grub screw (if fitted. Up for Switchcraft, down for Cannon, neither for Neutrik

12. Tighten the cable clamp. It's different for each brand and model, so do what seems logical!

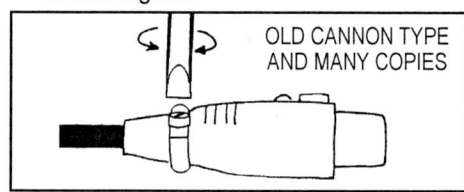

OLD CANNON TYPE AND MANY COPIES

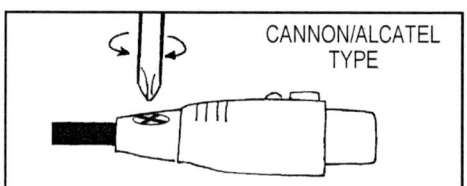

CANNON/ALCATEL TYPE

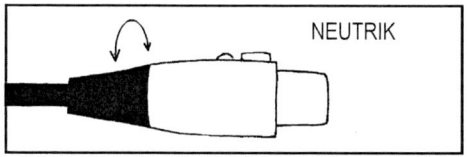

NEUTRIK

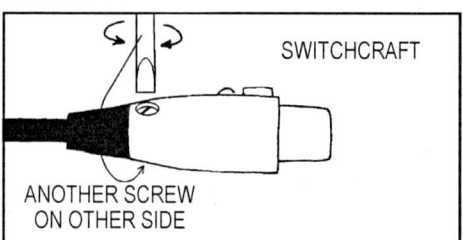

SWITCHCRAFT

ANOTHER SCREW ON OTHER SIDE

SWITCHCRAFT GRUBSCREW UNSCREWS UPWARDS TO LOCK

The new XLR connector from Amphenol has no screws, and uses alligator-like plastic jaws to hold the cable. Assembly is a bit different to before:

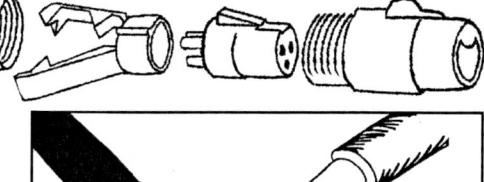

1. Cut the lead to the length you want with the snippers

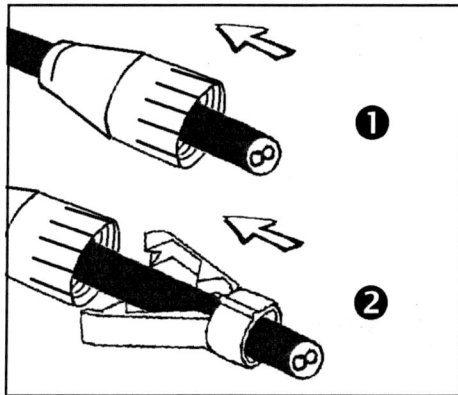

2. First slide the plastic/rubber boot backwards over the lead, followed by the green or purple plastic jaw clamp backwards over the lead

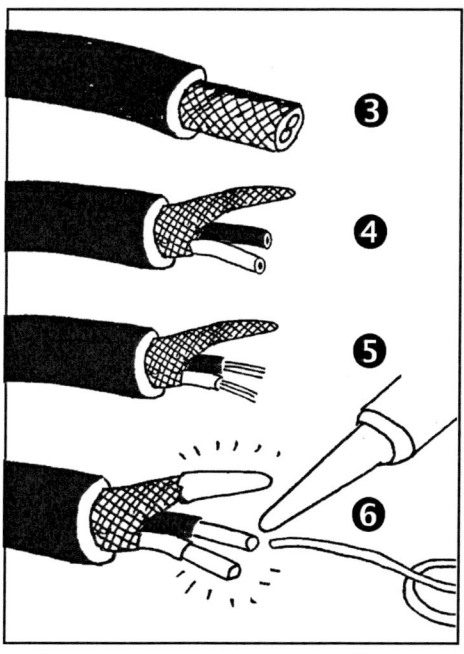

3. Strip and pre-solder the wires as you did in the previous example

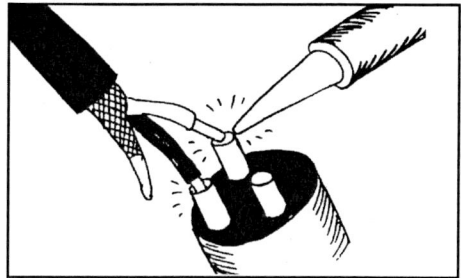

4. Solder the pre-soldered wires to the pins using your previous colour code. Braid is always Pin #1.

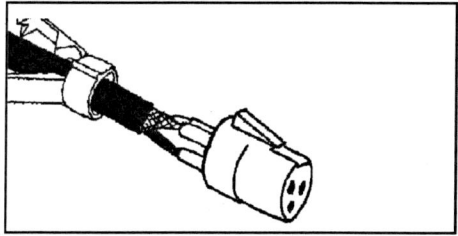

5. The soldered assembly should look like this

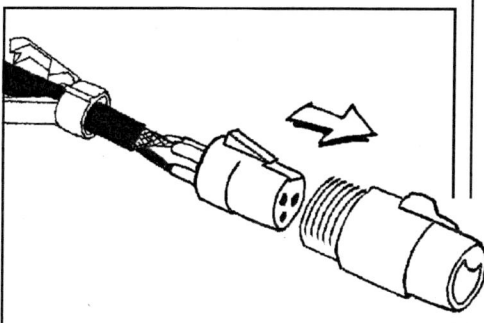

6. Slide the assembly into the alloy shell. Note that any ridges on the parts will line up with the slot inside the shell

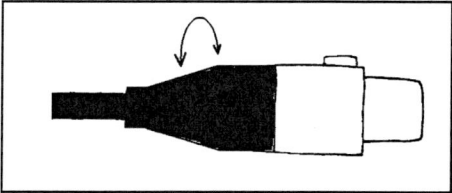

7. Finally, screw on and tighten up the big plastic/rubber boot onto the rear of the alloy casing. This clamps the jaws down to grip the cable securely

Apart from the jaw clamp, these new XLRs look and work like an updated version of the original ones which came on my guitar amp back in the '60s!

ORIGINAL 60'S CANNON FEMALE XLR

As an alternative to *soldering* XLRs, you could always use the new Insulation Displacement Connectors (IDC) from Amphenol, Neutrik, Switchcraft and others. No soldering, just push the wires in and twist up the cable clamp hard. They're worth checking out, although for heavy duty Live Sound use a soldered cable is still preferred.

The first thing that you notice about soldering is that you need three hands! One to hold the soldering iron, one to hold the connector, and one to hold the solder! One way around this is to wedge the connector into the pliers so that it sits still in the jaws. Another is to use some locking pliers to hold the connector, like some Vise Grips or similar.

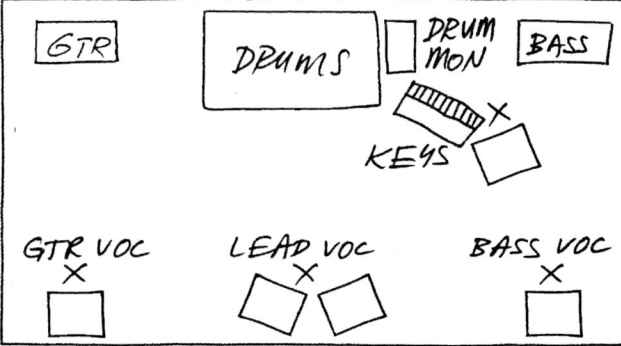

The easiest way, though, is to insert the connector into an opposite style connector mounted to a workbench, or to a piece of plywood for a mobile unit. All you need is a small piece of ply, and mount a female and male XLR, and a jack socket, onto it *(see Right)*. Now you have the ideal third hand. It's cheap, easy, and it will fit in your briefcase.

Whenever you solder, be quick! Have the soldering iron against the plugs for the absolute minimum time. As soon as the solder melts and flows, pull it away so you don't overheat and melt the plastic the pins sit in or the sheathing.

Hint: a tiny blob of hot solder already on the iron will speed up melting the solder on your connections to be joined.

For 4 core 'Star Quad' type cable, from Canare and others, twist the four centre wires into pairs of the same colour, and wire up as you would normally.

Note: Despite the four individual wires, it's still meant to be a single balanced lead, not a cheap 4 way loom!

## Stage Layouts and PA Riders

If you are working with a band regularly, and they get to do some supports for bigger shows, or a set at a weekend festival, their management will have to supply a stage layout plan for the band, so that the stage can be setup ready and changed over easily. And who are they going to ask? Why, the sound person, of course...and that's you!

### K.I.S.S.

This doesn't mean that you have to put on makeup and sing 'I was made for loving you baby', but stands for Keep It Simple, Stupid! You're not writing a 'no expense spared' PA rider, but something to help the crew get your show on the road as quickly and as painlessly as possible. So don't turn it into your dream PA 'wish list' or it will instantly go to the bottom of the 'too hard' pile! It doesn't have to be fancy - hand drawn is fine, but it ***must be easily legible*** as it may be faxed several times.

Here is a quick checklist of the information you need to supply:

1. A basic hand drawn stage layout showing where the drums go, and how many there are. ***Make a special note if the drummer is left handed!***

2. Draw on this layout where the Guitar, Bass and Keyboard amps

go, and whether they are miked up or DI'd. If you need 8 Keyboard DI's, then *now* is the time to mention it, not 5 minutes before the band walks on!

3. An Input List, showing what will be miked up, how many microphones, and whether a boom stand or straight stand is required for vocals.

4. The band's basic Monitor requirements. eg. Drum monitor; Lead Vocal wedges; Keyboard monitor, and so on.

### MONITORS

DRUM MON - KICK, SNARE, LEAD VOCALS, BASS

LEAD VOCAL (CENTRE) - JUST LEAD VOCAL

GTR VOCAL - ALL VOCALS, SOME KEYS

BASS VOCAL - ALL VOCALS + KEYS + GTR

KEYS VOCAL - ALL VOCALS, ALL KEYS + GTR

5. Finally, write the band's name, your name, and your contact details - phone number, email address, website, etc.
Keep plenty of copies in your briefcase, so you can hand them out to whoever needs them.

## THE TURBO HEMI ALLSTARS

Contact 1   Duncan Fry (Front of house) 5555 6789
Email: dunk@dunkworld.com  www.dunkworld.com
Contact 2   Daddy Warbucks (Manager) Phone/fax: 5555 1111
Email: typicalgreedymanager@hatemail.com

It's also worthwhile scanning it and saving it as a small .GIF (Graphic Image Format) file that you can email to production companies if necessary.

Don't get too specific as to brands of mics, brands of effects etc. You're not the one calling the shots at these gigs. If say that you must have a 'Widgetronix ZX 1500' reverb or the band won't go on, then guess what? The band won't go on!

If your band starts doing a lot of this type of work, then a neater, more professional sheet will probably be a good idea. Draw it up on a computer, and save it as a .PDF file (Portable Document Format) so you can email, fax or print as many as you'll need. Still keep it simple, though. Remember it's important information for the stage crew, not a puff piece for the band's fan club!

### The PA Rider

Touring with the band on their own, either at home or overseas, picking up production as you go, is of course a different matter. Then you *will* be creating a 'PA Rider', a complete list of what you expect the production to consist of.

This is where you can be much more specific about the equipment.

You've really got two options:

1. You can make it a wish list, and add in all those things that you've always wanted to try;

2. You can stick with what you are used to using, as you will have enough on your hands without learning how to use a new system

---

TURBO HEMI ALLSTARS
INPUT LIST:
1.   Kick
2.   Snare
3.   Snare bottom
4.   Hi hats
5.   Rack tom 1
6.   Rack tom 2
7.   Floor tom
8.   Overhead L
9.   Overhead R
10.  Bass            D.I
11.  Gtr Left
12.  Keys 1          D.I
13.  Keys 2          D.I.
14.  Gtr vocal L
15.  Lead vocal Centre
16.  Bass vocal R
17.  Keys vocal Rear R

Please Note: Round base straight stand needed for Channel 15 Lead Vocal

Band will supply its own Super Widgetron paralytic tube comprequalizer for lead vocal

---

Personally I'd suggest a little of both. Although it's good to try out new things, when you arrive at the venue, dog-tired and with 11 hours solid work ahead of you, it's always a relief to have some familiar equipment!

If the band is big on five part harmonies, then the monitor system is going to be crucial, and you should be very specific about what the band will need.

However it has been known for promoters to take the lowest bid on production, from a company who looks at the rider and says "Sure, we can supply that, no problems." Trouble is, when you get to the gig, the system is not at all what you requested.

What are you going to do? Not play? With the audience clamouring at the doors and the promoter tearing his hair out and threatening to sue, I don't think so! They've got you over a barrel, so all you can do is chalk it up as one of life's little learning experiences and make the best of it.

Always keep in mind though, that if you're travelling overseas, some esoteric pieces of equipment just aren't available in some countries, so make sure to put 'Widgetronix ZX 1500 *OR EQUIVALENT*' Then they'll have to get back to you and work out an equivalent acceptable product if it's not available.

If it's a *truly* indispensable item, crucial to the band's performance, then my advice is getting your own and taking it with you.

Even so, you'll probably end up using some very strange equipment from time to time, but hey, nobody ever said this job would be easy!

## Black Box circuit

Here's a diagram of a pad circuit you could make up should you need to plug the output of an amplifier into a DI that doesn't have a speaker level input

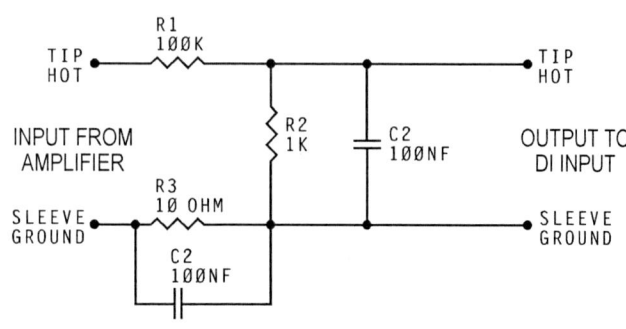

*Channel marker sheets*
Use these to mark your desk settings on when 2 or more bands are using the same mixing desk. Make some copies and keep them in your case.

## Connector Wiring

 *(FemaleXLR/EP and Speakon line connectors illustrated)*

### XLR Wiring

**Standard**
Pin # 1   Earth/Ground
Pin # 2   Hot (+) Signal
Pin # 3   Cold (−) Return

**Old non-standard**
Pin # 1   Earth/Ground
Pin # 2   Cold (−) Return
Pin #3    Hot (+) Signal

Check polarity carefully if you are making any **Balanced to Unbalanced** connections.
• If you're using XLRs as Speaker Connectors, use 3 core cable and connect all 3 pins.

### EP Multipin Wiring

**EP** and **AP** series connectors are a popular multipin speaker connector made by Amphenol / Cannon.

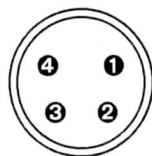

**EP 4 / AP 4**

Pin # 1   Low −
Pin # 2   Low +
Pin # 3   High −
Pin # 4   High +

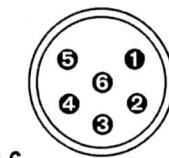

**EP 6**

Pin # 1   Low −
Pin # 2   Low +
Pin # 3   Mid −
Pin # 4   Mid +
Pin # 5   High −
Pin # 6   High +

**EP 8**

Pin # 1   Low −
Pin # 2   Low +
Pin # 3   Low Mid −
Pin # 4   Low Mid +
Pin # 5   High Mid −
Pin # 6   High Mid +
Pin # 7   High −
Pin #  8   High +

### Speakon® Connectors

The Speakon connector is a heavy duty speaker connector developed by Neutrik

**2 Pin Speakon Wiring**

Pin 1+   Hot (+)
Pin 1−   Cold (−)
Same body profile as the 4 Pin version, and fully compatible, except that only Pins 1+ and 1− are present

**4 Pin Speakon Wiring**

Pin 1+   Hot (+)
Pin 1−   Cold (−)
Pin 2+   -------
Pin 2−   -------

*2 way*
Pin 1+   Low +
Pin 1−   Low −
Pin 2+   High +
Pin 2−   High −

**8 Pin Speakon Wiring**

*3 way*
Pin 1+   Low +
Pin 1−   Low −
Pin 2+   Mid +
Pin 2−   Mid −
Pin 3+   High +
Pin 3−   High −
Pin 4+   ------
Pin 4−   ------

The 8 Pin Speakon can also be set up as a 3 way with 2 sets of Low connections, or as a 4 way, similar to the EP 8.

---

### Balanced Jack
Tip: +, Ring −, Sleeve Ground

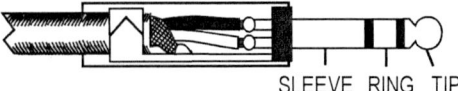

SLEEVE   RING   TIP

### Unbalanced Jack
Tip: +, Sleeve Ground

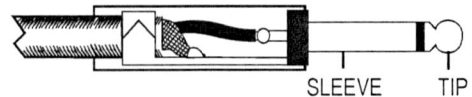

SLEEVE        TIP

Note: A stereo insert jack 'Y' lead can be wired either Tip In, Ring Out, or Tip Out, Ring In; there is no fixed rule. Luckily the required connections should be printed near the insert socket on the unit you're plugging into. If not, swap the In and Out ends around. One way will work, the other won't.

**Rules for Singers**

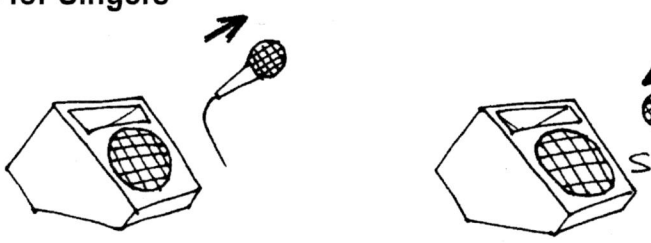

1. Keep the blunt end of the microphone pointed away from the speakers at all times.

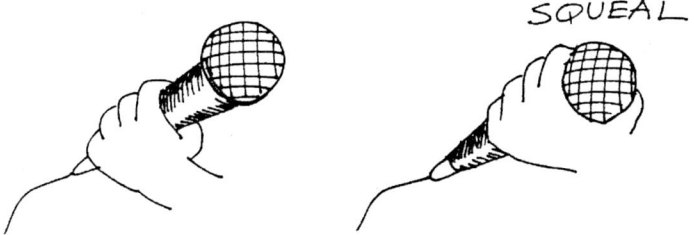

2. Don't cup the basket of the microphone in your hand.

3. Don't use the sidefill to lean on

4. Don't jump on the monitors or their owner may find a new place to put your mic stand!

## *Trivia*

A page from the original service manual for the RE 201 Space Echo. They sure don't write 'em like this anymore!

SECTION II:  HOW THE ECHO CHAMBER "RE-201" OPERATES

2-1     GENERAL

Echo chamber, Model RE-201, is consisted of 2 major separate sections:
1)  Mechanical Section to control the drive of the magnet tape, and
2)  Electrical Section of which the control devices are mostly concentrated at the front panel.

2-2     TAPE RUNNING SYSTEM

The figure below shows roughly the setting of the magnet tape.

When the power turned on, the Pinch-Roller moves toward the Capstan and the tape pinched between these two starts to run by the driving force from the capstan and pinch-roller.

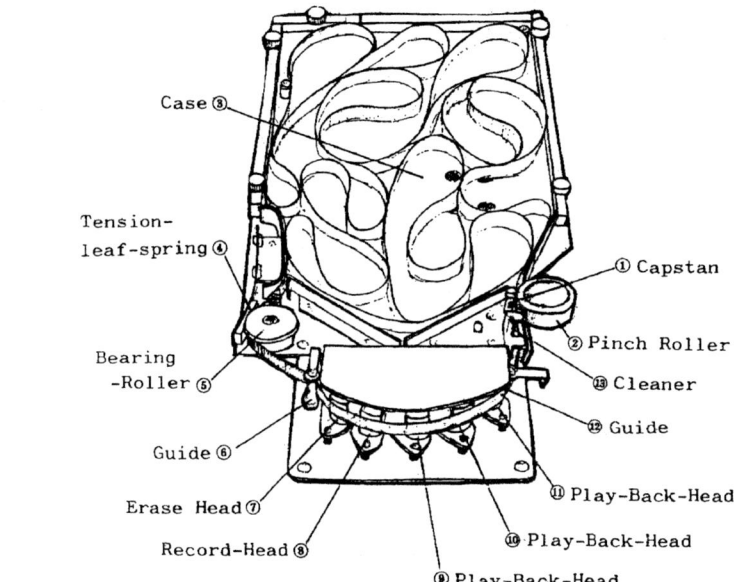

After entering into the chamber, the tape accumulates its own slacks and select its way till exit where it meets the tension-leaf-spring (4) which governs the feeding tension of the tape to the heads (7) - (11) passing over the bearing roller (5). The Guide (6) next is to assure of the right pass way of the tape to the heads (7) - (11).

RE-201 features a five Heads design, of Erase Head (7), Record-Head (8) and Play-Back-Heads (9) (10) (11).

Erase-Head (7) makes the tape ready for recording by the Record-Head (8) of the new sound fed into this unit, and this recorded sound is played back either by one of the play-back heads or in any combination of the selected heads from (9) (10) (11) by the Mode-Selector on the front panel.

## 'Words you'll need to know', 'Words you never dreamed you'd need to know' and other Technical Stuff

Although I've done my best to keep to my promise of all hands-on and no unnecessary technical stuff, there are words and concepts of which you'll need to be aware. Also, those of you using this book as part of an audio course might need some technical details and hard-core info that is not immediately applicable to actual mixing. So here goes:

### Active
An electronic circuit that uses power to drive it, and is capable of gain as well as attenuation. For example, an Active crossover, an Active DI.

### Amplitude
The level of a signal (i.e. its volume), usually measured in dB or volts. The following diagram shows the relationship of amplitude measurements:

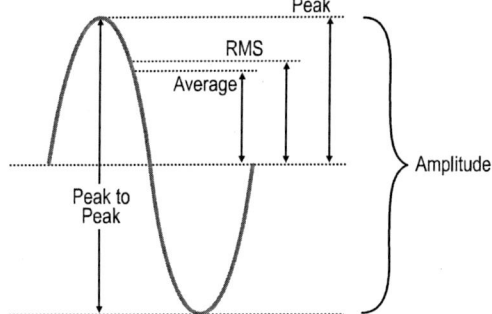

RMS = 0.717 x Peak

Peak = 1.414 x RMS

Crest Factor = Peak value divided by the RMS value

### Attack Time
The time it takes for a signal processor such as a compressor/limiter or noise gate to start to work, once the threshold has been reached.

### Attenuation
A big word simply meaning turning it down

### Balanced
A way of organizing cable wiring to reduce noise. It consists of 3 wires; Positive + and Negative − signal lines shielded by an Earth/Ground braid. The signal lines are opposite polarity, so any noise occurring in them is cancelled out at the Balanced Input. This Balanced Input can be Transformer Balanced, or Electronically (Differential) Balanced.

### Bandwidth ('Q')
The space between two frequencies which are the upper and lower limits in a circuit. For example, the bandwidth of a filter in a Parametric Equalizer can range from 3 octaves through to 1/20th of an octave. *See also Frequency Response*

### Bi-amped
An active 2 way sound system, with an active crossover feeding a Low amp and Low speakers, and a High amp and High speakers. The next step would be Tri-amped, a word hardly ever used, for an active 3 way system.

### Centre Frequency

The Frequency at which a filter is most effective. This can be the designated slider frequency on a Graphic Equalizer, or the frequency dialled up on a Parametric Equalizer.

### Clipping

The 'squaring off' of a sine wave. This occurs when the signal has increased past the point where the unit can reproduce it accurately. For example, an amplifier will clip when it can't produce any more voltage no matter how much you increase the input, and a tape deck will clip when too loud a signal is recorded.

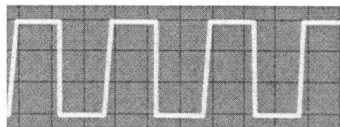

### Compressor

A variable gain amplifier whose output voltage compared to its input voltage decreases as its input level increases past a set threshold. In other words, a device to stop a signal getting any louder than a threshold that you set.

### Crossover

A crossover splits up the audio signal into different frequency bands for different speakers, and can be a 2, 3 or 4 way depending on the type of system. It ensures that the LOW speakers only get the LOW frequencies, the MID speakers only get the MIDs, and the HIGH speakers only get the HIGH frequencies.

An Active crossover comes BEFORE the amplifiers, and needs one amplifier per frequency band; a Passive crossover comes AFTER the amplifier, and is usually mounted inside the speaker cabinet.

### Crossover Frequency/Crossover Point

The transition frequency from one frequency band to the next.

### Damping Factor

Put simply, this is a measure of how well the amplifier controls the movement of the speaker cone. Bigger (200 or more) is better

### dB

The decibel. A unit of comparison for audio levels. For example: +3 dB is Double the Power; +6 dB is Double the Amplitude, 4 times the Power; +10 dB is 10 times the Power; +20 dB is 10 times the amplitude, 100 times the Power.

### dB SPL

The Sound Pressure Level, a way of measuring the loudness of speakers. It follows the same ratio as above, but substitute SPL for amplitude. 1 dB SPL is the smallest change in loudness that the human ear can detect, while a 10 dB change is perceived to be twice as loud.

### dBu (used to be dBv)

0 dBu = 0.775 volts

### dBV

0 dBV = 1 volt

### Decay time

In Reverbs, this refers to the length of time it takes for the reverb signal to die away to its lowest level (the noise floor of the system). In signal processors like compressors and gates, see Release Time.

### Digital

The representation in Binary code (0s and 1s) of a series of samples of an analog audio signal. Generally the higher the sampling rate (number of samples) the better. Has to be converted back to analog for us to be able to hear it. Its advantage is that it can be stored and manipulated and copied without any loss (theoretically!). Digital mixers, digital delays, digital reverberation etc etc.

### Distortion
Any modification to an audio signal which produces harmonics that were not present in the original. An essential part of a guitar amp, to create new sounds, but not something you need in a live sound system, which needs to accurately reproduce whatever goes into it.

### Dynamic range
The difference between the softest and the loudest sounds. A wide dynamic range is fine for CDs, but we use a compressor to reduce the dynamic range in PA systems so that the soft parts can be louder, and the loud parts don't get too loud.

### Equalization (EQ)
We use an Equalizer when it's necessary to modify the sound. This can be for two reasons; one, as a creative tool to get the sound we want; and two, as a control tool to remove frequencies that are causing problems. So, as a creative tool we can add more LOW into the Kick drum to give a pleasant 'Thud', and as a control tool we can pull out the frequencies in the vocal monitors that are making it squeal.

### Equal Loudness Contours

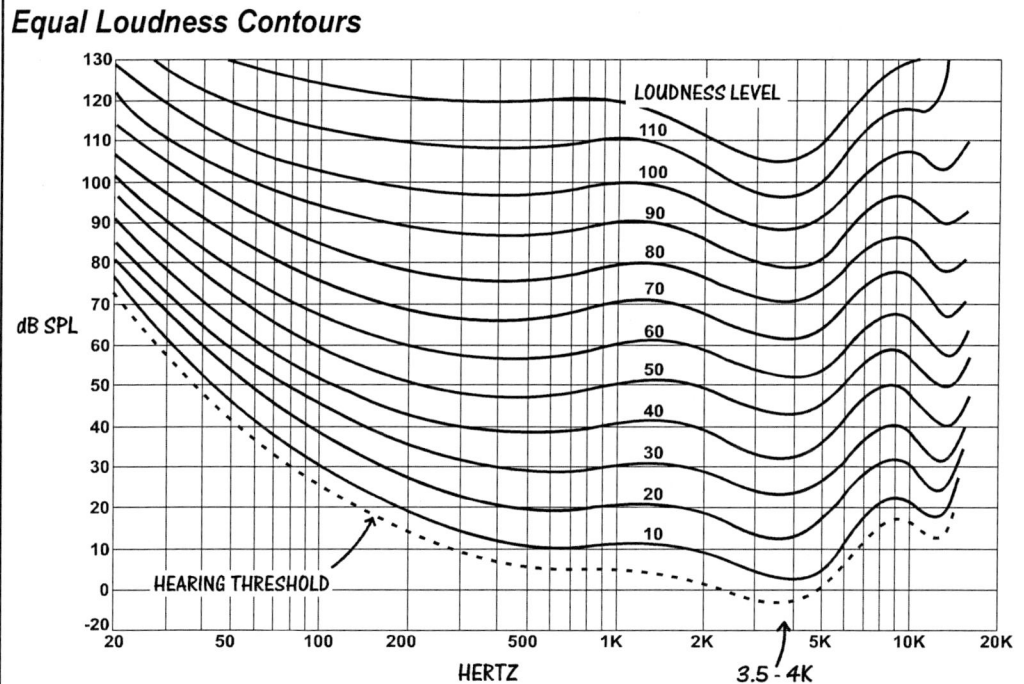

Equal Loudness Contours show you the sensitivity of the human ear at different frequencies. As you can see, it is most sensitive at 3.5 to 4KHz, less sensitive at high frequencies, and much less sensitive at low frequencies. Squint your eyes a bit and it looks like a typical consumer EQ curve. Can 500 million car stereos be wrong?

### Fader
A slider that controls the level on a piece of audio equipment, such as a Mixer (at the bottom of a channel) or a Graphic Equalizer (one of 30 similar ones, one for each Frequency)

### Feedback
*(Full name - Acoustic Feedback)* This refers to the squealing sound that seems to come out of the sound system all by itself. It is caused by the room, or the area in front of a monitor, being more sensitive at certain frequencies. This causes a peak in the response which is

picked up by the microphone, through the speakers, causing a bigger peak which is again picked up by the microphone, goes through the speakers... and so on.

It can usually be cured by pulling down the appropriate frequencies on the equalizer just enough to stop it. You can see it on a spectrum analyzer as a line of LEDs that disappears off the top of the display. Can also be automatically controlled by a Feedback Eliminator, which is an automatic Parametric Equalizer.

### Frequency Response

This is the amount of sound between the Highest Frequency and the Lowest. It can refer to individual pieces of equipment, individual speakers, or the complete system. A frequency response plot or a spectrum analyzer will show you the amount of each frequency in dB.

### Front-of-House (or House)

The house is a term for the venue, thus Front of House, often abbreviated to FOH, is the whole area in front of the stage (as opposed to Backstage).

### Gain Reduction

The amount that a compressor/limiter has reduced the level compared to what the uncompressed level would have been.

### Haas effect (Precedence Effect)

How the difference in level of 2 identical sounds from 2 sources makes the closer one seem to be the only one. The closer one arrives first, and takes precedence over the other, providing the arrival time of the second is less than 35 seconds after the first. This is the way stereo imaging works, with sounds arriving at different times at each ear.

### Headroom

The difference between the normal operating level of something and the maximum operating level before clipping.

### Hertz (Hz)

Cycles per second; the repetition rate of a wave is its frequency, measured in Hertz. The higher the note, the higher its frequency.

### High Pass Filter

A filter which rolls off (reduces) all the frequencies below it *(also known as Lo Cut).*

### Impedance

In speakers, the resistance of the speaker to the incoming signal; in electronics, the resistance of the input circuit to the incoming signal. It is measured in Ohms (Ω). The signal has to push against something to keep it stable, so an output is usually a lower impedance than an input. Balanced microphone lines are essentially Low Impedance circuits, unbalanced guitar or other instrument amplifier inputs are High Impedance circuits.

### ISO standard frequencies

The International Standards Organization has split the 20Hz to 20 Khz response of the human ear into these standard third octave frequencies, for consistency across various measurements and brands of Graphic Equalizers. If you need a frequency in between them, then you should use a Parametric Equalizer.

### Kilohertz  (KHz)

1000 Hertz  (1,000 cycles per second)

### Line Level

This means a signal level of 0 dBV (1 volt) or thereabouts. It is used to distinguish between microphone levels (around -40 dBV) and signals from tape decks, effects units, active DI boxes, mixing consoles and other electronic equipment.

### Limiter
A limiter is a compressor with a high compression ratio (10: 1 to Infinity: I) thus maintaining a constant output level despite any increase in input level above the threshold.

### Low Pass Filter
A filter which rolls off all the frequencies above it *(also known as Hi Cut)*

### Mixing
The art and science of using a Mixer, which is a device for combining audio signals of very different levels, and then sending this blended composite signal to amplifiers and then speakers

### Octave
A musical term for comparing frequencies. An octave higher means the frequencies are doubled; an octave lower means the frequencies are halved.

### Ohm (Ω)
The unit of electrical resistance or impedance

### Parallel wiring
A method of wiring, especially for speakers, where the + and – terminals on the amplifier are wired to the + and – terminals on the first speaker, then on to the + and – terminals on the next speaker, and so on. The most common method of speaker wiring

### Passive
A device that needs no power to make it work. For example, a Passive crossover, a Passive DI Box

### Phantom Power
DC (Direct Current) power sent down microphone leads in order to supply power to condenser microphones and active DI boxes. 48 volts is the official standard, but can be as low as 12 volts and still work acceptably

### Power amplifier
A unit that takes the medium level signal from a Preamplifier and amplifies it to high levels so that it can drive a speaker. It can be a separate unit, or built into mixers, or in some cases built into the speaker cabinet.

### Preamplifier
This is the first stage in the amplifier chain, and amplifies very low level signals from microphones up to medium level to drive power amplifiers

### Release Time
The time it takes for a signal processor such as a compressor/limiter or noise gate to stop working and return to normal once the signal has dropped below the threshold.

### Rack Unit (RU)
The standard to which all equipment is built. 19 inches wide by 1¾ inches high. Everything that you screw into a rack is built on multiples of this, i.e. 2 rack units (2RU), 3 rack units (3RU) and so on. Awkward to convert accurately to metric, but 482mm by 44 mm is usually accepted as being close.

### RMS
Root Mean Square. RMS = 0.717 x Peak The only amplifier watts that mean anything. *Also see Amplitude*

### RT60

The Reverberation Time of a room - the time it takes in seconds for a sound to decay by 60dB; the longer the time, the more reverberant the room

### Series wiring

Another method of wiring for speakers, where the signal goes from the source through each speaker one after the other and returns to the amplifier. When wiring up 2 speakers in Series, the + terminal on the amplifier is wired to the + terminal on the first speaker, and the − terminal on the first speaker is wired to the + terminal on the second speaker. Then the − terminal on the second speaker is wired back to the − terminal on the amplifier.

### Signal to Noise ratio

The difference between the level of a signal and the level of noise in a circuit, measured in dBV. Higher is better.

### Sine wave

A representation of a single tone. 1 KHz (Kilohertz) is a commonly used test tone.

SINE WAVE

### Speed of Sound

In Air at Sea Level, 21 C (72 F) sound travels at 344 metres per second, or 1130 feet per second. The warmer the air, the faster sound travels through it, as warm air is less dense.

### Threshold

The level at which a signal processor starts to act. On a compressor/limiter, the level above which the unit starts to compress; on a noise gate, the level below which the unit shuts off the signal.

### Transient

A sudden sharp peak of energy in a signal, such as the 'crack' of a snare drum or a breath 'pop' into a microphone, often reaching 20 dB or more over normal levels. The better the headroom in a system, the better it will cope with these transients without excessive compression or distortion.

### Unity gain

When the Output level is the same as the Input level.

### Wavelength

The distance covered by one complete cycle of a specified frequency as it moves through the air. Wavelengths of some different frequencies are:

| 100 Hz | 3.4 metres | 11 feet 4 inches |
| 500 Hz | 1.7 metres | 5 feet 8 inches |
| 1 KHz | 340 mm | 1 foot 1 1/2 inches |
| 5 KHz | 170 mm | 7 inches |
| 10KHz | 34 mm | 1 1/2 inches   (Imperial conversions to nearest 1/2 inch) |

### Z

Single letter abbreviation for impedance, more common in the USA than anywhere else. Don't ask me why the letter Z was chosen, unless someone wanted to make sure there was always something starting (and ending) with a Z at the end of lists like this!

For those of you who'd like to know more Technical Information on all this and more, the industry standard reference list is on the Rane Website - www.rane.com. Put a couple of weeks aside to read it all!

## Some final words

Well, that's about it from me! I hope I've kept to my promise of lots of hands-on advice, and not too much technical stuff (well, as little as possible, anyway).

A lot of books on sound squeeze all the sense of enjoyment out of mixing and replace it with endless pages of technical and acoustic theory that would choke an anaconda. Who wants to get bogged down reading that? Not me! I want to know what each knob does and when to turn it, so I've tried to write the sort of book that I needed when I started.

Mixing Live Sound can be a lot of hard work and late nights, but it can also be a whole lot of fun, and that's what I've tried to get across in this book.

Let me know if I've succeeded.

All the best

Duncan R. Fry
July, 2005


PS. If you'd like to read some other books *after* you've read this one, here's a short list to choose from:


**Practical Guide for Concert Sound**, Bob Heil, Melco Publishing 1978.

Fascinating classic stuff from an industry pioneer who did concert sound for The Who and others. Long out of print, I bought mine at a street market.

**Concert Sound and Lighting Systems**, John Vasey,  Focal Press 1989.  ISBN 0-240-51798-9

A good overview of the whole industry, including *(gasp)* lighting!

**Making The Connection** - The Fender Pro Audio Primer, Tom Butler, Fender Instruments Corp 1994. Their order code: #991-7000-000

An easy to read, not too technical look at Live Sound. It's a little Fender biased, but with 70 Fender logos on the cover at least they're up front about it! Worth reading.

**Live Sound Reinforcement**, Scott Hunter Stark. Tech-Access Publishing 1993.

A pretty good overview of live sound systems. Not *too* technical. Now reprinted by MIX bookshelf.

**Sound Reinforcement Handbook**, Hal Leonard Publishing 1987.

Known to most people as the Yamaha book. It's chock full of detailed and accurate info, but it's not a particularly easy read. Whenever I look something up in it, I end up thinking *'well that's a whole lot more than I needed to know!'* A comprehensive general reference text, though.

**Live Sound for performing musicians**, Peter Buick, PC Publishing 1996. ISBN 1-870775-44-9

A UK oriented overview full of technical formulae that most musicians wouldn't understand if it jumped up and spat in their eye! Good MIDI section.

## Technical Reference books:

**Sound System Engineering**, Don and Carolyn Davis, Howard W. Sams Co Inc 1975/1987, ISBN 0-672-21857-7

**The Audio Cyclopedia**, Howard Tremaine, Howard W. Sams Co Inc 1979. ISBN 0-672-20675-7

Can't sleep at night? These two will fix that! They both make the Yamaha book look like a tabloid newspaper! Seriously though, these two are great technical references for anyone designing and installing professional sound systems.

## *About the Author*

LIVE SOUND MIXING is the result of author Duncan Fry's years of experience mixing sound on all kinds of PA systems - big and small, good and bad. In the early 1980's, dissatisfied with the equipment often available, he joined up with Colin and David Park to form ARX Systems, a company dedicated to making unique products for the Pro Audio industry.

When he's not mixing or manufacturing, he likes to put on sunglasses, fake beard and spinning guitar, and play some boogie.

There is a LIVE SOUND MIXING homepage at:

**www.dunkworld.com**, where you can read 'Old Dunk's Tales from the Road' and order books, t-shirts, caps and associated merchandising online

THE AUTHOR ON STAGE AT THE HOLLYWOOD BOWL - PRIVATE CONCERT!

This picture was taken during a tour of the Hollywood Bowl one year. I was unable to resist the large sign saying 'Do not get up on the stage' so naturally I jumped up there! It looks so empty in the picture that it's always reminded me of those people who hire out Carnegie Hall for a concert and no-one turns up!

Hence the caption 'Private Concert!'

# Index

## *Illustration and Photo Credits*

All illustrations and photos by the author except as follows.

**Front Cover:** Frank Park/ Pages 79 and 140 Colin Park/ Page 96-97 Peter Twartz/ Pages 94-95

**Special Note:** Page 142 'Fools Guide to Fuse Replacement' This is not original but an old photo-copy I've had for years. I still can't find anybody who knows where this historic classic comes from, but I've included it in the interests of safety. I'll be more than happy to credit its source in the next edition if the originator gets in touch with me.